Naked (in Italy)

A Memoir About the Pitfalls

of *La Dolce Vita*

M.E. Evans

Capybara
Media

Published in the United States by Capybara
Media, an imprint of M.E. Evans LLC. SLC, UT.

This is a work of nonfiction. Names of both people and places have been changed, time has been condensed, and identifying characteristics tweaked. All of the stories here were written from memory and my own perception of events. I accept that others may remember things differently. I drink a lot of wine so it's entirely possible that none of this is true.

First edition
Copyright © 2019 M.E. Evans
Cover design by Trev Poulson
Cover photo and author bio photo by Duston Todd
Edited by Lucy David

ISBN-13: 978-1-7334155-0-7
Library of Congress: 2019914566

For Francesco, Oliver, and Leo.

Contents

"The gentle reader will never, never know what a consummate ass he can become, until he goes abroad."

—Mark Twain, *The Innocents Abroad*

Preface

From what I could gather from the conversation between my boyfriend and his mother, American women give birth by pausing to squat on a sidewalk somewhere on their way to work. They push the baby out and immediately resume walking, briefcase swinging in hand, Starbucks in the other, rushing to their 9 a.m. meeting as if nothing happened. The newborn is dragged along until the umbilical cord finally snaps and the infant bounces away to raise itself entirely. As an American woman I was taken aback; my God, I thought, I had no idea we were so *efficient*.

I sat at the kitchen table between my Italian boyfriend, Francesco, and his mom near the sink, trapped in an awkward place where her insults had to pass through me to get to him. All of the blood in her body had rushed into her face as she listed off the many reasons American women make terrible mothers. She lifted a saucepan in the air like she was about to bludgeon me with it, then turned and chucked it into the soapy water, sending a tidal wave of suds crashing onto the counter. When she turned her back to violently scrub the dishes, I snuck out the sliding glass door.

From the balcony, I basked in the moonlight. I could see Francesco and his mom through the glass, and tried to tune out the soundtrack of audible disappointment playing inside. I fantasized about making a full escape by climbing off of the balcony to the parking lot below. I wasn't that high up, maybe ten feet, so if I fell the worst thing that would happen is I'd break both of my ankles. Then I could drag myself to the road and call a cab to take me to the airport, and bank on the kindness of airport employees to cart me around in a wheelchair all the way home to Salt Lake City. I leaned over the rail and looked down on the laundry lines—the same ones that every apartment had in that tiny town in southern Italy—at the threadbare floral sheets that quivered in the warm air. I spotted my black lace thong that I hadn't washed or hung there and thought to myself, *not today motherfucker, not today*, and snatched it off the line in an act of defiance. I felt bigger. I wash my own goddamn undies! It was a small act but putting my underwear in my pocket energized me, like I'd regained a little bit of myself, a little autonomy. It was sad what my life had become: one big panty grab for power.

The woman who lived in the apartment just across the parking lot, the one whose son asked me, "Do you know how much Francesco's mom hates you?" pretended to sweep her balcony but we both knew she was just eavesdropping, and how could you not? It sounded like someone was being murdered over here. The screams were so shrill that every syllable echoed like a siren punctuated by heaving sobs. And it all started because Francesco wanted to marry me.

I liked the balcony. The laundry smelled "fresh" and "clean" as advertised on the Italian version of Tide. It reminded me of my grandma's house, the laundry that hung in her backyard that I used to play in. I missed her and, surprisingly, I missed home. I never thought I would but the more his mom yelled the more I missed people who might be on my side. But whose fault was all of this anyway? Maybe it was mine because I just couldn't fit in or live up to their expectations, or maybe it was hers because she'd always been an asshole. But hadn't she earned the right to her feelings and her method of expressing them in her fifty-something years?

Still, I caught myself fantasizing about the day she'd be old and frail and I could do what everyone else did: hire a foreigner to take care of her. Oh, the irony, oh the glory, oh my God what is *wrong* with me?

Something crashed in the kitchen. "She'll divorce you!" she shouted. And I thought, what a stupid stereotype. Then I shrugged because, yeah, *maybe.*

My boyfriend sighed, signaling defeat, and I wanted to scream, *"Why do you always give in?"* I wanted to charge in there and tell her that we were adults and we could make our own fucking decisions. But I couldn't. I'd lost my voice and my gumption to vulnerability.

Not being able to communicate was a bitch.

An elderly man that everyone called the Frenchman, maybe because he's French or maybe he ate at a French restaurant once—entirely possible because that's how nicknames worked there—left the apartment building with his poodle, Sofia. He looked up at me and we both smiled, even though I knew that he knew and he knew that I knew that he knew because everyone knew everything all the time and it was fucking suffocating. That's how things were in the small village. Gossip was currency and it kept you in either humiliation or check.

I talked to myself, out loud because I'd become my own sounding board and my own best friend, like that one homeless man who stabbed me with a spork on a bus when I was a teenager. For the first time in my life I could truly empathize with losing one's mind.

I'd moved to Italy for the rolling green hills, cheap Chianti, and sexy Italian men with their rolled *r*'s and majestic chest hair. But Italy wasn't rainbows and unicorns all the time. Sometimes it was falling down, agoraphobia, and a future mother-in-law who brandishes saucepans at you.

Stripped

"We showed up in Italy having shed so many things to journey for something new, selfish for some and obvious for others. We were personally naked of our perceived selves, our societal places, our birthrights, and cultural burdens. We all met in this state of invention, this unique opportunity to decide in each moment as to what exactly we wanted to put forward. Little demigods creating a new personal universe."

—E.S.

Baggage

September 2009

A sweaty taxi driver who talked with his hands and smelled like eggplant deposited me and all my baggage in the middle of the street in front of my new apartment in the San Lorenzo area of Florence, Italy. It was sometime around noon on my twenty-eighth birthday. This is where I'd live for my first semester of grad school with four other women I didn't know. My ankles wobbled on the cobblestones because I'd strapped my feet into six-inch stiletto sandals in the airport in an attempt to look "more put together." That was at least half of the point of studying abroad, to become some magical better version of myself. Sweat ran from the crease of my butt down the back of my thighs and I thought, I hope that guy can't see it. The guy in question, the one I didn't want to judge me, was bedraggled and openly pissing into a potted plant a few feet away.

While I stood there among my explosion of shit, people just wove around me like they would a pothole. A group of gorgeous Italian men in pastel summer suits sauntered past, making aggressive eye contact with me until they disappeared into the San Lorenzo leather market at the end of the road. I could smell the market, that distinctive musty scent of skin soaked in a chemical bath. The sun beat down on my back and my thighs kept dripping sweat like my vagina was crying. I needed to get out of the sun.

A woman in platform pumps and white linen pants with sunglasses the size of two microwaves raced across the cobblestones like a goddamn Olympian, and I thought, If she can do it, so can I. I took a confident step forward, my ankles buckled beneath me like they were made of paper and I landed flat on my back on the sharp, stabby rocks, hard. My dress was up around my hips and my thong was on display. Someone in the distance giggled. I reached up, unbuckled my shoes, and threw them towards the sidewalk. I hopped to my feet, kept my head down and dragged my bags, one by one, to my apartment door, barefoot. I could feel all of these eyes on the back of my head and wondered, Did people stare this much back home? And how is it possible that nobody has offered to help?

I used my *Secret Garden* key and stepped into what appeared to be a giant bat cave. Dark, damp, stone, and a single staircase that shot up into oblivion. I couldn't find the light, so I pulled each of my bags up four flights of stairs in the dark, taking one bag, one flight at a time, still barefoot, cursing, grunting, heaving in the oppressive heat and humidity like a burrito that had been wrapped in aluminum foil and put under a heat lamp; for a brief moment, I ugly cried.

At the top, I gently pushed open the front door of my new home and called inside, "Anyone here?" Silence. *Thank God.* My body hurt, I had a bruised ass, and my feet were filthy. I'd gone feral and I didn't want to meet my new roommates looking and smelling like an injured swamp rat. Plus, it gave me time to explore alone.

The apartment was quaint. There was a small kitchen with a tiny balcony, living room with a loveseat and a dining table for four, two bathrooms (each with a bidet) and three bedrooms for five women. All of the beds had been claimed except for a twin bed in one of the shared rooms furnished with white Ikea furniture. I heaved my bags up onto it and checked the tag on the designer luggage on the other bed. Amy Hess, Georgia. *Should be interesting.*

Twenty minutes later, I stepped out of the shower and felt human again. I pulled on a simple dress and flat, sturdy sandals like a normal person and sat down at the bistro table on the balcony to write lofty romantic things in my journal.

... Laundry hangs in the gardens below. The smell of marinara mixes with the earthy scent of mildew from the green patches that cling like a Pollock painting to the exterior walls of this hundreds-of-years-old apartment building. Everything is perfect.

I left the apartment to grab an espresso at a nearby bar. Afterward, I wandered around San Lorenzo for a little while, careful not to go too far and nervous that I'd get lost because I seem to be missing that part of my brain that tells direction. My mom always jokes, "You couldn't find your way out of a paper bag," which is one hundred percent true. Utah, where I'm from, has a numerical grid system, so if you can count, you can get anywhere. But names of streets? I can't remember the name of anything, including my own if I've had too much to drink. I popped into a Wind store, an Italian version of AT&T, to buy a little disposable cell phone that looked like it was from the nineties and a phone card with sixty minutes of talk time. I sat on the steps of the San Lorenzo church and called my mom.

"Hi Mom, I'm alive," I began. Our conversation was quick because it was evening in Utah and she was already lit.

"Be safe," she said, her voice spiked with mourning and enveloped in booze like it had been after 5 p.m. for a year, ever since my brother died.

"I'll be fine," I said, "I love you." I felt guilty for leaving after everything that had happened but I had to.

I shook my head to clear it, the way you shake an Etch A Sketch to erase it. I called my dad but he didn't answer because he was still mad at me for "ruining my entire life" by moving to Italy for grad school. Which was fine, because I was still mad at him for being mostly absent for the first nine years of my life, and judgmental as fuck for the past eighteen.

For most of my childhood, my dad wasn't around. Both of my parents have conflicting stories about why. Mom says that he just took off and didn't want to be involved. Dad says that he wanted to be there but that Mom moved so much he couldn't find us. Regardless of the reason, I didn't start seeing him consistently until the fifth grade when he randomly popped into my life after a very long hiatus. I had a lot going on that year. My mom and stepdad were heading towards divorce, I'd had my first panic attack, and I'd recently started an environmental group called the Fluorescent Fireflies, inspired by a book on forest conservation I'd checked out of the library. I spent a lot of time at the city building in Sunset, attending meetings and bothering the mayor and city council. On one occasion, I insisted on strict laws for littering: a two-thousand-dollar fine or jail time.

"Well, that does seem high," a councilwoman said, "but we'll talk about it and see what we can do."

I nodded, as if to say my work here is done, gathered my graphs and charts, and exited the premises. On my way out, a local reporter grabbed me for an interview. The journalist, a young woman, was completely convinced that the seeds of world change had been planted by my Democrat, tree-hugging parents.

"My mom doesn't like reading," I told the reporter, "But she really likes music and cartoons."

"Maybe you got it from your father?" she asked.

I scratched my nose. "I don't really know him. I met him a few times but haven't seen him in a couple of years."

The story ran in the newspaper a few days later titled, "Fireflies Have Been Sighted in Sunset," and detailed how a group of ten-year-olds was trying to change the world. It also mentioned how I wanted to have a parade made entirely of garbage to be recycled so people could get a good look at how much crap we were throwing away.

Later in the week, as though summoned forth by the reporter's questions, my dad resurfaced. My mom mentioned his return in passing, the way someone might say, "Brush your teeth" or "Dinner's in the microwave." Mom was the kind of woman who could survive a genocide and talk about it as if she'd accidentally bought a moldy loaf of bread at the supermarket. "Shit happens," she'd probably say. I was supposed to match her blasé attitude, so as my body heated up like I'd just jabbed a wire hanger into a live power outlet, I kept the electricity below the surface.

I'd only seen my dad a handful of times since I'd been born, and only remembered the meetings vaguely as if every encounter had happened in a dream.

"Okay," I said flatly, though I definitely didn't feel okay. I didn't want anything to do with him. Why would I? He didn't want me. He was practically a stranger, and being sent off to stay with him was scary.

The next day, I moved out of my mother's house and into the shed while she was at work. I built a fireplace inside with cinder blocks and Indian clay that I dug from our own backyard, which left a massive crater in the center of the lawn. I even cut out a chimney hole in the shed wall with power tools. Surprisingly, the chimney mostly worked, though it was a little smoky. I dusted off my hands and moved my stuff in, throwing a mattress on the floor and a rocking chair in the corner that I'd borrowed from Mom's living room. Then I stocked up on canned stew, cute pasta in alphabet shapes and powdered sugar from the grocery store just up the street. I "accidentally" dropped most of the cans to get them for half-price because I needed to save money now that I was on my own.

I put my groceries away on a shelf that used to hold the gas cans and lay on my mattress, staring at the cobwebs that decorated the ceiling and basking in the glory of living alone. Unfortunately, my independence lasted less than three hours. After my mom came home from work she made me move back into the house and return the tools to the shed. I was told that I would be going with my father for the weekend in just a few days' time.

The night before I went, Mom had her best friend over for drinks. They sipped rum and whispered in the corner like I wasn't sitting on the carpet watching TV less than five feet away. Then Mom walked over and popped something into the VCR.

"I want you to watch this, okay?" she said.

I nodded, and then she went into the kitchen to chain-smoke and drink with her friend. The film was *Not Without My Daughter*, supposedly based on a true story about an Iranian man who takes his American family for a "visit" to Iran and then essentially kidnaps them and holds them hostage after turning into an abusive lunatic. After the film was over, I stared at the screen wide-eyed, wondering why in the hell I was being forced to see this man. As I sat there horrified, Mom walked back into the living room.

"Oh, it's over already? Anyways, your dad is a really nice person but these are your father's people, so, you know, don't get on a plane with him or whatever okay?"

The following morning, I paced the length of the living room, my heart pounding. When a car pulled into the driveway I rushed to spy through the blinds and there he was: a cross between Count Dracula and a silverback gorilla, getting out of a black BMW in a black leather jacket. His unibrow furrowed as he made his way to our front door. Panic formed, peaked, and disappeared as I went numb (years later, my therapist would refer to this as "numbing out"). He knocked on our screen door, standing proud and tall, and I vaguely recognized his nose that curved out from his face like a ski slope—it was the same as mine—and jet-black hair. Mom, who had just put on a fresh swipe of frosted eyeshadow, opened the door and he stepped inside and leaned towards me.

"Hello Princess," he said.

His accent was strong and I struggled to understand him. He hugged me and kissed my cheeks, as his culture and affectionate personality required. I didn't like being touched by him; it felt invasive, and his stubble agitated my soft skin. The fact that I had his DNA meant nothing to me: he was just a strange man, from a strange place, who was overzealously attacking my cheeks with his big mauve lips. I glared at him. Less than five minutes later I was led to his luxury car and probably to my death.

As we sped down the freeway heading south towards Salt Lake City, my dad pulled out a brick-sized cell phone and began screaming in a language that didn't seem like it could be real. I hadn't met anyone with a cell phone before so I assumed that he was probably a drug dealer and most likely speaking in code. He hung up.

"Det vas yair grandma back home in Iran," he said.

Shit. He's totally kidnapping me and taking me to Iran. What am I going to do in Iran? Where is Iran? I have a grandma? I was a latchkey kid who had just found out that she had a little old foreign grandma. And it occurred to me, for the first time in my life, that I was half-ethnic.

For the painfully awkward and long drive, my dad rambled on speaking in tongues while I stayed glued to the window, watching the scenery. My mom never left the teeny-tiny town where we lived and I was amazed by all of the landscape I'd been missing. Everything was beautiful and new, and we were passing real cities like the ones I'd seen on TV, the ones I dreamed of being a part of someday.

We pulled up to a house and a little girl of about five years old ran out and crawled into the back seat.

"Hi Daddy!" she said enthusiastically.

"Hello, baby. How's my gill?" he asked.

"I'm good!" she smiled, and then she turned her focus to me. Her eyes were large and brownish-green and her round cheeks were rosy like she'd put on blush.

"Who's that?" she asked.

"Kuh-Lowy baby, dis is yair sister Misty, say hello to hair."

Her eyes grew huge. "I have another sister?" she beamed, clasping her hands together. It was weird but she kind of looked like me. I thought of how odd it would have been to see her in a mall one day and have someone point out that we could be sisters, unknowing that I was related to her. Strange. His interaction with her was natural and clearly he hadn't stolen her and fled the country, so maybe he wasn't so bad.

Another young girl, about my age with blue eyes and pale skin, walked out of the same house and hopped in the seat next to Chloe. She didn't look like me.

"I'm Ellen," she said in response to my expression. "Dad adopted me. I'm Chloe's blood sister, not yours though."

I nodded. The car lurched forward and we were off.

At my dad's two-bedroom apartment, my sisters took great interest in getting to know me, firing question upon question, while my father watched us over his cup of tea.

"You look so-a Persian, just-a like your ent," he said.

Persian? What the hell is Persian? Isn't that a huge cat with a flat face? I was something and I didn't even know what it was.

"You want to learn Farsi geyl, I teach you da Farsi geyl."

My dad tried to explain all things Persian to me, and that night we ate Persian food for dinner, a stew called *geymeh*. Chloe scooped spoonfuls of Greek yogurt into her mouth and smiled between bites. Having the other two there helped the transition, made me feel more at ease with all of the strangeness happening.

After dinner, we watched movies together on my dad's bed for the rest of the night. He put his arms around us and kissed us on the cheeks constantly, which kind of freaked me out. My mom wasn't the affectionate type but my dad gave cuddles in spades. I remember sitting snuggled against my dad, who I barely knew, while my little sister twirled my hair in her fingers, and my other sister whispered jokes to me under her breath.

It occurred to me in that moment that life with my mother was the exact opposite of what life would be like with my dad. I was a "free spirit" at home, spending most of my time alone either collecting animals or coming up with some kind of get-rich-quick scheme. For the first time, I felt different, strange, like I had been missing something that I never knew I needed. Not only was I sitting in my dad's apartment with my two new sisters, but I was also part of a culture that I didn't know anything about and that my dad was incredibly proud of. I looked like an aunt I'd never met. My dad spoke multiple languages and I had another grandma. My family ate something called *geymeh*. And just like that, my identity began to change.

I liked my new family, but liking them didn't make the fact that he'd bailed when I was younger any easier. From then on, I spent weekends with my dad, me bitter and him clueless.

Flash-forward almost twenty years later, to the day that I told Dad, against my better judgment, that I wanted to go to graduate school. It was at our usual place, a café that overlooked an organic market in downtown

Salt Lake City. I got there first since I lived nearby, but it didn't take me long to spot him over the aisles of cricket-gut protein bars and essential-oil douches. My dad is attractive and knows it, which puts a special pep in his step that's easy to spot from a mile away. His toasted brown skin that he refers to as "absolutely perfect" stood out in Utah, the whitest place on earth. He wore a tight t-shirt that showed off his muscular frame and strolled around like he owned the place, his shiny bald head thrown back, his chest up and out like a king penguin. He promenaded up the stairs, threw his keys on my table, and hovered pompously over two overweight teens with blue hair at the table next to us.

"Hi Dad," I said to distract him.

"Baby! How's my baby doing?" He pulled me into a tight hug, and kissed me hard on both cheeks, his scruff burning across my skin. I winced. He sat across from me, then turned back to stare aggressively at the table of teens next to us, again.

"Dad!" I shook my head at him.

He wore an expression that looked like "I smell poo," because he wanted the kids to know that he disapproved of their everything. He turned to me and crossed his legs.

"It's absolutely spectacular today, isn't it? Nowhere in the United States is as beautiful as this place, nowhere. Don't you think so, baby?"

My dad only speaks in hyperbole, like everything that he enjoys is factually the best in the world. The café he goes to is spectacular, his favorite restaurants are the best ones (even if nobody else agrees), and his DNA, the gift that he bestowed on you, poof, like magic, is something to be grateful for because that olive skin and the Persian genes are "perfect, baby." If only our genes hadn't been diluted by our white mothers (five kids, three different moms). We're the product of a man who is so proud of his Persian heritage, yet he cannot resist a blonde (he says it's because he grew up watching *Bewitched*).

When the waitress came over I ordered a soy latte and Dad asked for a black coffee, plain, on account of his diabetes. Then we stared at each other, cautiously. He waited for me say something that would set him off because I usually did, and I waited for him to hurt my feelings. I couldn't remember the last time I'd walked away from one of our encounters without an argument, without feeling deeply wounded. For the most part, I don't think he intentionally set out to be mean. But when you're not sure if someone loves you or not, it's easy to read into things and hard to let things go.

The first time I'd gone to Europe with friends, my dad had asked me suspiciously, "Where did you get the money?" (the subtext as I understood it was that if I could afford to go, I was clearly involved in some maniacal scheme, as if it had cost me millions to buy a plane ticket). Because of my dad's success in the money department, he has a weird concept of the denaro. Where I could travel in Europe for under two thousand dollars a month by staying in hostels and living on a loaf of bread and jar of Nutella, he couldn't do it for less than five thousand a week. So, in his brain, every time I went to Europe it cost me twenty grand.

He's also one of the few Persians who emigrated but still holds onto traditions from the 1500s, where all things modern or progressive are seen as some kind of personal attack on him and his way of life. Attending a dance club in one's twenties was basically the same as smoking crack in a garbage can. I was, for all intents and purposes, not what my dad considered a good kid. I had tattoos, listened to punk music, and dated a variety of mostly useless men (although two had gone to Ivy League schools).

"So, Dad, how's the family in Iran?" I asked.

Predictably, his face lit up and he launched into a story about his childhood pet chicken, nine brothers and my aunt, and sheep with huge asses.

"No, baby!" he laughed showing all of his teeth, slapping the table. "The sheeps in Iran, they have the really huge butts, you've never seen butts that big, I guarantee you that! It's so cute!"

He threw his head back and roared so loud that he shook his chair and every other human there turned to see who was having such a jolly goddamn time. I shelved Italy to the back of my mind, my palms sweating every time I considered breaching the subject. I needed his support but deep down I never believed I would get it. I'd always felt like I was putting myself out there only to have him shut me down, again and again. And every time it chipped away at me a little bit.

An hour later, when I could tell Dad was about ready to leave, after hearing about his pet chicken, the butcher, the baker, and the candlestick maker of small-town Golpayegan, Iran, the "best city in the world with the most educated people—"

I blurted out, "Dad, I've been thinking about grad school..."

His smile vanished.

"I think," he paused for a dramatically long time, his lips pursed, "you should be a teacher or get a job at a corporation and work your way up."

"A teacher," I cocked my head to the side. "Like for children? *Me*? And who works their way up in a corporation nowadays? This isn't the fifties; you can't start out as a dishwasher and end up owning a Hilton. That's not a thing."

He clenched his jaw to hold back whatever it was that he actually wanted to say. I was worried that he might devour me, or leave me on a cliff somewhere because only the strong should survive.

"I just don't understand why you'd be against grad school," I said, as deflated as a flaccid air dancer, face-down outside of a car dealership at the end of the day. He leaned forward, impatient for me to finish.

"Look, baby, no. These things are *fantasy*. You don't have the personality for these things. Lower your expectations." *Ouch*. Then he launched into one of his lectures, a confusing mix of ancient Iranian wisdom and an unusual grasp of the English language that sounded like: "If you ask a wasp to wear pants, he will become a blueberry Pop-Tart." Which I, of course, read as "you're worthless and I hate you."

I'd hoped that he'd be proud of me like my friend's parents who wouldn't shut up about how amazing she was for going to Ecuador to study rock formations for her *semester abroad*, which they emphasized and chased with a swig of California Sauvignon. I didn't give a fuck what anyone else in the world thought of me except for him. He was supposed to believe what I believed—that I was destined for something big in spite of myself. I slowly nodded.

He stood up and kissed my unresponsive face. "I love you, baby, I've got to go."

I stared vacantly at an event corkboard—Free Yoga and Reiki in the Park!—and tried not to cry into my latte.

* * *

The sun was setting and the Italians were on their way home from work as I made my way back to my new Florence apartment. I walked up the stairs again, this time without bags and without tears, opened the front door and heard voices in the living room. I leaned against the door frame and waved to my new roomates, who were cozied up on the furniture.

"Hi."

"Hi!" they said in chorus.

A woman in a bright yellow sundress said, "Eh, darling," and brushed her long black and blonde braids from her shoulder.

"I'm Kuhle," she smiled. She was a Xhosa woman from South Africa, here to study digital media. Next, a mousy girl whispered her name, Debra Darlington, adjusted her glasses and fell silent. A schoolmate later described her as "the kind of woman who would take a shit and turn around to look completely shocked by her own doody, every single day." Next, a Joan Jett look-alike who seemed about fifty put her hand up like she was asking to be called on. Her name was Karen, a painter, and she went to the San Francisco Art Institute, also known as SFAI. She went vegan at SFAI, and was in Italy on a full-ride scholarship and really loved her time at SFAI. Long live SFAI. A woman with blonde hair that bloomed over her small frame hopped out of her seat and shot her hand towards me.

"I'm Amy Hess, and I believe we're sharing a room." She had an ever-so-slight Southern way of speaking.

"Georgia," she winked at me, "Nice to meet ya, roomie." She was a jewelry designer and came to Florence to study new jewelry techniques. When she turned to go back to her seat, I noticed that she had the monogram *A.H.* in large, tan letters, sewn where you'd normally find a brand label. Amy Hess?

"Uhm, I'm Misty," I said, "I'm from Salt Lake City but I'm not Mormon—everyone asks—and today's my birthday. I just turned twenty-eight. And, I'm here to study painting although I've only ever done it as a hobby so I'm kind of hoping I don't completely bomb."

"Happy birthday!" they beamed in unison.

"Thanks!"

I took a seat. From the arm of the couch, I listened to the room. They talked about jobs they'd left behind, family and friends who didn't get why they had to move to Italy. In the pauses and the tones, there were also other reasons for moving to another country, bigger reasons than they were letting on, and I could hear the subtleties because we had that in common. But unlike my new roommates, I hadn't left an amazing career or a mortgage. I'd left a less-than-ideal roommate situation and a string of odd jobs that I took because they were "interesting," including:

A bartender in a Bosnian bar that definitely trafficked drugs or ran some kind of money-laundering scheme. People would often stop by with envelopes of money for me to "put behind the bar for the boss." All of my coworkers were illegal immigrants from Russia, Bosnia and Lebanon. We were expected to work fourteen-hour shifts. But being legal and unaccustomed to actual slavery, I quit after a particularly long sixteen-hour day. When I quit, the owner literally picked me up underneath my armpits and threw me out of the bar like a sack of potatoes. I sped away on my Vespa, flipping him off over my shoulder.

A lady pimp. One morning after too many mimosas, I somehow acquired the name "Big Mamma M," and agreed to act as a sort of "coordinator" in a sex-for-cash situation. Basically, I became a lady pimp for two of my friends, a handsome guy I nicknamed T-Bone, and a petite pixie of a woman we called Sparkles. It was a short endeavor but it taught me a lot about society and the economics of humping. Sadly, my pimp days were mostly unsuccessful and short-lived (partly because T-Bone wouldn't stop giving it away for free).

A dog sitter at a doggie daycare. Dogs are the greatest thing in the world, so what could be better than watching fifty of them at once? Turns out, everything. I hated it. The place didn't treat the pets like the gods that they were, the manager was a sadistic twat, and I had to leave before I got all stabby.

I kept all of this to myself, though. I planned to reveal these things in spoonfuls instead of buckets. I'd learned growing up that it was better that way.

"Would you guys be interested in going out for a drink?" I asked.

Kuhle smiled. "I'd love to, Angel, but I'm so tired. I'm actually heading off to bed now. And we have to be up early tomorrow." Everyone else agreed.

In bed, I lay in the dark with the cool white cotton sheets against my bare legs and stared at the ceiling. Melodic words that I couldn't understand hummed in the streets just outside of the windows, sentences that meant nothing, and I felt a jab of childlike vulnerability in my chest. I was living in a country where I didn't speak the language, in an apartment full of people I didn't know. I was alone and free and terrified. I'd actually done it. The vulnerability fled and was replaced by a conflicting feeling of self-possession and a sense of accomplishment. I had made the decision to move to Italy and I'd done it. My dad wasn't around to criticize me, my friends weren't there to distract me. I had no ties, no responsibility, nothing. And I was far from the bad thing that happened, far from where my brother had left the world, which helped lift my sadness just enough to make it manageable. I could be *anything* or *anyone* and it made me feel powerful and ravenous with ambition. A warm breeze drifted in through the white drapes and open window, along with the laughter and shouts of drunk Italian teens. I'd been so set on getting away from home, on packing, purchasing plane tickets, and telling everyone goodbye, that I hadn't actually processed much. I spent that first night tossing and turning, tangled in sheets, somewhere between exhilaration and anxiety.

2

Animal Sex

A my and I cut through the San Lorenzo leather market and booked it through the carts where rowdy vendors competed to sell Pinocchio puppets, leather jackets and silk scarves to tourists. They yelled "Good deal!" at thrilled American families while we huffed and puffed around them. A group of men whistled and called after us, *"Bellissima!"*, *"Bella!"*, and one, "I love you!" in between soggy air kisses. Amy seemed to float in her coral jersey dress, all color and joy. I looked like I'd just come off of a week-long crack bender. After falling on my ass, I'd boycotted heels and ditched my goal of looking more "put together," reverting back to my eight-minute morning routine. My long hair had matted into a rat's nest at the nape of my neck and my black leggings and wrinkled red plaid shirt were in stark contrast to Amy's polished vibe. We blurred past the merchant carts like a storm cloud stalking a rainbow.

We ran onto Via Guelfa and spotted the studio door right away. It was next to a café, Bar Maria and, because we both prioritized coffee over punctuality, we headed for the café first.

"Oh thank God," I tried to catch my breath, "I'm not a morning person and I feel like I'm fucking dying."

"Same, roomie," Amy winked.

The barista, a lanky man with salt-and-pepper hair, leaned against the counter. He sipped on what looked like a shot of liquor and laughed with a customer. A short, middle-aged woman with black hair pulled into a high ponytail yelled in Italian over the hiss of the espresso machine, "Stefano!"

The barista straightened up and sauntered over to us.

"*Ciao,*" he smiled.

"Ciao!" we responded with a wave.

"Dimmi," he said, inviting us to order.

I froze and just kind of stood there trying to remember how to ask for things. I pointed to a random *cornetto* in a glass case filled with other pastries and cookies.

"*Vorrei?* Cappuccino. Vorrei?" I asked. Which basically translated to, "I would like? Cappuccino. I would like?" And I sounded bewildered like I was asking him if eating was ok.

I'd traveled to ten other countries before coming to Italy but I'd never felt pressured to speak the language until now. Knowing that I'd be living in Florence for a while changed things. It was my home now and so I looked like a complete asshole if I couldn't speak Italian, which made me suddenly self-conscious and shy.

Amy pointed to herself. "Me, too!" she said, flashing her bright whites.

He chuckled like we'd just told him a hilarious joke. We counted out our euro coins slowly, holding up each one and examining it in the light.

"Ciao!" we yelled and left clutching our tiny cappuccinos in paper cups. The barista called out behind us, "Thanks, guys! See you again tomorrow!" In perfect English.

In the graduate studio, Amy and I made our way through our peers to two empty seats. The room was dreary and empty; nothing on the walls, just two ancient Mac computers in the back corner, plastic chairs and a red vinyl loveseat. The plaster walls were cracked, and in a few places crumbled into pyramids of heroin-like powder at the baseboards. It smelled like dust.

In the front corner of the room, an older, beanpole of a man gesticulated wildly at a blonde woman. His giant blue eyes, framed by round, red plastic glasses, were fixed on her face, his long slender hands twirling, rotating, and waving. In the US the only time you wave your hands wildly at someone while talking one inch from their face was right before you attack them, and his flailing gave me anxiety. The blonde woman, though, nodded politely and responded much more quietly than him, hands clasped calmly in front of her body. Though I hadn't spent that much time in Italy, I got the sense that she wasn't Italian. Her body language was just too different from his.

There were three men in our program, seated among the ten women. Two of the men, a bald, bitter-looking man and a kid that looked about twenty, surveyed the room, no doubt checking their options for getting laid. The third guy wore skinny jeans and a t-shirt under an unbuttoned flannel. He sat next to my roommate Kuhle on a red vinyl couch in the back corner, completely glued to his BlackBerry. He only looked up when someone said something stupid to stare at them bemused, before turning back to his phone. Kuhle bounced her legs against the side of the sofa, her hands folded in her lap, smiling. Occasionally, she reached into her purse for something. Her most recent excavation: a jar of Vaseline the size of a suitcase that she delicately dabbed on her lips. Amy flipped through her syllabus, two women behind me laughed together at something that was apparently hilarious, and I took mental notes on every person present. *Different from my friends back home. I don't know how to relate to them.*

The older gentleman finished aggressively gesturing at the Zen-like woman and walked to the front of the classroom. He cleared his throat and clasped his hands together in front of his chest. Amy turned and grinned at me. *Here we go!*

"Hello, new-eh students. My name-eh is Leonardo. I am the director of the program. I have-a been-eh here for many years but once I was like you. A student of deh art! Only not in Italy—I was in the United States and married, but dat's another story. That's a very important story. Perhaps-a we should start from deh beginning."

And he really did start from the beginning. Two hours later he was just barely wrapping up the first half. Leonardo was born and raised in Florence. According to him, he spoke *real* Italian, which he emphasized by speaking very slowly and enunciating "real," unlike the other Italians who apparently spoke a *dirty*, tainted, non-Florentine version or a local dialect. He fell in love with an American student studying in Florence (he shook his head and lowered his eyes as though he were mourning her) and moved to the United States to study art. They divorced, "tragically," because, he waved his hand, "you know how Americans can be, since all of you are American."

Kuhle piped up, "Actually, I'm from South Africa."

He waved at the air like he was brushing her words away.

"It's eh, deh same ting," he replied. "Now where was I? Oh yes."

After he returned to Italy he met and married a wonderful *Italian* woman. Leonardo then turned on the projector to show us pictures of himself and his work. He was an artist, a master of *filo* or string, and he used it in all of his work. This "string" he made himself out of acrylic paint which produced a sort of rubbery, plastic-like tube with little barbs coming off of it. It looked like plastic barb wire in primary colors. In the slides, videos, and photographs, we saw him in military garb, holding an AK-47, posing in front of a billboard of filo, with the filo running horizontally like a wartime fence. He posed nude with filo, made a bike with filo, painted a

21

portrait with filo colors stippled over it, thousands of installations, art pieces; an endless resume of a life wrapped in obsession. The nucleus of an artist is self-loathing but, it turns out, the mitochondria is all-consuming self-love.

My heart sped up when I thought about all of the things I could make that year and what it would mean to me to have that kind of freedom. I needed catharsis more than oxygen.

Leonardo sidestepped away from the center.

"And-a now-a, I-a give deh floor to you all to talk about the work that led you all to us here, to this program."

Wait, what? I grabbed my bag and ripped out the syllabus. Oh no! Oh fuck, no! We were supposed to present a sort of visual resume. Painting was a hobby of mine. I didn't have a lot of training and unless they wanted to see cellphone pictures of a few things I'd done while "drunk painting" in my friend's living room, I didn't have anything to show. My peers took hold of the projector one at a time and it was clear right away that I was out of my league. Kuhle attended film school in Johannesburg and showed clips from a full-length, HBO-quality film she'd made in South Africa. She was only about five foot one but she spoke with such confidence (in that posh South African accent of hers) that the entire room hung on her every word. She could have said, "I have to take a huge crap," and it would have sounded like a queen making a declaration for human rights. Grayson, the guy with the BlackBerry, got up as though he was pained by how boring it all was and did a quick presentation with slides of his photorealistic paintings that were disgustingly good. His self-portrait looked like it was breathing, like he'd trapped his twin inside the canvas. Grayson was completely unimpressed with himself, which naturally made him that much more interesting. Amy gave a moving TED Talk-style presentation about gems, soldering, and a variety of metals with so much passion that even I suddenly cared about different stones. I was next. I hunkered down in my seat and avoided eye contact in hopes of being overlooked and forgotten.

Amy finished and everyone clapped. As she made her way back to her seat, Leonardo scanned the room and his eyes met mine.

"Hey, you, what's your name? Did you go?" he asked, pointing at me.

"Me? No." I answered. My cheeks were flushed.

"Well, come on up-a here den!"

I slowly nodded and tried not to throw up as I made my way to the front. In high school, I frequently took a failing grade over an oral presentation, and at that moment I'd have chosen death by a pack of hungry boars over talking in front of all those people.

I stepped in front of the class and smiled and waved, which was weird and I immediately regretted it. I cleared my throat.

"Sooo, I don't have a slideshow because I lost my jump drive." *Oh, my God why are you lying?* "Actually, no, I didn't make one, honestly. Before I came here I painted a lot of animals having sex at my friend's house. I used acrylic. Like, animals having sex with humans, kind of against their will, you know, all rapey because Leda and the Swan, because literature. I'm also interested in sexuality, feminism and, uh, I like to read a lot, about stuff. Thank you."

Leonardo's eyebrows were fixed in a mountainous *m*-shape across his forehead and his hands were frozen like he'd tried to catch a hot potato. Nobody clapped.

"Okay," he said, "dat was *interesting*. Let's just go ahead and call it a day, shall we?"

I went back to my seat to grab my bag. I turned to Amy, who was throwing things into her backpack. "I have no idea what that was."

"You're crazy, roomie!" she smiled. "I'm off to jewelry design. Love ya, mean it!" And she rushed away with the rest of the class.

On the way to my next class, I spotted Grayson hunched over on the road near Piazza del Duomo in the Florence center. As I got closer I could see that he was photographing something. A dead pigeon that had been smashed by a bike or a car.

"For a project?" I asked when I reached him.

"I might paint it," he said, examining the image on his phone. It must have been satisfactory because he nodded to himself before turning to walk off, pivoting to call over his shoulder, "Gotta go to class! See you later!"

I wandered around the piazza alone, zigzagging in and out of the pods of tourists gazing up at Florence's famous cathedral of Santa Maria del Fiore, otherwise known as the Duomo, with their heads tilted all the way back and cameras jammed into their faces. It's one of the most visited places in Europe, and it was twenty feet away in the center of Piazza del Duomo, surrounded by apartments, restaurants, leather stores, pubs, and gelato shops. I sat on the steps of the cathedral to people-watch for a moment and think back on my first trip to Italy. I'd been there a few years earlier and sat in nearly the same place. It was less crowded then and there had been a lot more alcohol, public nudity, and petty theft involved. It was that trip that initially planted the seed for me to move to Italy one day.

I'd come to Europe with my friend Nathan. Like many Europe first-timers, we did the Paris–Florence thing, spending our first week in Paris then taking an overnight train to Florence. We booked a little "room" on the train with four strangers, each of us in our own little bunk bed eerily close to each other for total strangers. Two of the guys, super young Australian kids with matted hair and sunburned faces, had graduated from high school and were doing a celebratory three-month backpacking trip. The other two guys were in their thirties from somewhere. They had shifty

24

eyes and a vibe that read *murderer*. They didn't talk to any of us at all. Instead, they just stared at me in this uber-soulless sort of way. I was completely creeped out. Nathan stayed up all night making sure I didn't get stolen or killed while I zonked out. Even with the threat of imminent danger, I slept like a baby.

It was 6 a.m. when we got to our hotel in Florence, a sort of dilapidated shithole near the river Arno. The hotel lobby smelled like the BO that oozed from the receptionist, a plump Italian man who snacked on a plate of pastries as he checked us in. Nathan went off to nap while I went out to find coffee. I eventually wandered into Piazza del Duomo, where I stood in front of the cathedral in awe. It was so beautiful, the terracotta roof, the detailed green-and-white marble. I sat down on the steps of the Duomo as the city slowly woke up. Men and women in business clothes walked briskly through the square. Parents ushered their kids to school in little uniforms. People hopped on their bikes in skirts or suits to pedal to work.

After Nathan's nap, we ate pasta marinara in a restaurant near Santo Spirito and did some shopping near Piazza della Repubblica, where he developed a crush on an Italian woman who worked in the Diesel store.

"She's pretty," he said, four hundred times until he got up the courage to talk to her. Her name was Ilaria and she invited us to a concert that night.

"Wanna go?" Nathan asked.

"Yeah, why not?" I shrugged.

The concert was great, but hanging out with Ilaria was not. Turned out that she could inexplicably say, "Come to a concert tonight at this place," in English, but absolutely nothing else. For hours we just kind of stared at her across the table, as if our eyes might magically send words to her brain. Eventually, I excused myself from the table and headed to the bar. I had my first mojito there and fell in lust with the hot bartender who crushed ice cubes by hand with a wooden stick because handcrafted ice mother fuckers! I took my mojito outside into the small courtyard to get some fresh air. It was warm out with a cool breeze, and I was in Italy with a mojito and life was good. I leaned up against a beam and closed my eyes. Then someone poked me in the back and bent to sniff my hair.

I whirled around. "What the fuck are you doing?" A pack of Italian boys stood there with dim, smirky expressions. They laughed.

"It's like they've never seen a woman before," said an Italian guy sitting on a ledge behind me, kicking his Converse against the wall. That's how I met Sergio.

We went bar-hopping in Santo Spirito with Sergio and walked into a bar where an American woman was standing on a chair with her t-shirt pulled up, flashing her boobs to a crowd of Italian guys who had their hands in the air, all "praise the lord of tits!" One of Sergio's friends followed her around afterward, begging to buy her a drink.

"No thanks," she said, "I think I've had enough for the night. I'm going back to my hotel to pee and sleep."

"No, wait!" He dropped to his knees and cupped his hands. "Pee in my hands! Pee in my haaands!"

On our way back to the hotel, Nathan and I stopped in a small kabob restaurant to get a falafel sandwich. We were staring at the menu, trying to figure out what to order, when a redhead with loose messy curls walked in, unzipping her black leather jacket. She turned to us and asked in English, "Waiting to order?" We shook our heads. She winked at us, stepped forward and ordered in Italian. The guy behind the counter called her by name and said something funny; she threw back her head and laughed, leaned on the counter and spoke rapidly, rolling her *r*'s, and only pausing once or twice to check her phone. Both Nathan and I developed an instant crush. She was confident, American, and clearly lived in

Florence. That was the kind of life I wanted: a globetrotter, a cultured, bilingual boss. She grabbed her order and said, "Have a good night!" to us on the way out. My brain filed that scene under "to do."

Back at our hotel, I drunkenly babbled to a very sober Nathan about how I was going to move to Italy one day because it was amazing and romantic and *cool*. I talked so much that I worked up an appetite and realized that at 3 a.m. in a foreign country, I had no idea where to find food. The hotel didn't have room service because it was crap.

"I'll be right back," I said.

"What are you doing?" Nathan asked.

"Scavenging."

"Nooooooo!"

But I was already on my way out.

I tiptoed down the staircase that led to the lobby where that same receptionist, the only one, was asleep on a cot behind his desk. I could hear him snoring and there was the stink of garlic and sleepy breath in the air. When I got to the lobby, I peeked over the desk to make sure he was out cold. One leg hung off the cot, a small blanket was draped over his tummy. I quietly made my way across the lobby towards the kitchen where they served the worst breakfast in the world of porridge, damp bread, and bruised fruit every morning. But breakfast was included with our room so it wasn't exactly stealing because we'd paid for it and hadn't eaten it. At least, that's what I told myself when I pulled open the steel doors and stepped inside the walk-in fridge. I used the front of my shirt as a basket and filled it with fruit, *cornetti*, and a few slices of cheese.

I had to cover my mouth on the way back up the stairs because I kept giggling uncontrollably. Nathan wasn't that excited when I swung open the door carrying my bounty.

"You are fucking crazy, dude," he said.

"I think you mean 'resourceful'."

I sat on my bed shoving cheese in my mouth, grinning like an idiot, never wanting to leave. Pantry-raiding aside, I felt a pure, unbridled freedom unlike anything I'd ever felt before and I never wanted the feeling to end. *I'm going to move here.* I sighed and fell back onto my crumb-dusted pillow for some shut-eye.

* * *

On the steps of the cathedral, I watched Chinese tourists in matching hats follow their leader out of the piazza. Two Italian teenagers to my right smoked cigarettes and talked amongst themselves in a way that made them seem decades older than they were, with expressions best described as an adorable relaxed pessimism. Despite my disastrous first day of class, I still felt pretty good about my decision to move to Florence. I loved the city.

3

Dead Woman in a Sack

I walked into the graduate studio and beelined it for my space on the south side of the building. Grayson hummed and painted the dead bird that he'd taken a picture of in the piazza. An oil painting of a taxidermy deer head titled *Oh Dear* hung in his studio space. Kuhle sculpted her own face out of a block of clay at her desk, and Amy huddled over a pair of jade earrings with tiny tools that looked like they'd been borrowed from elves. My nose twitched from the chemicals that hung in the air: turpentine, varnishes, and gesso. My black ankle boots left footprints in the charcoal dust on the cement floor.

I spun around on my chair and zoned out on a paint smudge on the wall like I'd had a lobotomy. I'd read that JFK's sister had had one, and it basically turned her into a vegetable and she spent the remainder of her life in assisted living, staring off into space, just like me in the studio. I thought about his poor sister more often than was healthy considering I didn't know her. I put on headphones and listened to Bikini Kill and Bob Dylan and waited for inspiration. "Suck my left one," I sang as I scratched terrible ideas in my black Moleskine notebook.

Ideas:

Paint a tree?

Something Persian? ~~Why is my dad always mad at me?~~

Myself in mourning? ~~Why do people die?~~

What if I wrote poetry about paintings and then painted the poetry?←This idea is shit.

School had started just two days earlier but I felt decades behind and constantly lost. In addition to the projects I had to produce for my thesis for grad seminar, I also had four classes: intermediate painting, fresco, Italian and drawing.

Kuhle peeked into my studio space.

"Hello dawling," she smiled.

"Kuhle! Hey babe!" I turned off my headphones and threw them in my tote bag. "Whatcha doing?"

"I'd like to make a stew this weekend. What do you think? I don't like the food here so far, it's a bit bland. And I'd like to make something South African."

"Oh! I like that. You should. I don't know anything about South African food but it sounds like something I'd be into."

"Lovely!" She twirled her braids and smoothed the front of her purple dress. She had paste or something on her cheek.

"Babe, you have like clay right here," I pointed to the side of her face.

"Eh, shame, I'm such a girly girl back home but I feel like I'm going to turn into a real mess here. I'm covered in filth. How are you doing, Angel Muffin?"

Angel Muffin? I smiled. "I'm a little freaked out, honestly. Like, I don't know if I belong here or what I'm doing."

"That's life, darling. None of us know." I nodded because it sounded true. I glanced at the clock: 18:50. I counted the time on my fingers,

"Twelve, thirteen, fourteen, oh, FUCK!" I jumped up. "I have to go to class!"

"Go! Go! See you at home," Kuhle laughed. I grabbed my tote bag with my charcoal and pencils and headed out the doors and into the night towards Via Sant'Antonino.

Professor O'Connor, the drawing professor, gestured in slow motion for all of us to gather around him in a half-moon in front of the whiteboard, so we could all see what he was about to do. There were two other grad students in my class. Violetta, a woman whom I hadn't spoken with yet, and Grayson, who had somehow walked in right before me, both stood across from me on the other side of the semicircle. Everyone else was female and practically an infant: eighteen, maybe nineteen years old, with round cheeks, glowing complexions and optimistic expressions. Behind us, easels were set up in a circle around a metal chair.

"The kind of technique we'll be practicing in this class," Professor O'Connor said, "involves never taking your pencil or charcoal or whatever from the paper. The idea is to sketch out shapes by continuously moving your hand." He pointed in my general direction.

"You, there."

I looked at the girls on my left and right.

He stepped closer, wagging his rough pointer finger in my face. "Yes! YOU THERE! Come here and draw a sack."

"Me?"

"YES!"

I cleared my throat and smiled nervously, "Uhm, what kind of sack?"

Professor O'Connor pursed his lips, then spun around to the board. He made an exaggerated air drawing with his hand around the entirety of the whiteboard.

"Any sack, maybe a sack with a body inside, or presents! Come on then! Draw us a sack! Maybe a woman is trapped inside! Ah, YES! Now, that would be fun!"

Would it? Grayson smiled at me, at Professor O'Connor, then back at me with judgmental fascination. Professor O'Connor turned around and handed me the red marker. I took it reluctantly as if he were handing me a fresh turd. I was panting at that point, sucking in tiny gulps of air. I slowly brought my marker to the board and drew a basketball-sized circle, and the marker squuuueaked all the way around. How do I trap a woman inside? I stared at it. Then added a square on top, like a pumpkin, then a little wiggle for the "string," where it was supposedly tied to stop the kidnapped human from escaping.

Professor O'Connor stepped back to examine my drawing with his hand on his chin.

"What is *that*? That's not a *sack*!" He pointed to it. "Does this look like a sack, anyone? Anyone?" He snatched the marker out of my hand and went to the board where he drew wildly. "You can draw a sack like this, maybe with a woman's leg popping out the top or an arm trying to get out of the side. Your sack doesn't look anything like a sack!"

I'd offended him with my inability to properly contain a body. He exhaled. "All right, fine, everyone, go find an easel."

I took the easel closest to the doorway, next to Grayson. Our model, a thin, thirty-something man with wavy black hair, shuffled to the center of the circle, kicked off his slippers, dropped his robe and sat on the chair naked. He let his legs fall slightly apart, just enough for us to fully capture every pillowy dimple of his balls. He yawned, and his uncircumcised penis flopped to the side like it was playing dead.

Grayson leaned over. "His penis looks like a deflated balloon," he murmured. The female students, many of them in their early twenties and who had never seen an uncut willy before, whispered amongst themselves.

"What's wrong with his wiener?" a young girl to my left asked.

"Nothing," I whispered back, "He's not circumcised."

"Ooooh," she said, "Italians aren't?"

"I don't think most people are. I think it's mostly a Muslim or Jewish thing and I don't know why people in the States do it. I read somewhere that people used circumcision in the US to make masturbation more difficult."

"I had no idea," she said, still staring.

"All right, get to it then," Professor O'Connor said briskly.

The room came alive with circling arms and the low hum of scratching in unison. Every arm moved and I scribbled wildly too. I could smell my charcoal stick as it zoomed around the paper. I tried to capture the essence of the bored naked man by waving my hand like the other students, all "hocus pocus," but without the same result. The professor circled us, yelling things out like, "Keep your hand moving!" and "Don't focus on the details, just map out the shapes."

He paused next to me, bent down into my ear and asked,

"Are you *enjoying* yourself?"

I leaned away from him. "Huh?"

He looked right into my face. "Are you enjoying yourself?"

"Uhm, not particularly," I mumbled under my breath.

He asked me again every time he looped around, "Are you enjoying yourself now?" I finally stopped and turned to Grayson.

"Is it just me or is he fucking taunting me?"

Grayson replied in a sing-song voice, "Are you enjoooooying yourself?" and grinned widely. "Let's go get *un espresso.*"

At the bar across the street, Grayson and I drank our thimbles of espresso standing at the bar like everyone else. The barista was cute, we agreed.

"So where are you from?" I asked.

"New York. You're from Utah, right?"

"Yes."

"What's that like, dumpling?"

"It's fine. So, what brought you to Italy?"

"I needed to get away," he said, playfully, like he was making a joke.

I nodded and finished the last drop of my coffee. "Me too."

After class, I walked home in the dark eating a mini pizza that I'd bought for one euro. The merchants of the San Lorenzo leather market were locking up their carts, shop owners pulled iron gates down in front of their stores, groups of Italian men and women of all ages, dressed fashionably in black, stood in clusters talking outside of a restaurant across from our apartment. The electric air enlivened the city.

When I walked into our bedroom, Amy was studying Italian in bed. I stripped down to my underwear and crawled under the covers.

"Long day, roomie?" Amy turned on her side to face me.

"Hmm. *Weird* day."

"Oh my lord tell me about it," she laughed. "This place is crazy! But it's amazing, isn't it?"

"Yeah, it really is."

Kuhle opened our door and came into our room. She sat on the end of my bed.

"Do you guys mind if I hang out in here for a minute? Debra is already asleep." She lay down next to me and rested her head on my hip.

"Darlings, it's a dream, isn't it? I mean, are we really here?"

"In bed?" asked Amy.

"Shame, you know what I mean," Kuhle said.

"So, what brought you guys here?" I asked.

"Well, that's a loaded question," Amy threw back her head. "Ha! I'll need a few drinks in me for that conversation. No, but really, I guess I'd been wanting to learn new jewelry techniques for a while. Plus, I feel like I'm getting older, I'm thirty-four and if I want to have kids I'd better get to it. I guess it's a last hoorah before I reach the point of no return."

"I feel like I'm on a journey to meet myself for the first time and to figure out who I actually am. I'm figuring me out." Kuhle said.

"I hear ya," Amy said, stretching out.

"And you, Angel Muffin, what are you doing here?" Kuhle asked.

"I don't know."

But I did know. There were a lot of reasons.

It was June of 2008 when I decided to do something different with my life. Obama had just secured the Democratic nomination, Silvio Berlusconi was Prime Minister of Italy and thirty-four people had just been hospitalized in Utah after their "indoor BBQ" imploded. I sat in a strip club in Salt Lake City, watching a tan brunette, Diamond, vigorously dry-hump the stage. She jumped to her feet and grabbed onto the pole, crawled up, and slid down in a split. I tossed a handful of bills at her feet. She winked at me and came over to chat. She had two kids and a degree in accounting. Sir Mix-a-Lot started playing.

"Five bucks for the Running Man," I said, with a grin.

"You're on," she responded, and jumped up and started to run in place, laughing out loud. I'd always enjoyed strip clubs—the elegance, the grit, the raw economics. We high-fived and I threw ten bucks onto the stage.

My phone rang. It was my mom, calling to say hello. I mouthed, "My mom," to Diamond who mouthed, "Ooooh," and crawled towards a man on the opposite side of the stage.

"I'm at the strip club," I told Mom. "Diamond is currently taking money out of some guy's hand with her butt."

"You there alone?" she asked.

"Uh-Uh. My friend and his friends are in the bathroom, probably doing blow," I said. I finished off my vodka soda, the ice cubes clanked against my teeth.

"Well, don't do too much cocaine," my mom said, "You know it ain't good for ya."

"Ok, Mom. Thanks."

The thing about my mom is that she never really felt the need to parent. She kept us alive, made us go to school, but other than that she just believed that everything would be fine, often in spite of myself (or in spite of my two younger brothers). And sometimes we were (but often we weren't). There wasn't a lack of love, just a lack of good old-fashioned know-how. You can't focus on others when you're in survival mode, so insecurity begat insecurity for over one hundred years because that's what happens when children have children. Rinse and repeat.

The strobe lights slowed the action in the room down to a crawl. Dollar bills seemed to freeze mid-air, the faces of customers blinked behind the darkness and then appeared suddenly. The beading sweat of my cocktail stuttered down the side of my glass onto my hand. The smell of cheap musk and Jim Beam wafted around the stage.

Diamond twerked for a small group of leering man-boys that had just sat down next to me. They peacocked for each other, tried to sit taller, to seem nonchalant about the taut, bouncing buttocks two inches from their faces. The eldest-looking one, maybe twenty-two, wore outdated Levi's and a black shirt. He caressed his chin-strap of patchy fuzz as he turned towards me.

"So you're here alone?" he asked.

The overconfident (deeply insecure) cock of his head and aggressive smirk instantly gave him away. I knew his type. He was the kind of guy who watched too much porn and finger-banged anyone unlucky enough to go home with him like he was sending a goddamn telegram to her ovaries.

"No, there's a group of really coked-out defense attorneys around here somewhere," I motioned towards the bathroom.

"You a lesbian?" He looked from me to Diamond.

"I just really like strip clubs. It's more entertaining than a bar and the dancing is coo—"

"Got a boyfriend?" he interrupted.

"No. And I'm not looking."

"What a bitch," he scoffed to his friends.

"It's true," I winked at him proudly.

Diamond collected wads of cash from the stage, smoothing out the wrinkles before adding the bills to the phonebook-sized stack she kept folded on her ankle. She stepped into a floor-length, sheer black dress.

"Hey thanks," she said, reaching for her plastic heels.

"Have a good night!" I waved, and hailed the waitress—a silicone-enhanced blonde—for another Ketel One greyhound. I finished it and ordered another. Then another. I sat back and felt guilty. Tomorrow I'd be hungover. I knew I was partying too much and hadn't done anything productive in months. My head spun. I needed to move on to the next phase of my life.

The following morning, I felt the way that people feel when they are out of options and experiencing regret. It's a shitty feeling-cocktail of dread, dehydration, a slight unspecified fuzziness, and dull muscle pain mixed with what-the-fuckery. At twenty-seven, I'd already finished my second useless bachelor's degree in sociology, which I thought would have been a lot better than my first degree in literature because it involved some math. After graduation things got really confusing. I'd gone to college. Twice. After that, what was there? My parents were well-intentioned but simply couldn't tell me anything that didn't suck. My mom never went to college; instead, she drove forklifts, worked in construction, and stripped to put food on our table, so anytime I talked with her she was all, "You have a really nice body, you know," or, "Have you considered welding? Those people make soooo much money!" My father studied engineering and political science, but he's a businessman, and wealth seemed to top his list of priorities.

Growing up in Utah, I never quite felt like I fit into a world of strip malls; instead I fantasized about being a woman known for a sort of vague, unnamed success, the kind who wears a silver mane kept loosely and stylishly in a French twist, paints nude models and throws parties with friends named "Gregory" and "something, something, the Third."

There weren't any people like that in my family. My father brought a foreign language, culture and food from Iran, but my great-grandfather allegedly smoked all of his millions away in random opium dens, leaving my father a total hater in the fun department. My grandmother on my mother's side was an excellent artist but she smoked Virginia slim cigarettes, drank hot toddies, and said things like "Eat shit, fuckwad," in Utah vernacular. I knew what kind of person I wanted to be but without a goal list, I was well on my way to becoming my biggest fear: mediocre.

I'd always had a thing for lists. If I could stay occupied, if I could keep moving, then I didn't have to think about how overwhelming it was to actually be alive. I loved college because it was essentially just a big list. Every time I finished a class I'd get to put an *x* next to the class number. I'd repeat it a few dozen times until someone eventually handed me a degree. Inhale. Check. Exhale. It was like an orgasm but without the messy clean-up.

Sprawled out on my mom's doody-colored carpet in her guest room, I wrote down my five-year plan in a black Moleskine notebook:

Learn one foreign language
Learn how to cook
Live in a foreign country
Go to graduate school
Learn how to paint better

After an hour or so on Google, I found a graduate-level art program in Florence. I applied as an art history student and was accepted a few weeks later. Then I changed my focus from art history to fine art, overly confident of my own creative abilities but dead set on living the kind of life that was decidedly more "me."

Things got complicated when my mom found out that my younger brother Mitch had been crushing up pills and shooting them into his arm. The thermal shirts that he'd been wearing in July were kind of a dead giveaway. I wrote the art school to defer my attendance and put off Italy to be a better sister. As children we were close—I watched him, gave him his nebulizer when his asthma attacks swept in during the night. I fought with daycare providers when he'd cry in the toddler room on the other side of the building. But I was only four years his senior, and there was only so much I had control over. Things changed when I turned twelve and became a self-involved asshole like twelve-year-olds do, and so helping him kick drugs was a chance for me to make up for all the elder sibling torment. My mom and I focused on getting Mitch clean and into culinary school because being a chef was his dream.

Just a few months later, he did get clean. He started culinary school at the Salt Lake community college the last week of August in 2008 and was loving it. Staying was totally worth it. He was finally doing well and could work towards his aspiration of becoming a chef. In his resource writing class, he wrote an adorable essay about how I was one of his heroes because I had helped him to change his life.

Then, unexpectedly, on September 23rd, 2008, my little brother, the one with the golden curls and ocean eyes, went to sleep on the floor of a new friend's home, and never woke up. A doctor had prescribed him Valium for his panic attacks but had failed to inform him, or any of us, that he couldn't drink alcohol while taking it. A pill that was supposed to make him feel safe when he was scared had slowly suffocated him while he slept.

The cliché "there are no words" exists because really there aren't enough words in any language to describe how heartbreaking it is to lose a sibling; to know the crushing internal pain. Then, on top of the pain, sat the guilt. I was in San Francisco at a birthday party the night he died. I was the one who had asked the doctor to prescribe him something for his anxiety. I didn't know how to live with myself. I could have done more or done less; either way, I was convinced that it was entirely my fault.

By early 2009, I didn't want to move to Italy for self-improvement anymore. I needed to move for self-preservation.

I thought about all of the things that led me to Florence, to that bedroom, lying next to Kuhle with Amy on the other side of the room. But I didn't say them out loud, not yet. Not because they were secret but because I couldn't think about them. It was easiest to push my brother's face out of my mind, to bury his memory because I felt ashamed, responsible and broken. And, like both of my parents, I'd never been good at dealing with feelings. We were all quiet and I assumed that they were reflecting on how they ended up in Italy too, the many reasons, both said and unsaid, that would lead a person across the Atlantic to pursue a new life essentially from scratch. Turns out, we all need a break from our demons once in a while.

4

Paint Me a Thousand Vaginas

October 2009

Leonardo asked if he could speak with me after our weekly graduate seminar class to talk about "something very important." Grayson stood behind me, listening with his usual level of amusement like he'd just stepped into a circus and was seeing clowns for the first time. I shifted my weight back and forth while I waited for whatever Leonardo had to say.

"What I wanted to tell you," Leonardo gestured like he was cupping someone's balls, "is that you're just-a too-a fiery," he continued, "for most of the professors here. Trust me, you-a need someone who can-a calm your fire. So, for your major professor, I have selected someone for you."

I crossed my arms. From what I understood, Italians were supposedly pretty feisty themselves and I hadn't done anything particularly intense since I'd arrived. By the way he cautiously measured his words, you'd think that I'd tried to stab him.

"I'm assigning you to Demyan," he continued. "He'll be able to manage you."

"'Manage' me? I don't know what that means exactly. Can you tell me why I need to be 'managed'?" I stepped closer to him, which prompted him to step back. I rolled my eyes.

"I don't understand. Have I personally offended you in some way? Is this about the animal sex? It was a bad presentation! I get it! I'm *sorry*!"

He waved me away. "It's-a for your-a own good-a. You have-a to-a trust-a me," he said, and walked off. I stood there dumbfounded until Jenny, a ceramist and self-confessed hippie yelled, "Hey, do you like my balls?" and held up a ceramic sphere she'd been working on. I gave her a thumbs up.

"What was that all about?" Grayson asked. "This entire thing is fascinating."

I threw up my hands. "I honestly don't know. It's complete bullshit. What does 'a-too-a-fiery' even mean? Do you think I act too fiery?

"I mean, you're not a *complete* crazy person," Grayson said, sarcastically. I pretended to be offended. We wandered over to Violetta's space to watch her mold wax into figurines. I told her about my chat with Leonardo.

"I think that you frighten him," she teased and you could slightly detect her Russian accent. I'd just become friends with Violetta during our Intermediate Italian class and already loved her. She was a Californian who'd studied engineering at Berkeley, whose family had moved to the US from Uzbekistan as refugees when the political climate became unsafe for the jewish community. She continued to mold her wax ball, her head down, and then glanced up through her long eyelashes.

"But really," she said, "it seems that he's not used to women who say what they think. Don't you agree?"

"But we've only been here for a couple of weeks and I've never really talked to him. It's baffling."

She smiled and her dimples showed. "I'd take it as a compliment," she said, reaching into her giant tote bag and pulling out a chocolate bar.

"Here," she handed it to me, "this will make you feel better."

I perked up.

I begrudgingly emailed my assigned professor that night before bed and was surprised when he responded ten minutes later. He asked to meet in the studio the next day so we could "get to work immediately." I'd never met Demyan, never even seen him, but a few of the other grad students had him for classes and I'd gathered that he was an eastern European artist in his early forties, "brilliant and talented," "sexy" as two students put it, and "scary as shit." According to student folklore, he made people cry, *often*.

While waiting for Demyan in the studio, I Googled artists, how to write an artist statement, and trolled images for inspiration. At exactly noon, right on time, Demyan glided into the studio. He was attractive in his fitted trousers, a v-neck t-shirt, and Chelsea ankle boots. His messy dark hair was chin length and hung in his dark, brooding eyes. He had an air about him, like smoke from smoldering coals.

He narrowed his eyes to inspect me as I greeted him with my hand out. He smiled, which hardened into intense focus. Was he disappointed already? He took a seat. I scooted my stool in front of him, crossed my legs, and waited for him to speak.

"So, tell me, what do you do?" he inquired, crossing his legs.

Nothing. I was a fraud posing as an artist in hopes of learning cool skills that I'd probably never use until my forties after going through a divorce. I was confused. I cleared my throat and leaned forward. I avoided crossing my arms because I'd read that people cross their arms when they're insecure.

"I'm sorry? In general, or in this studio specifically?" I asked, to buy more time.

He narrowed his eyes.

"I suppose that you can tell me what you do in general though I'm more concerned with what you do here specifically?" he purred, a smirk flickering across his lips.

"I went to school for lit and sociology. I liked writing about people." I'd just read about Sophie Calle the day before in the library. I went on, "So, if I could combine art with that, um, Kant, the kingdom of ends, morality, sexual fluidity, and that stuff. The little human in the jar that wants to die, Sybil of Cumae? Soo, um, yes." I had just successfully and weirdly name-dropped all the things that had been of interest to me in the past decade.

He moved his hair out of his face. "Uh-huh. And, who is your favorite painter?"

I didn't have a favorite painter on standby. It would be too obvious to pick Michelangelo or Donatello or any of the Ninja Turtles so I fumbled for someone who I thought would make me seem more artsy and less generic, less like a fake. Then I remembered the gallery with Leonardo the week before and the artist who seemingly painted nothing but abstract genitalia. Jesus, how long had it been since I'd had sex?

I blurted out his name. "Burri!"

He sat back in his chair and looked amused. "Why?"

My foot tapped against the metal of the stool. "Vaginas?"

"I'm sorry?"

"He paints penises and vaginas and I studied sexuality at school so that's interesting to me." What the fuck was I saying? *Penises!*

Demyan moved in closer, his lips curled up. He ran his hand through his hair again and watched my face, seemingly amused.

"Is that what you think? I've never heard that before. Interesting take on his work." He stood abruptly. "Take me to your studio space."

He strode purposefully into the other room while I trotted behind him.

45

My studio space was composed of three wooden dividers, the same as everyone else's, only all of my three makeshift walls were bare except for one large oil painting I'd taped crookedly to the center, an outline of a nude model bent over. He shook his head, one hand resting on his hip and the other holding his long bangs out of his eyes. My peers had already painted a few impressive pieces. Grayson had painted about fifty, ranging from deer heads to rolls of toilet paper. I'd scribbled out a few cartoonish images that were on the floor tucked mostly out of the way: a tree in the middle of an empty field, a doll wearing a plague mask, a dramatic piece of a girl crying on a Persian-inspired chair that was supposed to pay homage to the crappy feelings I was currently harboring towards my dad. Even looking at it made me feel pathetic. Just how badly did I vie for his approval, knowing full well that I'd never get it?

"What have you been doing these past few weeks?" he asked, turning towards me.

"We've seen a lot of churches?" I stammered, "I've been collecting ideas fo—"

"You need to get started. Just paint *something*. This isn't terrible, this *thing* of the woman bent over, although that is not at all what a vagina actually looks like up close. You know that, right? I mean, you have seen one, I imagine?"

"Yes, I do. I have one, so..."

He stepped right up to the canvas and stared at the nude figure's lady cave, straight into what looked like a hot-dog bun that had fallen slightly open.

"The other things are, well, I don't know what it is that you thought you were doing. You like Burri, so pull from that inspiration. Why don't you paint vaginas? Paint eleven vaginas this week. You could use the practice." He pointed at the hot-dog bun hoo-haw.

46

"Eleven vaginas? Human vaginas? Like, just a floating vagina?"

"Why not? And the more detail the better." He smirked again. His constant shift between cold, intense stares and random smirks freaked me out. I couldn't read him and being near him felt like little spider legs were dancing up the nape of my neck.

"I want this entire studio space covered in work by the time I get back," he said. "You've been here for long enough. I'm a little frustrated by how little you've accomplished in these first few weeks here."

Vaginas. I wasn't opposed to vaginas.

"Okay," I responded.

He left and the doors slammed behind him.

I stared at my easel. But *whose vagina?*

The next day, I went to the studio to Google and print porn. The images weren't the best quality, so I took awkward pictures of my own vagina, too. I had no idea how intricate female anatomy was until I'd tried to sketch out the curves of my labia on an oven-sized canvas. It was a little off-putting to stare at my own vagina for hours on end because it's the kind of thing you start to overanalyze.

A guy in our program, Senza Capelli, with whom I rarely spoke, muttered in passing, "Painting nudity is so freshman year of art school."

"I'm basically a freshman, asshole," I called after him.

Every evening for a week, I stared into *Hustler* centerfolds of women all spread-eagled. My eyes had started to cross, my wrist cramped and my feet hurt from standing in boots all day, bundled up as if I was preparing to trek across Siberia. It had been raining nonstop for weeks, water collected in ponds all over the city and the school refused to turn on the heat.

One day I was sitting there, shading a clitoris, while swaddled in a dusty blanket thinking about pictures of Van Gogh in his twenty layered sweaters and nodding emphatically to myself, *yeah, me too*, when Grayson danced over to my studio space.

"I'm going to YAG tonight, this gay club nearby. Do you wanna come?"

"Yes, absolutely. Get me the fuck out of here," I said. I threw down my paintbrush, grabbed my bag and followed him.

A movie screen covered the back wall of YAG where the music video for Lady Gaga's "Bad Romance" played. Grayson and I beelined it for the bar. The bartender, a slight man in a t-shirt and skinny jeans leaned across. "*Dimmi.*"

"*Per me*," I thought for a second, "*un vodka soda con* lemon. Er, *limone.*"

The bartender nodded.

Grayson leaned forward flirtatiously, "*Un mojito per favore*," then turned and surveyed the dance floor.

"Let's go join that gaggle of gays," he suggested.

We grabbed our drinks and headed over, wedging ourselves beside a group of drag queens. We danced together and then the group of men next to us started dancing at us. One of them, a tiny pocket-sized Italian guy in a blue tank top walked towards me like he was on a catwalk, pivoted, and flipped his head in my direction. He wanted to have a dance-off.

I downed my drink. Then I pranced toward him, flicked my hair, spun around, touched the ground and shook my ass at him. The crowd of men erupted in cheers and the guy in the tank top hugged me. Then it was Grayson's turn: he started with a pirouette, shimmied his shoulders, tossed his head back, and did a body roll. The crowd erupted again.

Grayson and I went back to dancing. He leaned over and leered, "Are you enjoying yourself?"

I pretended to dry-heave. "Oh, God. Please stop."

"It's fascinating that everyone is actually insane. Like this is a place for real-life crazy people."

I nodded. "That seems accurate."

"And what is going on with all of the professors? It's like they want to kill you or screw you."

"Is that what it is? I just assumed that they can easily spot frauds."

"No, I don't think that's it. You have weird pheromones or something. I mean, I'm gay and not at all attracted to your, uhm"—he glanced down to my crotch—"but still, a very small part of me kind of wants to have sex with you."

I laughed. I'd never felt attractive. As a kid, I idolized women who didn't look anything like me, blondes with milky-pale skin, like Madonna. My olive skin and dark hair seemed boring. It was death by comparison. I wondered if other women felt that way, too.

"If you do warm up to my anatomy, I can paint you a portrait," I humped the air.

"I feel like your vagina paintings are legitimately giving Leonardo a heart attack. The other day he asked me, 'But a-why she is a-doing dis?'"

"Poor guy. Next time tell him it's his own damn fault for assigning me a professor to calm my fire."

"You scare people."

"Clearly."

I adored Grayson and not only because he wasn't afraid to aggressively dance-battle but because I liked how he made me feel about myself when I was around him: safe. And I didn't feel like I needed to make myself small around him. Unlike a lot of people in my life, like Leonardo who wanted to tame my fire, my mom who had too many of her own problems to think about mine, and my dad, whose personality was just so big that he unknowingly dwarfed everyone around him, Grayson made me feel like I could be big and he encouraged it.

A guy walked up behind Grayson and dry-humped him. I used it as an opportunity to go pee. When I came back they were making out.

"I'm heading out," I interrupted, "Have fun."

"See you tomorrow, sweet pea," Grayson called after me.

I winked at him and headed into the empty streets. I would have never walked across town at 2 a.m. alone in Salt Lake City but in Florence, I happily meandered alone in the dark and the rain and felt fine. While Florence isn't a blissful utopia (there's crime and shit happens), there was something about the place that never felt scary. For the most part, nobody bothered me and I could concentrate on my thoughts instead of looking over my shoulder. It was empowering to enjoy the night and the solitude.

In my Italian class at a bright and shining 9 a.m., our teacher, "Shocked Priscilla" as we'd nicknamed her, wrote verb conjugations on the board. She was a pretty Florentine woman with a sort of innocent kindness about her that we unanimously adored. Anytime we fed her a little tidbit of Americana she'd gasp in shock, hence the nickname. I was slightly hungover and tired because I'd been out till late at YAG the night before. Grayson sat next to me, all fresh-faced and exuberant somehow.

I leaned over and whispered, "Did you go home with that dude last night?"

"Sì," he answered, waggling his eyebrows.

"Who did you go home with Grayson?" Violetta giggled.

"Grayson, you get more action than a post office," Amy said, "and I'm jealous."

Shocked Priscilla turned around. "Okay, let's practice now. Everyone tell me what you ate for breakfast this morning."

"*Ho mangiato* oatmeal," a woman in our class said.

Priscilla put her hand on her chest. "But-a what-a is oat-a-meal?"

"It's like mush made from oats," Grayson explained. "You eat it with fruit or sugar and milk."

Priscilla put her hand over her mouth. "*Ma, no! Really?*"

We all nodded our heads that yes, it was a real thing that people ate.

Amy ate yogurt, Grayson had a chocolate *cornetto* with coffee, and Violetta hadn't had breakfast because she was running late. I'd done my homework and practiced my verbs and I knew what to say. I repeated the line in my head over and over until it was my turn: "Oh mangiato, oh mangiato, oh mangiato."

But when Priscilla pointed to me, my brain turned off and I became really defensive, my face all squished into a pout.

"I, uhm, I…" And my cheeks turned pink. In English, I said, "I ate a cornetto, too. And a cappuccino. And yogurt." Priscilla smiled and told me how to say it in Italian: "*Anch'io, ho mangiato un cornetto, un cappuccino, e un yogurt.*"

I nodded. "Yep, exactly. That."

Grayson shook his head disapprovingly at me.

After class, I waded through the marshy roads towards the studio to kill some time until drawing that evening. I thought about my night out with Grayson and how the way we see ourselves is so rarely the way that other people see us. At least, it was for me. Back home, people described me as "confident" but the truth was that I typically sought easy victories and stayed within my comfort zone, and when you play to your strengths all the time, it's easy to give the impression of fearlessness. That's why art school and Italian were so hard for me; I was completely out of my realm of expertise and put in a position, daily, where I couldn't do anything right, my shortcomings were put on display and I couldn't bullshit my way out of it. Shame, really, because I'd mastered bullshit at age five when I realized that adults weren't smart, trustworthy, or consistent.

My coat pocket buzzed. A text from Demyan: "I'm swinging by." *Fuuuck.* I kicked up the pace and jogged the rest of the way to the studio.

Demyan marched straight up to my vagina (the one that was hanging on the wall, not the one packed away in my thong). He inspected it so closely that he was practically standing inside of it, and I stood next to him all, ta-da! I did it!

Demyan cleared his throat. "What is this, exactly?"

"It's a lady bit?"

He shook his head. "This looks like a piggy bank opening. I want to take out my change and shove it in there." He jammed a hand into his trouser pocket, pulled out a one-euro coin and banged it against the painting repeatedly. *Clack, clack, clack!*

"This is a children's savings account, not a vagina."

"If you put coins in it that's just asking for a yeast infection," I mumbled under my breath.

He cocked his head to the side. "And where is the other important hole?" he asked. "What goes next to the vagina? Where is the *anus?*" He pointed to the painting with both hands, "There should be a vagina here and the anus next door, it's clearly supposed to be right here. Right. Here." Demyan jabbed the canvas with his finger, *tap, tap, tap.* "Try again. I think you can do better."

He smirked, and this time I glared back in defiance but I kept my mouth shut. Mostly because there was something otherworldly about him, like "I'm actually four hundred years old and I maintain my youth by drinking the tears of idiots and bathing in the blood of virgins" otherworldly.

Demyan left. I balled up my fists and exhaled. A familiar darkness swept in and whispered *you're not good enough*; it was the same voice that showed up anytime I hung out with my dad. I grabbed a bottle of wine that I kept behind some blank canvases and took a swig straight from the bottle. I walked over to Grayson's space. He was staring at his painting of a stack of toilet paper.

"Hi," I waved dolefully.

"Hello, doll face."

"I'm pretty sure I'm going to fail," I said, running my hands through my hair. Then I told him what had happened with Demyan and he listened attentively.

"Hmm. Let's talk about it on the way to drawing," he said.

We walked along Via Faenza, around ancient buildings and statues created before telephones or penicillin. We stepped over dog shit, which littered the sidewalks, and dodged Italian businessmen in slim-cut suits who played an aggressive form of sidewalk chicken.

"Maybe I shouldn't be here," I said self-consciously, "I don't know what I'm doing."

A bus passed by and nearly hit my elbow because the street was so narrow that it barely fit and even the slightest mistake—a texting driver, a sneeze—could have killed us.

"What if I did an installation about people getting hit by a bus?" I joked.

Grayson exhaled, "Don't *try* to make art, just make art."

"What? That doesn't even make sense. You're speaking in riddles."

"Let things come to you; stop trying so hard. You do this thing where you have really good ideas until you try to force it. Just stop trying and do what you like."

"Fiiiiine. But—"

"*Mamma mia*! Look at the little shorts on him. What do you think he'd do if I just latched onto his back like a baby monkey?" He pointed to an Italian jogger wearing toddler-sized Spandex. I laughed and grabbed

Grayson's hand and we interlocked fingers. He was right: I needed to get out of my head, to stop trying to strong-arm everything into place. I would try to let go and *enjoy* myself.

5

Obituary

The studio was empty and quiet in a post-apocalyptic kind of way. Often, we forgot to turn on the lights. It was October and everyone had gone on a trip for fall break, except for me and Grayson who stayed in Florence. Amy went to Venice, Jenny went to Croatia, Violetta was in Russia, others went camping or to Switzerland. I stayed behind to work on my grad projects because the first semester was almost over and I had so much to do. I had abandoned painting for installation and digital media and stuck to things that I knew: being a complete weirdo. And I was having a glorious time.

I set up a sign in the main building one afternoon: Video Project: Need to Interview Women on Their Bodies. I sat and waited. A group of undergrad women walked by and paused in front of the sign. One of the women, a blonde, smiled and said, "I'll totally do it." She sat down across from me, the white wall behind her acted as a backdrop. I pointed the camera at her and held up a sign that read: Describe an Orgasm. She looked directly into the camera and leaned forward.

"An orgasm is an intense full-body experience," she annunciated slowly. "It's hot, painful, delicious, euphoric, and wet... " End recording. The next woman sat down and when I showed her the sign, she blushed and said, "I wouldn't know, I'm saving myself for marriage."

"Oh, totally respect that," I replied. "It doesn't have to be an orgasm related to sex though." And then she just stared at me, baffled.

"I've never, uhm, done *that* either." Then we looked at each other awkwardly until she got up and walked away, and I thought, *never?* No shower heads, no vibrator, no finger DJ, *nothing?*

For another project, I made little journals for the women in my program. I wanted them to write about anything related to the female body; how they viewed themselves, their secrets, their sex life. What do we tell ourselves that nobody else gets to hear?

I was editing my orgasm video in the studio when I heard quick footsteps behind me and I thought, This is how I die, right here in Italy, murdered in the empty art studio. But then Demyan came into view, which was somehow worse.

"I thought I'd swing by to see what you're working on now," he said. I stood up and leaned back on my desk. He searched the walls for paintings that weren't there anymore.

"So, okay, please don't kill me, but in the process of mutilating porn star clitori, I became interested in some other things related to the female body. I've started some projects but nothing I can show you yet. I need some time."

He stepped uncomfortably close to me and lowered his head like he was going in for a kiss. I held my breath.

"Fine," he smiled playfully, "I'll wait until the show next month. But I'm expecting to see something thoughtful and interesting."

I nodded. "Okay."

"Enjoy the break," he said and lingered, still close to me. I could smell him, the soap on his skin. Then he straightened up and sauntered off.

I turned back to my computer and typed "Oh-Oh-Orgasm" in a twenty-sized font, the sign that would hang above my video at the show. Grayson popped into my space.

"Demyan wants to put the sex on you," he said.

"I think what you mean is Demyan wants to murder me, in a secret cave somewhere. Which is similar but different."

"Not true," he said, pivoting and walking off. "Don't leave, I'll be back."

I remembered that I'd picked up a letter that morning from the main building, which I'd thrown in my bag to open when I had time to read. I fished it out and looked at the name on the return address again. From Mom to me. I ripped it open and dug inside to pull out a small, rectangular newspaper clipping. A note fell to the ground. I picked it up and flipped it over.

Misty,
Here's the one-year anniversary obituary of your brother's death.
Love you, Mom.

My brother's sparkling eyes shone, even in gray newspaper print. His curly blond hair and a huge grin. I couldn't swallow and my hands began to tremble. Why would she send me this?

I hung the obituary up on my studio wall, slumped into my chair and stared at it. I remembered the last time I saw him alive, in a café in downtown Salt Lake City. He had a beer, I was with a friend and distracted. I gave him money from his student loan because he didn't have a bank account and I never saw him again.

Grayson danced over, "Want to go to lunch Pean—" He stopped short when he saw the obituary. "What's that?" he asked, pointing.

"My mom sent it to me in the mail. I don't know why..."

"Who is it?"

"My little brother. He died last year."

"My mom, she dead, too," Grayson said in his fake Italian accent, a thing that he did sometimes for fun or when situations were awkward or uncomfortable.

"Lunch?" he asked.

I nodded.

In the only Chinese restaurant in the center of Florence, Grayson and I ordered hot-and-sour soup, vegetable fried rice, and sweet-and-sour tofu.

"So," Grayson asked, "what happened to your brother? If you don't mind talking about it."

"I don't mind," I took a sip of water.

Then I explained it, all of it, from the very beginning.

My little brother Mitch had been a sick baby and was often in the hospital. I loved him so much that I wanted to be a nurse so I could spend more time with him. Then he became an annoying little brother and we fought constantly, then a nerdy teenager who embarrassed me. He was angsty and sensitive, and I was self-involved and tormented him.

"He never had very many friends and I wasn't very nice to him," I said. "I didn't understand anything about social anxiety back then." I thought about the time that I told him to stop wearing Wranglers when he was ten because he "looked like a fucking nerd."

I told Grayson how after years of being picked on and outcast and trapped between his drug-addict father and our mom, who'd ended up in a bad marriage, Mitch had turned to drugs.

58

"Tough love doesn't work," I said. But then he wanted to get clean and he came to me and Mom for help. We were so proud of him.

"He wanted to open a restaurant," I told Grayson. "He'd been in school for one month and I went out of town to San Francisco to visit a friend for my birthday. And I got a call at 5 a.m. from my mom telling me that he had died at some stranger's house. That was the worst morning of my life. And I spent the year after that mostly drunk, bawling, and hating myself." I said this flatly. I pictured my brother trying on his chef coat for the first time and quickly pushed it out of my head.

"I'm sorry," Grayson said.

"Thanks. And your mom?"

He told me how his mom had died when he was a kid from cancer. And how his dad had raised him and his brother.

"I don't think people are ever the same after someone that close to them dies."

He was right. It took a lot of energy every day to not think about him, to not think about every single thing I could have done differently and better. When I let the thoughts in, my brain was overtaken by this insidious dark cloud of shame and regret and a chorus screamed, "IT'S YOUR FAULT! YOURS!" If I hadn't gone out of town. If I'd only stayed in Utah. If only. I winced and pushed the thoughts away and spooned more rice on my plate.

"So, are you ready for the show?" I asked.

"Yeah, I'm not doing anything particularly special for it. You still stressing out?"

"Not as much," I said and stretched my arms above my head.

A few weeks later, I finished my "pieces" exactly three hours before the doors to our fall show opened. I displayed two videos: my *Oh-Oh-Orgasm* video and a black-and-white video of me convulsing or something. I actually don't know what the point of the second video was. I was still trying to figure that out.

I'd collected the body journals from most of the women in my grad program, including Kuhle, Amy and Violetta. A few women had written about what it meant to be a woman to them, a few described recent sexual adventures in explicit detail (including double penetration), and one woman wrote a moving entry about her struggle with body dysmorphia.

I taped up photocopies of the journal entries and looped the videos on repeat. I stepped back and felt okay for the first time: I was a goddamn *genius.* Then it hit me that people were going to actually see all of this and *judge me.* Or worse, what if people didn't want to see it? What if they skipped over my space altogether? What if Demyan told me that he hated it in front of everyone? *Oh fuck.* What had I done?

In our apartment, we listened to music and drank wine while we got ready. Our room smelled like soap and perfume, and we smelled like perfume and Chianti. Amy pulled on a red-and-gold dress that Violetta had made for her out of silk scarves and finished straightening her wild blonde curls. She looked like a completely different person with long sleek locks. Kuhle wore a deep purple dress, Debra Darlington was nowhere to be found and Karen had already left for the show because she was always early. I wore my standard going-out outfit: a black dress and black booties. We took a collective deep breath, clinked glasses and left.

The studio had been cleaned and transformed into a gallery. Instead of turpentine, it smelled of bruschetta, and works of art hung on studio walls orderly and with purpose. I hugged Violetta, then hid in the bathroom because I'd started to freak out a little. I breathed in slowly, held it for ten seconds, exhaled slowly, and repeated 3,456 times until the crippling fear subsided.

I meandered around the room, pausing at Amy's intimate photographs of eyes, arms, torsos, and bodies; Jenny's large monochromatic painting of two women embracing; and Violetta's tiny wax objects. Since I lacked any real talent I'd convinced myself for the sake of self-preservation that if people didn't get my stuff they just didn't get *real* art. As people trickled in off of the street to peruse the studio I hovered by the wine, out of sight of my own work. I was afraid of the crinkled noses, the narrowed eyes, and yet, more than being an object of derision, I was worried about being ignored.

An hour into the event, Violetta came up next to me and waved her glass of wine towards the other side of the studio, which was blocked by the beam I'd positioned myself behind.

"Wow, look at your studio space!"

Panicked, I stepped out from behind the wall. Ben the librarian sat cross-legged on the floor, wearing my headphones, watching the entirety of my video. Five other people stood behind him, reading each of the journal entries. The tension melted away from my back and chest. But then Demyan entered and my throat closed up a little. He started at the space furthest from mine and worked his way down. He spent a lot of time with Kuhle's sculpture and Grayson's paintings until he finally reached my space. He put on the headphones, listened to the orgasm video and read the journals.

I walked right up to him. "You've found my new work," I said, smiling and tilting my head. I was flirting, *why* was I flirting? The answer: to reclaim a little power. It didn't hurt that he seemed to ooze sex, leaving a trail behind him like a snail.

He grinned. "Yes, it's interesting. You could have made some small adjustments but it's not bad. Keep it up."

He took a sip from his wine glass, brushed his hair out of his face, and walked away, leaving me somewhere between triumphant and confused. What small adjustments? I rolled my eyes, *whatever*, and wandered off to see Grayson's pieces.

We'd found a rock-and-roll pub called Angie's through our school's nude model, Lorenzo. He'd promoted his club nights while sitting awkwardly on a metal chair with his elephant trunk resting nonchalantly on his leg. "If you like-a to-a dance-a, I make deh music-a. Come!" And a few of us were able to take him seriously while sketching his foreskin.

Angie's had a specific odor, somewhere between a stripper's sweaty, yet fragrant thigh towards the end of a long, lucrative shift, and a men's urinal. Angie's wasn't classy or even hygienic but the place was full of chill locals, alternative types who were too awkward to spike my vodka with rape meds. The other popular dance clubs like Thrice were packed with perverts who slicked back their hair, wore too much cologne, and preyed relentlessly on barely conscious American teenagers. They were mosquitos, rather than men.

Lorenzo was in the DJ booth in the back room, next to the makeshift dance floor. Soft-core seventies porn played on a small TV on the back wall. He played Depeche Mode then Fleetwood Mac and "Bad Romance" by Lady Gaga. It instantly felt like a home away from home; like the subculture clubs in Salt Lake, it felt dangerously safe.

Kuhle, Grayson, Jenny, and I were on the dance floor grooving out to MGMA.

"I'm going to get a drink," I yelled over the music.

"I'll come, too," said Grayson. He followed me to the bar where the bartender, a rugged hottie, was making a drink for a couple of women.

"Oh, he's cute," Grayson commented.

I agreed. I walked up to him and leaned over the bar to rest my palm on the back of his hand. "Hey honey." He looked up at me and I locked eyes with him. "Can I get a vodka soda and whatever my friend wants?"

"You most certainly can," he said in an Australian accent.

"Which part of Australia are you from?" I asked.

"Melbourne."

"Never heard of it," I replied with a wink. He slid our drinks towards us. I threw ten euro on the bar.

"It's only six euro," he smiled.

"Keep the change. What's your name?"

"Damian."

"Keep the change, Damian."

Grayson held up his mojito. "Cheers."

"Cheers," I took my drink. Damian stared at me with a crooked smile. I grabbed Grayson's hand and led him back to the dance floor as Damian watched. I could feel him scanning us.

"Also, if I were you, I'd have sex with him immediately," Grayson said.

"Yeah?" I asked.

"Yes. He looks dirty in a hot way. The things I would do to him." He twirled. Students poured into the bar and before we knew it, we were packed in like sardines. I went back to the bar to grab another drink.

"Damian," I called as he went behind the bar, "could I grab another drink?"

"Absolutely. So, can I ask what you're doing here?"

"Dancing."

"Yeah, I can see that. In Italy. You studying?"

"Yes."

"And before studying?" he asked.

"A little of this, little of that. A little bartending, too."

"Really?"

I nodded. He maintained eye contact while he slid my drink over to me, slowly. I tried to pay him but he waved his hands in the air. "This one is on the house," he said.

"Careful with that," I held the drink up, "I'll drink you dry." I paused and thought about what I'd said. "Because apparently, I'm a vampire."

He laughed.

"You should come back here and help me," he said, motioning behind the bar.

"Bartend?"

"Yeah, we're slammed. That would be helpful."

I thought about it. "Sure, why not?" I slid behind the bar and took orders from an endless line of nineteen-year-olds who'd already had way too much to drink. I gave them advice, too, like, "Make sure nobody drugs this," and, "If this is your first time drinking, remember that the alcohol hits you later so pace yourself," and, "Remember the buddy system!" For every five drinks we sold, Damian and I would take a shot of vodka straight from the bottle, and before I knew it, I was seeing double and struggling to find the right words. At some point, I slipped in a puddle of vodka and fell backward, and when Damian leaned down to help me up he grabbed the back of my head and kissed me. That sobered me up. I got to my feet and awkwardly mumbled something about needing to get back to my friends. Damian was hot and a hot mess, which was the exact opposite of what I wanted. I'd done the whole emotional wreck/borderline alcoholic bartender thing before and already knew it wasn't my cup of tea. But I was open to being his friend. He was rough and tumble, which reminded me of friends back home, and there was something familiar about his unique form of disaster. That didn't stop me from sleeping with him though. Twice.

The next day, I woke up to Amy packing her suitcase to go back to Georgia for three weeks for Christmas break. I'd planned on staying in Italy because I'd heard that Florence was supposedly filled to the brim with spiced wine in December. But as I watched her clean out her closet, I started to panic a little. What would I do in Florence, alone? I stretched and reached over to turn on the room heater I'd borrowed from the studio by shoving it up in my sweater and waddling out the front door. Our school controlled our housing and heat, and the cheap bastards kept the thermostat at a very frugal sixty-five degrees for four hours per day; the rest of the time the temperature dipped to a chilly fifty. So, for most of my day, my nipples were harder than the tip of an iceberg, my skin was permanently goose-bumped and I could see my breath when I got up to pee in the middle of the night. And, given how much debt I took on to go to that school (debt I will surely die with), it seemed a little unfair to die from hypothermia.

I sat up. "Are you getting ready to leave already?"

"Sure am," Amy replied. "See you in our new apartment after Christmas break?" She gently laid a stack of coral and pink jersey dresses on top of her monogrammed jeans.

"Yeah. You excited to go home?" I asked.

"I am. I miss my boyfriend."

Kuhle opened our bedroom door and came bounding onto my bed. She had decided to stay in Florence instead of going back to South Africa for the break. But she had a boyfriend by then, a Nigerian man who spoke Russian fluently and had studied medicine in St. Petersburg. While she cozied up next to me, he slept soundly in her room.

Kuhle rolled herself up in my sheets and stuck her tiny feet in front of the space heater. "Shame. It's freezing in here!"

"I'm honestly tempted to go home just for the heat," I said.

Watching Amy pack, I remembered that I had a life outside of Florence, people that had meant a lot to me before I'd left. Did I want to go home? It seemed unlikely that in just a few months, my life in Salt Lake City and the people in it would have faded into the background of my existence. But I had to adapt to so much in Florence that it had happened quickly and silently. I'd be lying if I said that's not what I'd wanted: to grow, change, and escape. Still, I missed familiarity, I missed the idea that I could exist without expelling an enormous amount of energy. That I could buy tampons, for example, without flipping through a translation book and gesturing wildly towards my vagina, or thinking back to lessons with Shocked Priscilla. It sounded awesome to have a conversation without needing to summarize my life for context because with every new friendship in Florence, we all had to do the "I was born and raised" song and dance, which was fun but sometimes it's nice to just be known. Even if the person everyone knew was quietly taking a backseat to the person I was becoming. I also didn't want to be alone for weeks in a foreign country. I could leave but not be left. However, going home meant going back to a family that I didn't fit into, a dead brother, old habits, and feeling caged in by expectations. There's a downside to knowing the same people for decades—they unintentionally hold you to their idea of you.

I lay there by Kuhle, the heater beating against us, her tiny cold feet practically on top of the red-hot coils of the heater. Amy carefully put her jewelry into a case and called a cab in Italian.

"See you after Christmas, roomies!" She hugged us and walked down the hallway, pulling her luggage behind her.

6

I Like You

I stood on top of a booze-soaked table with Amy to my right and a guy from our program called Benedict on my left in the back room at Angie's. My feet tapped to the beat of Depeche Mode's "Personal Jesus," with spilled cocktails, cigarette butts, and hepatitis squishing under the weight of my soles. Kuhle was out on the front line, hands on the ground, ass in the air, twerking her peers into submission. She was lethal on the dance floor and we watched her lovingly from our perch. The walls vibrated as hordes of college students filed into the small space all at once to hit the bar and shake one out.

It was the end of January, and I'd been back from Christmas break for three cold and soupy weeks. The rain never seemed to stop, and the constant overcast painted the city monotone. The hangovers didn't help. Since returning, I'd been going to Angie's twice per week, sometimes more. Some things had changed but others had stayed the same since we'd all gone home and come back. Amy and I had moved out of student housing and into our own two-bedroom apartment in Piazza del Duomo, numero 7 (for the same price we'd paid for five of us to live in a student apartment).

My new classes were screen-printing, creative writing, an independent study with Mario and grad seminar with Leonardo, who still turned crimson and backed away from me every single time we interacted. Demyan was still a major pain in my ass, and yet I'd started to like him in a sort of twisted, masochistic, "I have Daddy issues, please approve of me" kind of way.

Benedict yelled above the crowd and the music, "I want to date an Italian girl while I'm here. At least one."

"So ask someone out," I shouted back.

"Easier said than done."

"Not really," I replied, with alcohol-infused confidence.

A smoking-hot Italian man floated past us in a black peacoat with his collar popped all mysterious and smoldering. He had short espresso hair, peppered with a little gray on the sides, and olive skin with a thick five o'clock shadow. He sipped something brown, whiskey or rum, and casually scanned the room over the top of his glass. He waded through the drunk students to the opposite wall and turned to face our side of the room.

"Watch this," I told Benedict, and as soon as the Italian's dark brown eyes hit mine (I was standing on a table and knew at some point he'd notice the weirdos who appeared to be surfing on humans), I pointed drunkenly at him (like a total dildo), and then to myself to communicate that I wanted him to walk his adorable ass from the wall to me. He smiled and began walking towards me but was interrupted by a pretty blonde student who twirled her hair and arched her boobs forward. He explained something to her and she moved away, then took another step in my direction but Kuhle jumped in front of him with an epic full-body shimmy. He pointed to me, she threw back her head and laughed, and pushed him towards me. He arrived at my feet.

I bent down. "Hi. What's your name?" I shook his hand.

"I'm Francesco."

"Um, do you speak English?"

He nodded.

"Great! Come and get my number before you leave," I said. Then I stood back up and went about my business. He lingered for a split second, his eyebrows knitted together. Then he appeared to decide something and walked off. I thought, *I'm so badass*, because vodka.

But then I thought it'd probably be easier if I just gave him my number because we'd probably leave soon, so I hopped off of the table, walked behind the DJ area and snatched a pen and paper from nude model Lorenzo. I marched over to Francesco who was talking with people he clearly didn't know.

"Here." I handed him the paper. "But don't call until Thursday because I'm busy."

He accepted the piece of paper with a nod and a smile. I returned to my friends, who patted my back and high-fived me as if I'd just taken gold in the 100 meters at the Olympics.

"Are you fucking kidding me! That was great!" Benedict yelled.

I puffed out my chest and felt smugly proud of myself for doing something as incredible as drunkenly handing a stranger my phone number in a bar.

I danced to MGMT with Amy and Kuhle. Francesco nodded to me when he left. I stomped my feet and shook my hair and laughed. I noticed something in that moment—I didn't care if he called or not. That was a new thing for me. Back home, I serial-dated or purposely dated people who I knew would never work out because commitment scared me but so did loneliness and I'd found that nothing quieted a tantruming mind like lust. The fact that I felt so okay without someone on the hook was unique. Suddenly, even the thought of a *real* relationship made me a little anxious.

I was happy and for the first time doing everything that I wanted to do. I didn't want to lose that. I didn't want to get sucked into another person, into their life, into their expectations. In every relationship, one person is engulfed and turned to dust. I'd seen it in my childhood. Each time my mom dated, married, or remarried, she changed and I felt a little less important every time. I'd seen glimpses of it in myself, in my friendships back home. My friend Giselle always said, "You see your friends through rose-tinted glasses." And what that translated to was this: I habitually dedicated myself to friends, often at my own expense, while I slowly suffocated below the surface. Things were great and I didn't want to fuck up a good thing.

One week later, on Thursday, I swung back and forth in my rocking chair in the place I now shared with only Amy. The sound of shouting outside, bicycle bells, the general bustle of tourists and the pungent stench of horse shit floated up from Piazza del Duomo, which was right outside my window and fifteen feet from our front door. We basically lived in Florence's version of Time Square and we loved it. Amy and I regularly sat at the restaurant under our apartment and drank wine while we watched bitter Italians ride kamikaze-style on bikes and talked about our lives back home.

My phone rang.

"Hello?" I answered hesitantly, because I didn't recognize the phone number.

"Hello. This is-a Francesco." He paused. "I don't know-a if-a you remember me but-a you told-a me to call-a you?"

I panicked. "Uhm, I need to call you back!" I said and hung up on him. I tried to remember what he looked like. It had only been one week. Exactly one week. What day was it? Thursday? Seriously? Francesco had called me on Thursday afternoon, five days after I'd met him, *exactly* as I'd instructed. Unlike other guys I'd given my number to in the past, he didn't text me, "Hey, remember me?" the next day; he didn't wait for three days and try to hook up. That in and of itself was sexy as hell.

I called Grayson. "So, the guy that I gave my number to the other night—remember, I told you about it—should I go out with him?" I asked. "What are the odds that he's homicidal? Is it stupid to meet a random guy at night?"

"Yes, go. He might make you dead but maybe he won't. Isn't life fun?"

"Yay, a romantic night in an abandoned warehouse," I sighed.

"Let me know how it goes. Don't die."

"Okay." I hung up.

What did he look like? I remembered giving him my number, I remembered a generic idea of him. I knew that he looked *Italian*. I wasn't big on blind dates or stranger-danger dates but I was curious. What kind of guy did this—waited to call, wanted to go out with someone who'd drunkenly summoned him from atop a table? I needed to know. And curiosity often did it for me.

I called him back.

"Hi. It's me. So, um, yeah, we can go out. I live in Piazza del Duomo. Do you want to meet me in a wine bar downstairs from my apartment?"

Americans, I've heard, have a reputation for being sex-crazed lunatics. So, he most likely thought that I'd picked a place near my apartment for easy access to my bed. Unfortunately, I didn't choose the downstairs wine bar so I could easily whip out my vagina; I chose it for safety in case he was a *psycho* because as a woman, I have to wonder, Will he kill me, though?

I didn't really know what to expect but I hoped it would be better than my last and only real date I'd been on since I'd moved there. The cute barista, Alberto, who worked at the café across from the school asked me out when Grayson and I popped in for an espresso on our drawing break.

71

I said, "Sure," because I'd been eyeing him for weeks and making mildly perverted comments about him to Grayson.

The next day, Alberto picked me up from my apartment, dressed as a snowball. He wore a white tracksuit, white sneakers, and held a white leather wallet in his left hand. This immediately put me on guard because what kind of nutjob goes monochromatic on a first date? I texted Grayson, "He's dressed like he's on his way to his own baptism," frowny-faced emoji. Alberto took me to Kitsch for an *aperitivo*, basically, a buffet-style pre-dinner snack that comes with a cocktail for around eight euro each. We ordered two mojitos.

"What are your plans after this?" I asked him.

He leaned in flirtatiously. "I have to stop by my stepmother's house to pick up my laundry but then I'm going home to relax a little, maybe with some wine." He waggled his eyebrows. Ew, I thought, your mom still does your laundry?

"Didn't you say you were thirty-eight?" I asked.

"Yes," he said, his gaze dropping to my lips. Every ounce of attraction I'd felt for him went out the fucking window. No, nope, no way. Maybe I didn't make the best decisions or have the world's highest standards, but there was no way in hell I could sleep with someone who had that kind of relationship with a parent. I love my dad, but if he scrubbed my Calvin Klein boy shorts, I'd be scarred for life.

When I first landed in Florence, I thought, *sexy Italian men*, but realized that Italy and I had a different definition of "sexy." The accents, yes; the passion, absolutely, but there was nothing even remotely hot about a grown-ass adult letting his mom fondle his man-panties. Italian parents are incredibly dedicated and I admired that especially because my upbringing was so hands-off. It's awesome to be super close to the human who birthed you. But some men take it too far, and these men have a name: *mammoni*, or "mamma's boys." This kind of guy expects his mom to dote on him as if he were a toddler. Mamma cooks all of his meals, washes and irons his clothes, and cleans his bedroom. She also schedules his appointments and picks out his outfits. To be clear, being a *mammone* isn't the same thing as simply living at home. Most of the Italians I'd met seemed like normal, responsible adults who were forced to live at home because unemployment was high and wages were low and that totally made sense. Shit, I didn't even care if he lived at home just because he really loved his family and wanted to help his parents. But *mammoni* is some next-level shit that I couldn't get behind. And I wanted to tell him to wash his own stuff and let his elderly mother take a fucking nap. She'd earned it. But I didn't. I just pretended to yawn and asked to go home.

Hopefully, my date with Francesco would be a step up from that but I wasn't optimistic. I already had a backup plan to meet Grayson at YAG if things tanked. Around 7 p.m. I pulled on a pair of black snakeskin leggings, black ankle boots, and a black knit sweater. I didn't brush my hair but I shook it around a bit and put on a coat of mascara while dancing to the Yeah Yeah Yeahs.

"Maaaaaps, they don't love you like I looove you." Lyrics that were meant to make people stay. I stared at myself in the mirror, thinking, OMG I'd do me. My ass looks amazing in these pants. I shook it a little. I felt sexy in that way where I kind of wanted to sleep with myself, which my friend Jerome calls "clexing," or wanting to clone yourself for sex. The hotter we women feel, the more we want to go down to bang town.

I put on my jacket in the living room. Amy smiled from the dining table where she was arranging photos for a class. "You excited for your date?"

"Not really," I said, "I'm always disappointed and I'm not relationship material anyway. I'm not meant for them."

"No! Come on, roomie!" she urged. "You don't believe in fate or that there's the right guy out there for you?"

I shrugged. "Sure, Plato's version."

In Plato's *Symposium*, the soulmates myth is that every human originally comprised two halves, two people in one. One day, humans tried to overthrow the gods (unsurprisingly because we can't have nice things) and Zeus was obviously pissed and severed humans in half as punishment. So humans roam the earth for eternity searching for their lost other half.

Amy walked me downstairs ("In case he's a serial killer") to the teeny-tiny restaurant next door to our apartment, which was terrible all around. It was one of those tourist traps that served frozen entrees, and it was owned by a really angry Lebanese man who yelled at people for talking too loud. The angry owner seated me and Amy at a little table in the back of the restaurant against the exposed brick wall. He rolled his eyes and scrunched up his angry little face when I said I didn't need a menu, "Just wine glasses, *per favore*." Amy waited with me until Francesco showed up. He was late. We drank wine.

"What are you doing for your end-of-year project?" Amy asked, sipping her Brunello.

"I'm going to take photos of myself, stick them to a wall and title the piece *I'm Stuck*. It will be brilliant."

"You're crazy," she laughed, shaking her head.

"Or what if I drown myself and title it, *Why Don't I Know What to Do?*" I smiled and scanned the door for signs of Francesco.

"Ha! You'll figure it out. You always do." She smoothed her cashmere turtleneck and leaned on the table with her right arm, delicate but with purpose.

Francesco strolled in ten minutes later. He was cute, really cute, and warmly greeted us by shaking Amy's hand and then mine. I invited him to take a seat across from me. Amy gave me a thumbs up—"See you later roomie!"—and left. I wanted to meet up with Grayson so I decided to quickly get a rundown of how much Francesco sucked so I could leave. I turned towards him.

"So. Francesco." I began. "Do you live with your parents?" I sat up extra straight.

He sat back in his chair and answered, "No. I've lived in Florence for three years and my parents live between Naples and Rome. I live with roommates."

"Oh. Nice. Do you do your own laundry?"

"Yes-a. Who else would do it?"

He had a great smile and I noticed that his canines were vampire-ish in a sexy, primal sort of way.

"I'm sorry, just one second," he said.

He raised his hand to a waiter who immediately came over to us. He ordered a glass of wine, "*Posso avere un bicchiere di vino rosso? Chianti. Di casa va bene. Grazie.*" He turned back to me. "Sorry. Who would do my laundry?" he said, seemingly amused.

"I don't know, someone's mom? Do you work in Florence?" I finished my glass of wine.

The waiter brought Francesco's wine over and I asked for another for myself by pointing to his glass and saying, "*Anche per me.*" He swirled it, smelled it, and then took a sip.

"Sì. I'm an engineer. I finished my master's degree-a in dee spring. This job I began a few months ago. So you like wine?"

"Yes."

"My family makes wine."

"With their feet?" I asked, wide-eyed and interested.

"No. Not with our feet."

"Oh." I said, a little disappointed. "What's your favorite book?"

"My favorite book, it must be *The Unbearable Lightness of Being*."

I scooted back a little in my chair and my heart fluttered a little.

"That's weird, that's one of my favorite books, too..." I trailed off. *Oh, shit*. I might actually like this guy.

He asked me a few basic questions about my life but I avoided saying anything about myself more than "I study art here," because my family was too weird and complicated for a first date. *Well you see, my parents were never married, they just had a one-time fling when my dad first arrived in the US from Iran; he didn't speak English and she was like seventeen. I am the eldest of seven half-siblings, we're relatively close. No, there are three moms, oh, and my mom had three kids with three different guys, and last year my little brother died, and while I might seem okay, I spend a lot of time crying in the shower and binge-drinking my feelings away.* There was no point in frightening him before I knew if I liked him or not. I asked him about his family. He explained that his mother was a Bible teacher, his father a policeman. Of course they were.

"My mother is Chinese," he added.

"Really?"

"No. Not really." He laughed and shook his head like he couldn't believe that I'd fallen for it.

I learned that he grew up in a small city called Cumino. He did part of his master's degree in Madrid and spoke Spanish, English, Italian, and French. His parents were still married, like pretty much everyone's parents in Italy. He ran through empty fields without shoes as a child and loved to cook. Was this guy for real?

"So you're Catholic, right?" I bit my lip and fidgeted with my hair.

He shook his head. "No, not religious at all. My parents made me do my Confirmation, and I was one of the little children who assisted the priest but then I grew up and stopped believing in all of it. Religion is a business like any business."

"Gay marriage?" I asked.

"One of my best friends is gay," he said. "Am I interviewing for a job?"

"Maybe."

"Do you have brothers or sisters?" he asked.

"Yeah," I thought about it and decided that yes, it was best to just let him have it. Scare him off so I could go have fun. "Like a million. I'm the oldest; I have two brothers on my mom's side, one recently died, three sisters and one brother on my dad's side. Plus a stepbrother and sister."

He stared at me, not in a judgmental way but more like I'd piqued his interest as though I'd just told him that I could talk to cats.

"My parents were never married and it seems like my dad came to the United States to breed," I added, "and I'd rather not talk about my dead brother."

I downed another glass of wine and ordered yet another. The alcohol was starting to take its effect and I couldn't take my eyes off of his chest muscles, which seemed to throb through his sweatshirt. "Did you know that babies pee in the womb?" I asked.

"What?" he chuckled. "No, I had no idea."

What was I doing? I was nervous. I took a swig of wine and set it in front of me.

"Do you believe in fate or soulmates?" I asked, fully aware of the fact that it sounded like I might propose any minute or put him in my basement to "put the lotion on its skin."

He thought about it, then leaned forward, squaring off his shoulders.

"Sure, I believe in fate. Plato's version."

It was *unsettling* the way he responded exactly as I had earlier in my apartment with Amy. I chugged my last glass of wine.

"I should get going," I said, standing up abruptly, but not in a casual sexy way, more like an "I have explosive diarrhea" kind of way. I'm a nervous person and sometimes that can come off as cool and elusive but it's really just awkwardness.

"I'll walk you out," he offered.

I paid for our wine by practically throwing euro at the mean owner before Francesco had a chance to even think about it. Francesco followed behind me as I went to my apartment door, two feet to the right of the restaurant entrance. We both paused there, long enough for our eyes to follow the green, pink, and white marble of the neo-Gothic facade of the cathedral from the cobblestones up into the dark starry sky.

"I uh, can't believe you live in deez piazza," he said.

"It's gorgeous," I said into my purse, where I had turned my attention.

"Want to go for a walk-a?" he asked while I fumbled for my keys.

"No. Can't. Call me if you want to see me again. I had fun." I strained to push open the three-hundred-year-old door that weighed two hundred pounds.

"Okay, I had-a fun too. I'll-a call-a yo—"

"Okay! Great!"

I panicked and slammed the door in his face.

I ran upstairs and burst into our apartment where I performed a little victory dance for Amy, who strained to do the superman pose on her yoga mat.

"How'd it go, roomie?" she asked, shaking from exertion.

"I could marry him." It slipped out.

"Wait, what!" She dropped to her knees.

"He's actually perfect. And, oh shit! I just slammed the door on him!"

"You what?"

"I said goodbye really fast and then I kind of slammed the door in his face. I panicked. Anyway, he's perfect. But he's probably not going to call again."

"You always find the right one when you're not looking," Amy said. "God works in mysterious ways."

"Or," I teased, "the universe is just fucking with me."

7

Put the Sex on You

Francesco called and asked me to dinner.

"I already have plans," I said, "but you can come over here if you want. I'm having some friends over from my program."

"Sure," he replied.

I immediately went out with Jenny, the ceramicist from school who'd moved into the apartment directly above us, to buy something to wear. I decided on brown strappy heels and super-tight blue skinny jeans. But later that night when it was time to shower and get dressed, I looked in the mirror and declared that I would not change out of my sweatpants or unravel my hair from its three-day bun. As crazy as it sounds, it's kind of like the sweatpants were acting as some kind of hideous security blanket that would somehow protect me from disappointment. The thought of taking them off irritated me, and I felt momentarily defiant. Like, if he doesn't like me in sweatpants, I don't want to know him.

At ten past six Kuhle arrived and sat next to me on my bed.

"Isn't Francesco going to be here soon?" She eyed my hair and outfit.

I nodded and fell backward.

"I'm excited to officially meet him. I honestly can't even remember what he looked like, I was too busy"—her accent changed from British to American-style slang—"twerking that ass."

"That you were," I agreed.

"Shame, Angel Muffin, what are you doing? Put on some normal clothes, you look actually homeless," she laughed. After some prodding, I begrudgingly complied. Truth be told, I didn't *really* want to smell like a badger and look like a vat of grease for a guy that I liked but I didn't want to care how I looked either. Since it seemed like I'd found the perfect guy for me, I took it as some kind of deranged personal challenge to fuck it up. I'd never worn a lot of makeup but I put on less than usual, and I didn't even shake out my hair but left a tangled mess.

Violetta came over, followed by my friend Elisa, a woman in the art conservation program who'd taken a short break from motherhood for the first time in her adult life to explore a new career in restoration. She cut my hair and talked about her children. We took spread-eagle nudes of me sitting in a chair while she stared into my crotch as if it were the most natural thing in the world while delivering sage advice on dealing with intense college professors. This was the weird and private world I'd grown to love. We were drinking wine and talking about Francesco when my doorbell rang at exactly seven o'clock. All of the women stopped talking and Elisa asked teasingly, "Is that him?"

"Who is it?" I leaned into the speaker.

"It's-a me." I buzzed him up, cracked the front door, and went back to the living room and my glass of wine because waiting for him at the door like a normal person somehow seemed desperate. Francesco found us in the living room.

"Hello everyone," he said, smiling and holding out a box of ice cream treats. "These are so good, you have to try them." And just like that, he won over the room. Well played, *Francesco*, I thought. He took a seat next to Violetta who immediately turned to face him, eyes narrowed playfully.

"So," she began, "what did you study and what do you do?" When he said he was an engineer, her eyes widened and she smiled. "Oh! Me too! I studied software engineering at Berkeley."

He explained that he worked for a defense company, that he "unfortunately" designed weapons. He had a master's degree in microwaves, or something, and I couldn't stop thinking about burritos because burritos go in microwaves and you cannot buy burritos in Italy.

As ten minutes turned into an hour, I watched and waited for his confidence to waver; for him to say something arrogant or offensive, but he didn't. He just sat there, polite and sincere, in a navy blue v-neck sweater, with his chest hair exposed, majestically billowing in the crosswinds of the open window.

"Excuse me," he said to Violetta, then turned to me. "Sorry, but where is your bathroom?"

"Oh, I'll show you," I stood and motioned for him to follow.

He passed the bathroom and went to my bedroom.

"Is this your bedroom?"

"Yep," I said.

Then he walked next to my bed. "It's nice."

I sauntered over to him; he turned, grabbed me, and kissed me hard and passionately. It was a nice kiss but I hadn't made the choice to sleep with him yet, so I put my hands on his chest and backed away.

"Okay, Casanova," I said, "the bathroom is over there." I pointed, and he laughed. And when the bathroom door closed behind him, I ran back to the living room to mouth "He kissed me!" to everyone. He left twenty minutes later because he said he "had to work tomorrow."

Francesco texted me the next day while I gossiped about him to Violetta in a little Peruvian restaurant run by a man who looked like the spitting image of Einstein.

"Can I take you to dinner?" he wrote.

"Yes," I texted back.

Then I didn't hear from him for days, and started to suspect that he had a wife or girlfriend because what kind of guy only texts once per week? Married dudes, that's who. So I called him one night before bed and asked,

"Listen, do you have a girlfriend? It never occurred to me to ask before and I just realized that I'm an idiot. So, do you?"

He laughed. "No, of course not. Do you have a boyfriend?"

"No. I don't. If I had a boyfriend, I wouldn't have been at a bar giving out my number to perfect strangers. I only make terrible decisions when single."

"Well, I'm *flattered* to be one of your terrible decisions," he teased.

Two nights later he picked me up in his car and took me to a restaurant called Giuggiolo in the Campo di Marte neighborhood.

"I chose this place," he explained, "because you asked me if my family made wine with their feet. Giuggiolo has a little wooden grape press, and I wanted to show you."

At the restaurant, he ordered wine from the waiter as soon as we sat down. A large Italian family sat next to us. They leaned over the table to scream-talk at each other. Someone's toddler was hiding under the table, laughing, with the family dog. It was a common scene in Florence, the children, the pets under the table no matter how fancy the restaurant. It felt like real life, less rigid.

Francesco explained a boring work project and I tried to explain a series of grotesque paintings I was working on for a school project ("Portraits of women, but like unattractive on purpose"). We hadn't slept together but it was pretty much all I could think about. I didn't want a relationship and I assumed he didn't either—he'd asked me out three times, but didn't call or text otherwise—so I took it upon myself to put his mind at ease.

"Just so you know," I began, "I like you a lot, but I'm not looking for anything serious." I fondled the stem of my wine glass and waited to read relief in his face.

He leaned forward and fixed his brown eyes on mine. His face was stern.

"If you're just looking for sex," he said, "you might want to find someone else. Usually, that's what I'm into but I'm not interested in that with you."

"Oh," I stammered, "okay."

He grinned and sipped his wine.

"What would you like for dinner?" he asked.

"I'm vegetarian so anything without meat is perfect."

When the waiter returned he ordered in quick bursts of Italian that I couldn't understand. When the food arrived I stared at my plate for a minute. Risotto with ham and a side of raw ham.

"So, you know that vegetarians also don't eat pigs?" I smiled. "Or does it mean something different in Italy?"

He brought his hands to his head, "*O Dio!*" He looked around for help. "I'm so sorry! I'm so stupid. Let's change it! Let me change it!"

"No," I said, "I'll eat around the pancetta in the rice but you'll have to help me out with the other stuff. Also, pigs, are animals. So are cows. Chickens. Plants, however, are pretty much never animals where I come from."

"Yeah, yeah, I get it." He gave me a playful eye-roll.

As we wrapped up dessert with a tiramisu, all of the wine I'd drunk hit me. He talked about physics and doing his master's degree in Madrid but

I'd stopped paying attention a long time ago. All I heard was "blah, blah, blah," while I imagined myself straddling him, slowly peeling off his shirt.

"I should probably get home," I practically purred.

He signaled the waiter for our check.

Back at my apartment, I invited him upstairs where I ushered him into my bedroom the way that someone might trap a small animal to play with. I closed the two French doors dramatically while he stood in the center, flummoxed. I locked the doors. I walked around him to switch on the glass chandelier lamp beside the bed. Then I kissed him deliberately and hard. He pulled away, smiled, and leaned in to kiss me again. I backed up and slowly unzipped my jeans, shimmying out of them while he stared at my black thong, wide-eyed, and hungry. I pulled off my drapey blouse and, in one motion, unhooked my bra and threw it. He stepped forward, lifted me off the ground and set me on the bed.

"You're perfect," he whispered. I pulled off his t-shirt to reveal a sturdy body, bulging pecs, and muscles that formed a deep-cut *v* that pointed south to his penis park. His chest was shapely under my hands, two rolling hills covered in a forest. He put his hand behind my head and pulled me towards him for a long, deep kiss.

The next morning, I woke to an empty bed. I threw off the burgundy comforter and went to the dresser to grab my towel from the corner where it hung. Words were scrawled across the mirror that hung above my dresser. With my red lipstick, he'd written:

You're beautiful when you sleep. Had to go to work –F.

On my way to the studio, I texted Violetta: "So, I put the sex on Francesco," to which she replied, "Oh good!"

I practically skipped into school where the administrator, Luca, came up to me.

"Hey Misty," he waved, "someone left this for you." He handed me a little paperback book, *La brevita della vita*. On the first page was a handwritten quote from the book:

Vivete come se doveste vivere per sempre, mai vi viene in mente la vostra caducità, non prestate attenzione a quanto tempo è già trascorso. Lo disperdete come provenisse da una fonte rigogliosa e inesauribile, benché nel frattempo proprio il giorno che è da voi donato a qualche uomo o attività sia forse l'ultimo. Ogni cosa temete come mortali, ogni cosa desiderate come immortali. —Un bacio, Francesco

Luca translated it for me. "It basically means to live as if every day is your last."

8

Breaking and Entering

I'd read that Carnival dates all the way to ancient Rome. It takes place every February throughout Italy but one of the biggest celebrations is in Venice, where hundreds of years ago the Venetian oligarchy began a month of celebration where common folk could eat, drink, and be merry. Masks provided a sort of temporary transgression from social norms. Basically, the masks made everyone equal, regardless of class or gender and I kind of loved it. How *sexy*. I'd chosen a gold mask because it matched the gold leggings that I'd recently bought from Calzedonia and apparently my goal was to drunkenly frolic in Venice with Amy, Jenny, and a few other women from school, dressed as an orb.

I threw underwear, socks, and makeup into a backpack and hoped that I'd packed warm enough clothes. Winter in Italy, I'd learned, felt colder than any winter in Utah because of the humidity and because nobody used heat for reasons I couldn't really understand. (Amy and I had yet to realize that the monthly heating bill in Italy was roughly the same price as a black market kidney, and so we kept our thermostat at a nice and toasty seventy degrees. We didn't find it suspect that every Italian we knew wore a parka to bed while we trotted around in our undies and tank tops.)

The day before we left for Venice Francesco offered Amy a ride to Ikea in his little Fiat, forty-five minutes away in Prato, so she could buy a desk for her room. I needed to wind down from a busy week of freezing to death in the studio while sketching out more of my grotesques that I'd recently titled *Tell Me I'm Pretty*. They'd said that they'd be back around eight, so the plan was to go out to dinner with Grayson and we would meet up with them later.

Grayson and I went to a Florentine spot for pizza and beer to plan our spring break vacation, a road trip south to Rome and the Amalfi coast. We sat across from each other and mutilated two margherita pizzas.

"Can you drive a stick?" he asked.

"Yeah," I said

"Well, I can't so it looks like you're going to have to drive. I feel like we're going to die on this trip. Also, aren't you going to Venice tomorrow?"

"I am. Wanna come?"

"No. You go and do Venice, I have a date tomorrow with a pretty Florentine guy."

"Grindr?"

"Mmm, yes. Also, where is Franny?"

"With Amy at Ikea."

"Ah, she trapped him into doing her bidding?"

"Ha! I guess so," I said.

We stopped at a little hole in the wall to buy a bottle of Chianti for two euro and wandered aimlessly around the dark, damp city drinking straight from the bottle. We rounded a corner and found an art walk near Santo Spirito and a row of little galleries open late to display some local art. We went into one gallery and silently paused in front of each abstract painting. Then we entered an impressive space that appeared to be an installation of someone's living room. It was so authentic! We paused for a long time on a painting above the fireplace, a modern Cubism piece likely inspired by Picasso. We noticed the family picture on a bookshelf, and another, and it clicked that we were actually in someone's home right about the time a couple came into view from what I assumed was their kitchen. I grabbed Grayson's hand and we ran outside cackling.

"And now we're breaking and entering," Grayson said.

"More like entering and admiring," I answered. "But to be fair, why was their front door unlocked?"

"Yes, let's blame them for not planning for crazy people to come and go as they please."

"Exactly!"

We walked to the Ponte Vecchio, still holding hands. We leaned over the wall to watch the river in the dark, the slow flow of tar-colored water trickling across the rocks. Standing there with Grayson, I felt calm and safe.

It was almost midnight when I realized that I still hadn't heard from Francesco or Amy. Ikea closed at ten, so where were they? I texted Amy. She responded, "We've been at the apartment waiting for you." I narrowed my eyes and my heart picked up the pace. I knew that wasn't true because why would they go home and not tell me? Something was up. I hugged Grayson goodbye and walked home in the dark, dodging water puddles. My mind raced with possibilities. Would he sleep with Amy? Would Amy sleep with him? No, I didn't think so, but I also had trust issues. I got home and found both of them sitting on the couch, talking.

"Hey, roomie!" Amy waved.

"Hey, babe!" Francesco got up and gave me a hug.

I was unresponsive and kept my arms by my side. I glared at him and Amy for a second, then walked to my bedroom, undressed, and climbed into bed. Francesco lay down behind me.

"*Tesoro*, you okay?" he asked.

"I have to get up early tomorrow to do some stuff before I go to Venice."

I fell asleep, livid and confused.

The next day, I stood in my studio space trying to sketch a grotesque of Violetta from a picture I'd taken of her. My charcoal-coated hands moved manically around the canvas, black water ran from Violetta's hair down to the bottom of the canvas, and my heart hurt. I texted Francesco.

"So, where were you last night?"

"We went to Ikea," he responded.

"And then?" I asked.

"Then we stopped and had a couple of beers."

"Why would you lie about that?" I texted, slowly, my hands shaking.

"I didn't lie. You never asked *me*."

"Erase my phone number and never talk to me again."

"Wait, no!"

I blocked him.

Jenny and I had some last-minute things to grab before we caught our train to Venice from Santa Maria Novella station. I ranted about my break-up with Francesco as we crossed Piazza del Duomo.

"They *lied* to me and—"

Mid-sentence I saw Francesco, sitting on a step, holding a guitar.

"Oh my God," I nodded in his direction so that Jenny would see him, avoided eye contact and practically galloped past him.

"Wait!" he called after us. He chased me through the piazza, strumming a guitar and singing at me.

I spun around and screamed, "Why are you doing this?"

"I'm trying to fix it!" he shouted back. He strummed the note of a flamenco song.

"Don't! You, you, fucking LIAR." I ran off, with Jenny running behind me until I lost him. When we finally stopped outside a clothing store, Jenny stared at me like I was the world's biggest asshole.

"What?" I asked suspiciously.

"You don't think that was, ya know, kinda sweet of him?"

"Not at all, it was mostly just embarrassing and I didn't know what to say."

We walked into the Zara store and started to rummage through clothing racks. I hated critique at school, public speaking, and being stared at in general. Serenading me in a public square packed with tourists seemed cruel, especially after being some sneaky asshole. I thought of my friends.

"I guess a lot of women would have liked that?" I said. Jenny nodded.

"Yeah, for sure. You didn't want to at least talk with him?"

I bit my lip, fingered a dress on display and tried to push the entire thing out of my mind. But I couldn't. I really liked him, and even though it was too soon, I kind of thought that I even loved him. But it's not like my panties were just gonna *drop* at the first strum of his guitar, anyway. Right? No. *Maybe*? No! Liars are the worst. Especially given my upbringing where my mom's boyfriends just came and went and we moved constantly and I couldn't depend on anyone. The last thing I needed was a partner I couldn't count on.

To make matters worse, Jenny and I didn't have seats on the train because two Italian businessmen had taken them, and the stewardess just shrugged and said, "Well, I guess you'll have to stand." So we found the car with the bar in it, pushed our backs against the wall, and sloppily drank wine that splashed everywhere while we wobbled uncomfortably at every stop.

I fell backward into a metal bar while complaining about Francesco. "Ouch. I mean, what a fucking dick!"

Jenny opened a tiny tin box and popped a Xanax into her mouth.

"I can't handle this train ride," she said, swallowing without water. "Getting tossed around like this is giving me anxiety."

She ran her hand through her sandy brown Rapunzel hair that fell past her waist, just above her bum.

"But are you *sure* that he meant to lie, or did he just not understand what was happening? I mean, his English isn't perfect and you didn't really give him a chance to explain himself."

It was a fair point. By the time we arrived in Venice, I'd accepted, for the most part, that it was probably a misunderstanding. *Maybe* I'd been a little too hasty when I broke up with him? Maybe I hadn't been fair.

When we got to Piazza San Marco, Amy and a few other women from our program were already there. I hadn't seen Amy since the whole thing happened. She was my friend, wasn't she? What the fuck? She looked at me with an "I'm sorry" face but I ignored her because I didn't know what to say yet. Then, when we all left to get dinner, she grabbed me at the top of a gold-and-marble staircase.

"Can we just talk?" she asked.

"You lied to me, Amy." I pushed past her and started down the stairs.

"I know! But nothing happened! He took me to Ikea and I was like, 'Let me buy you a beer for going to all the trouble.' Plus, you're dating him and I wanted to grill him. But then we took a really long time and I was like, 'Oh man, she's going to be pissed at us.' So I told him not to say we grabbed a beer."

"Why would I care if you two went for a beer?"

"Most women would care, I think. It was stupid. But be mad at me, not him."

"I dumped him."

"You didn't! Misty! No! He adores you! Seriously!"

I pouted for a second.

"Does he?" I smiled.

"Obsessed!" she laughed.

After a few seconds of awkward chatter, we hugged.

At about 1 a.m., I called Francesco from a bar in Venice, off-my-rocker-shitfaced, and surrounded by people in long-nosed plague masks and antiquated ball attire.

"It might have been a misunderstanding," I slurred into my phone, plopping down into a chair shaped like a throne.

"I didn't lie to you," he said, flatly.

"I'm sorry that I was a little bit *rash* about the whole break-up thing. Do you hate me?"

"No. But from now on, can you at least talk to me before you break up with me?"

"Yes. And can you promise to never chase me with a guitar again?"

"I will definitely never do that again, you asshole." I could tell that he was smiling.

"Cool," I pulled at my gold mask that I'd pushed back on top of my head like a gigantic headband. "I have to go because it's loud. Some guy is only wearing bubble wrap and Amy is currently yelling into a girl's TV costume about George Bush."

"Okay, would you like to do something tomorrow when you get back?" he asked.

"Yes, yes, I would." Then I hung up and teetered off to somewhere with Jenny and Amy that I don't really remember.

Francesco came over after soccer practice with the European Institute team the day I got back from Venice. We went straight to bed. He wrapped an arm around me and traced my forearm with his finger as I sunk deeper into him. "So," I asked, "what was it like growing up in Italy? As a little kid?"

"It was fun," he grinned. "I visited my grandparents a lot. My grandma used to read omens in the coffee grounds at the bottom of espresso cups."

"She was a witch? What was your favorite memory?" I tangled my hand in his.

"I don't know. Every year I would help my mother and grandmother to make tomato sauce. I used to stand on a chair at the end of the line. It was my job to add one basil leaf to each jar. I really liked that."

"Wow," I craned my neck to look up at him, "that is so *wholesome*. You're like from the Italian version of *Leave it to Beaver*."

"Leave it to what?" he asked.

I laughed. I adored him, and everyone else liked him too. Which had me thinking, why would someone so *normal* be so into me?

Unlike Francesco's family, mine required a complex series of illustrations on who begat who. I worried that Francesco was a little *too* different, which probably meant that he was hiding something. I slightly distrusted him on the grounds that I couldn't have nice things. Francesco and I argued *all the time*; for example, he had strong opinions about why my purse needed to match my shoes. Also, about my newly developed habit of peeing in dark alleys when bathrooms weren't immediately available. I had strong opinions about why I should be able to do whatever the hell I wanted because who the fuck cares what strangers think? He argued that he didn't care what they *thought*, as much as he cared about them seeing my vagina. And I was like, "If you've seen one, you've seen 'em all." But he passionately disagreed. I spent many glorious days fantasizing about stabbing him repeatedly with a fork.

Despite bickering like an old, crotchety couple, we worked. He was the yin to my yang, the hot dog to my pizza (an actual thing in Italy). I opened up to him, completely, like a fillet. I didn't have a lot of security growing up as my young mom tried to figure things out—but Francesco, he seemed like he'd never leave. He made me feel secure in a way I'd never known before. As the months went by I found myself droning on about *feelings*. And, I wanted to be better for him. I admired the way that little got to him. I wanted to be like that. I was both too proud and too delicate, like a wilting flower, and it made it hard for me to be vulnerable. And what is love if not painful vulnerability?

I told him about my brother Mitch, and about how one time Mitch's dad took me with him to buy an eight-ball of cocaine when I was six.

"He tried to spell it out, *C-O-K-E*, but I could read by the time I was four so I went straight home and asked my mom what 'coke' was."

He shook his head. "Your childhood stories are *really* depressing," he said.

I thought about it. "Nah, the coke story is funny in retrospect."

Francesco's ample chest hair and six-pack glowed in the lamplight. Outside, it rained ice water but our apartment was a cozy ninety degrees. I sat up and tugged on the rat's nest that had formed at the back of my head. Francesco pulled me over to him and smiled when I clumsily wiped a few messy locks out of my eyes. He turned his head to the side and gazed into my eyes.

"I love you," he said.

I smiled awkwardly, "Ah, that's sweet. I love you, too!" I flipped my ball of knotted hair to look adorable and seal the scene into his mind. I'd read somewhere that men are "very visual." Although I looked more honey badger than honey pot.

"No, *ti AMO*, not *ti voglio bene*." He leaned closer into my face so I could see that he was serious. I caught the scent of his Issey Miyake cologne and tried to be coy. There are multiple forms of love in Italian. *Ti voglio bene*, or "I want you to be well," is reserved for friends, grandparents, and your dog. The more direct version, *ti amo*, or "I love you," is reserved for romantic relationships. It's the big love.

"Oh," I smiled. "Um, yeah, *ti amo*, too."

And I did.

In the morning, like he had done every morning for the past few weeks, he pulled himself from my bed after one hour of sleep for work, drenched in my wet kisses and Burberry London-perfumed sweat. Only this time he left me chocolate on the nightstand in the shape of a painting tube with a note that said, *"per sempre,"* or "forever."

Naked

9

Spring Break (the Big Cheese)

Spring 2010

Grayson and I cruised south on the freeway in our rented Fiat with the windows down and the music up. I drove because Grayson couldn't drive a stick, and he was afraid he'd kill us both, and he somehow felt better if I were the one to accidentally do it. It was spring break and we had five days to run amok together, heading first to Rome and then to Sorrento, where we'd stay for a couple of days near the sea. The roads weren't as scary as I expected, though it seemed like the speed limit was more of a suggestion than the rule. Like everyone on the road seemed to interpret it as "You can go this fast *if you want*." But after a half-hour on the freeway, I pushed the gas pedal nearly to the floor and wove around other cars like we were dancing.

Neither of us knew what to expect on this trip. Grayson and I hadn't spent much time outside of Florence; we'd never driven in Italy before and had been told by our Florentine professors that everything south of Florence was a bog filled with petty criminals.

"They'll ruin your Italian!" Priscilla warned us, because of the dialects and accents.

"Watch your wallets," said Leonardo.

"They'll chain you in the kitchen and turn you into a housewife," an Italian guy I'd had a fling with years ago texted (he was from Milan). But Francesco told us that the south was a magical paradise worth visiting— after all, that's where he'd grown up. "It's different than central Italy or the north, not better or worse, just different. But in a good way," he explained. Francesco was more excited than we were because he'd be in his home town of Cumino while we were on our trip and he wanted us to stop along the way so he could buy us lunch.

"So," Grayson asked while I sped up to pass a Maserati (out of principle), "you excited to see the place that birthed our Franny?"

"I guess?"

It was late when we arrived in Rome and it took us a while to figure out the parking situation. Nothing seemed commonsense; some cars treated certain roads like one-way streets but others didn't. People would just stop in the road and cars jetted around them in every direction. There were signs *everywhere* but we didn't know what they meant so I just drove in circles until we could figure it out. I nearly hit a man on a bike, a woman on a moped, and three or four different cars.

"Oh my God, we are going to *murder someone!*" Grayson clung to his seat belt as I nearly clipped a van.

We were let into the apartment we'd rented by an older gentleman with silver hair and a round body.

"Giuseppe, *piacere*," he introduced himself.

"Grayson, piacere."

"Misty, piacere."

"*Misti?*" he repeated. "You know what that means in Italian, right?"

99

I nodded. "Mixed?"

"*Sì*," he chuckled.

Giuseppe showed us to our room and pointed to the bathroom.

"Everything you need-a is in dair," he said, smiling warmly. Then he doddered down the hall and disappeared into a room, quietly shutting the door behind him.

"Oooh, he lives here," Grayson said.

"Weird!" I whispered.

Grayson and I changed into our pajamas and jumped into bed. We lay there for a minute, staring at the ceiling. I let my body relax into the soft mattress and tried not to think of how many people had slept there before us or how many random sloughed-off skin cells lived deep in the fibers.

"Goodnight, Peanut," Grayson said.

"'Night."

And he turned out the light.

The next morning, we went into the kitchen to get a glass of water on our way out of the apartment. The sun had just come up and you could see a little bit of light peeking in through the drapes. Giuseppe was sitting at the table with a map stretched out in front of him.

"Come, come, sit!" he said.

Grayson and I looked at each other and did as we were told.

He went to the counter and came back with two espresso cups and two *cornetti* that he set in front of us.

"Okay, so this is what you need to see," said Giuseppe, leaning over the map. "Here," he marked a spot with an *x*, "here and here." We nodded and Grayson asked about the distance from the first *x* to where we currently were.

"Well," Giuseppe answered, "it depends." Grayson and I glanced at each other, thinking the same thing. How is distance subjective? Forty minutes later, the map was covered in ink marks and we knew every inch of Rome without ever having stepped foot out of the apartment.

Grayson began to nervously eye the door, then he cut in hurriedly, "*Grazie mille!*" He turned to me with the slightest hint of desperation, and said, "We should probably get a move on." I stood up, shook Giuseppe's hand, thanked him for the coffee and directions, and sprinted for the front door.

"He's very nice," said Grayson as we stepped onto the street from the apartment, "also he fully wanted us to live in his apartment for the rest of his life to look at maps together and we only have one day here so—"

"No argument here."

We walked to an intersection and I stepped into the street. "Watch for cars!" Grayson yelled as a businessman on a Vespa zoomed around me. I shrugged and kept walking.

He caught up to me. "So you've given up on stop lights, eh?"

"Exactly," I said with a wink.

"Which way should we go?" I asked.

"That way," Grayson pointed into the distance.

And we went that way.

This is where I'm supposed to write a beautiful description of the ancient city. I'm supposed to detail the way fresh spaghetti carbonara melted on our tongues, describe the mind-blowing impression the Colosseum made on us when it came into view off of the subway—the awesome remains of one of the most famous entertainment centers in the history of the world (beautiful and utterly barbaric; the Seaworld of the old empire, if you will)—and tell you how lovely it was to sit at a café, floating in the smell of espresso beans while the sun set, casting a Malibu-pink glow over the Spanish Steps. But everyone has already written about these things a thousand times. What I will say is that Grayson and I had really good conversations about life while we casually found our way from landmark to landmark.

I felt totally complete and filled with hope, all new and naked like a newborn baby. My future didn't seem untidy like it had back before I left for Italy, because now I had a plan and things were falling into place. I had a lot to be happy about: a super sexy boyfriend, a new best friend (though I feel he'd roll his eyes at that), and cocktails on the Tiber River. There are only a few periods in your life where you can actually feel yourself expanding. That day, and that year, was one of them.

Grayson and I hopped in the car and buzzed towards Cumino, a small city in Lazio. It was Francesco's hometown and we were going to meet him for lunch so he could take us to an "*agriturismo*."

"So it's essentially a restaurant on a farm?" Grayson asked.

"I don't know. Did you Google it?"

"Yes. It looks like an actual farm. Also, do you think they're going to hand us a fork when we arrive and just lead us to a barn full of animals?"

"I mean, probably."

Francesco was waiting for us outside in the parking lot with his friend. He lit up when I climbed out of the car and I noted that he's the only person in my life that was always puppy-level excited to see me, every single time. Which only made me suspicious because it's not like I deserved that kind of enthusiasm.

"Francesco, *piacere*," Francesco's friend introduced himself.

"So you're both Francesco?" Grayson asked.

"Yeah," he grinned, "but you can call me by my last name, Greco."

"*Due Franceschi*," Grayson purred, which meant "two Francescos." Then he leaned into me and whispered loudly, "What I wouldn't give to be sandwiched in between the Francescos."

A plate of cheese and salami came out, followed by vegetables and bread. Grayson and I both ordered pasta marinara. The Francescos ordered a pile of meat and a bottle of Montepulciano d'Abruzzo.

"So," Greco began, "what are you doing here?"

"Eating on a farm, mostly," I responded. He wasn't amused. "Sorry, in Italy? We were basically spending a year making art."

"Very cool," he said. "What do you do—"

"She carries a huge hunting knife in her purse! She says it's for cutting canvases!" Francesco interjected.

Greco looked concerned and glanced at my bag, so I reached in my purse and fished out my Smith & Wesson knife, a gift from my sister when I left for Italy so I could "stab rapists." But I mostly used it to cut canvas and other art material. I flipped the stainless-steel blade open and handed it over to him. He examined it and handed it back with an expression that I clearly read as, "This woman is insane and why is she dating my friend?" I mean, it was a fair assessment, I guess, and I wondered why Francesco had brought up something that would make me look like a notable whack job. Who was I anyway? Lady Rambo?

Grayson refilled our wine glasses.

"Well isn't this fun. You don't look insane at all," he said with a massive smile on his face, the same way he used to look at me when Leonardo would accuse me of being too feisty in the studio. It was a distinct look, wide eyes that expressed horror but a mouth curled tightly into a genuine grin. Grayson loved it when I made an ass of myself—when anyone did.

"So how are your parents?" I asked Francesco.

"Great! They love it when I'm home. My mom gets to cook for me so she loves it."

"'Gets to'? Lucky her that she gets to do more work."

Francesco laughed out loud but Greco seemed perturbed.

Outside when we were getting ready to leave, Grayson spotted a gorgeous mare in a pen, a Palomino quarter horse with long golden locks blowing in the wind, and took off towards the stable.

"Oh my God, it's *Amy* if she were a horse!"

Amy doesn't look like a horse at all; the opposite, really. Amy is tiny with delicate features but this horse somehow captured her spirit and her long blonde hair.

"Aww," I peeked between the wooden posts. "Look at the sad little horse next to the pretty Amy horse." It was actually a donkey but "sad little horse" seemed like a way more accurate description of this particular creature. Amy the horse stood tall and majestic as fuck, but the little sad horse seemed awkward in his own existence and upset about it.

"It's a *donkey*," Greco said.

"What's the matter, sad little horse?" I called to him.

"DONKEY," Greco repeated.

"I love him," I whispered to Grayson.

"They eat donkey in Italy," said Francesco.

Grayson and I slowly turned to him. "Why would you say that?" I asked incredulously.

"It's true!" Francesco said. Then he reached into a large paper bag he was carrying and pulled out a six-pound wheel of cheese twice the size of my head. He thrust it towards me.

"What is it?"

"A gift for you! Pecorino cheese. Oh, and this." He reached into his bag and pulled out a jar the size of a thermos.

"It's honey!" He presented it to me.

"Oh, wow, thank you," I said, struggling to hold the jar that was slipping through my fingers while the cheese wheel I'd shoved under my armpit caused a weird cramp as I strained to keep it there.

"Let me help," Grayson offered, taking the cheese off my hands so I could carry the honey.

I didn't know what to make of lunch. Had it gone well? Greco definitely thought I was insane and didn't think I knew what a donkey was. I'd enjoyed it and Francesco was adorable, even if he did gift me an entire wheel of cheese and a gallon of honey. Later when we talked about it and I asked him why so much cheese, he said it was the only size they had. When I asked him about announcing the knife to Greco he said, "I thought it was cool! I didn't realize everyone else didn't think it was cool, too!" Which clearly shows how terrible Francesco is at reading a room.

Grayson and I pulled back onto the freeway with full bellies and headed towards Sorrento. He turned on the radio and Madonna was playing "Like a Virgin," and he started dancing in the passenger seat like he was grinding while on an elliptical. I shifted into fourth gear, sped up and changed lanes. A gust of wind blew my hair unexpectedly in front of my face and temporarily blinded me. I shook my head and leaned back in the seat to pin my hair behind my head.

"Do you think it's possible to eat an entire wheel of cheese over the weekend?" Grayson asked.

"We can try."

"No, but that was really sweet. Also, I wish he were my boyfriend and not yours but I'll live, I suppose. Although, I'd be more than happy to take Greco and—"

"I know you would. Greco didn't love me."

"IT'S A DONKEY!" No, he didn't."

Grayson and I were sitting on the patio of a restaurant in Sorrento, eating *gnocchi alla sorrentina*, a type of dumpling made with flour and potatoes, tossed in red sauce and smothered in mozzarella cheese. We'd arrived an hour earlier, starving, and stopped at the first restaurant we'd seen. The waiters zipped around the tables, as we zoned out and watched them, tired from the drive.

"Is it just me or are all of the waiters attractive?" he said.

"I was just thinking the same thing."

Our waiter stopped at our table. "Is everting *va bene?*" he asked in an Italian–English mashup.

"*Sì,*" Grayson answered. I nodded.

"So, are you here on vacation?" the waiter asked.

"Sì!" Grayson said again, more flirtatiously than the first time.

I chewed and nodded again.

The waiter gestured back and forth between Grayson and me. "How long have you been together?"

Grayson's eyes got big. "Oh, no. No, no. We're not together."

Then things got super weird. The waiter leaned down next to me. "So you're single?"

"No, I'm not. I have a boyfriend."

"But he's not here?"

"Not physically, no. But he's here in spirit. Like Jesus, I imagine."

The waiter stood up and walked away without a word. A moment later, I felt a whoosh behind me and a firm tug on my hair. I saw the waiter whizz by out of the corner of my eye.

"Did he just pull your hair?" Grayson asked.

"Yes! What the fuck? Is that some kind of mating gesture here? Who is this guy?"

We both turned and the waiter was standing against the wall with two of his friends, staring intensely at our table.

"I'm going to get murdered."

The waiter and his friends came across and loomed over us.

"Where are-a you staying?" he asked.

"I have no idea," I said.

"A little hotel right down the street and—"

"And we won't even be there because we're so busy. Can we get the check, please?" I turned to Grayson totally shocked, and leaned in so I could scream-whisper, "Are you *trying* to get me killed? This dude is pulling my hair! He seems rapey as fuck!"

"Yeah, poor judgment on my part. They definitely seem like the kind of guys who would kidnap and murder a woman. But they're probably not going to come over."

"*Probably?*"

"I mean, they might. Maybe we should go."

Grayson came out of the bathroom naked. I'd been in bed for some time, texting with Francesco about the creepy waiters. He wrote back, "Douchebags." I looked up at Grayson who was still standing there.

"You're going to get cold," I said. He shrugged. In the program, it seemed like we'd all seen each other naked a thousand times and so I didn't think anything of it.

"Honest opinion," he put his hand on his hips, "Do you think it's a good size?"

I sat up and focused on his wiener.

"I think so? I'm not really a dick expert, Grays. I mean, it doesn't seem shockingly small or freakishly big. Yeah, it's a good size."

He was satisfied with that and went back in the bathroom to change into black briefs and a green t-shirt. He switched off the light, hopped into bed next to me and lay back. I snuggled down into the bed and rolled over to face him. Grayson typed something on his phone and I watched his face in the glow of the screen. I felt lonely, often, even when I was around other people, and it was rare for me to feel connected in a way that a lot of people do from just casual conversation with anyone and everyone. A lot of people I knew preferred superficial relationships, liked to keep the conversations light and people at a distance. Not me. Once I let someone in, I needed a deep connection, needed to know someone intimately and be known, and I felt like that with Grayson. A few times, I wondered what would happen if we were sexually compatible. Would we have worked as a couple? The answer was always a hard no. We had too many of the same issues and were damaged in similar ways, which were great for friendship but terrible for romance.

"'Night Peanut," Grayson said.

"'Night."

* * *

"I can't believe there are this many jellyfish here. If you fell in, you'd die a miserable death."

We were standing on the pier in Sorrento, the sun beating down on us, the waves rocking calmly against the wood, the jellyfish—hundreds of thousands of them—suspended in the water in this way that was elegant and timeless, like chiffon skirts swaying in an anti-gravity room. I leaned over the edge a little to get a better view.

"Don't do that," Grayson called over to me.

"I'm not going to fall in."

"I feel like that's something you would say right before you fell in."

He had a point, I wasn't exactly danger-adverse but in my opinion, I took calculated risks. Grayson was more convinced than ever that my so-called "recklessness" would get me killed. He'd seemed sure of it ever since we went to Capri for a couple of hours. We'd happened past an orange orchard that was thirty feet below us. The tops of the trees were just out of reach and we were both a little hungry and we'd wandered away from the cafés and restaurants. So I sat on the fence with my back to the trees.

"What are you doing?" Grayson's eyes were bugging out of his head.

"Feeding us," I said. I locked my toes on the lateral wood post and slowly fell back into the treetops, dangling upside down. I reached out and grabbed two oranges while Grayson loomed over the fence and squealed, "You're going to fall to your death!" and "How are you still alive?"

"I used to do this on the bars at school all the time when I was a kid, I'll be fine," I said, inhaling the delicious citrus smell. Then I sat up and threw Grayson one of the oranges, and we ate them on our way to the top of the hill where the cafés were.

I watched the jellyfish and felt calm. The way they were suspended in the water and allowed the waves to carry them relaxed me, the way they surrendered to the ocean. What would it be like to just let go and exist in the world that way? Grayson stood on the other side watching silently, too. I liked that about us, that we could be together without feeling the constant urge to pollute the silence.

Looking past the jellyfish and into the dark, I imagined a great white leaping out of the water and grabbing a hold of me, pulling me down in the darkness where I'd die from a bazillion jellyfish stings, loss of blood, or, if I were lucky, I'd drown. I shivered and retreated from the edge of the pier. I'd always been afraid of deep water; there's too much of the unknown down there, too much out of my control.

10

The End of Days

I admired a wall-sized painting in Grayson's studio space. It had transformed over the last few days from a traditional portrait of a happy, smiling family to a macabre circus scene, bright neon strokes smeared over the previous paint. The faces were now clownish, with bright red streaks for mouths. I got closer.

"Is that glitter?" I asked.

"Yeeeees," Grayson twirled, "I like it."

"Me too. I really love this. Is this the piece you're going to use for the final show?"

"I don't know. Maybe? It makes me feel bad," he gestured, "'cause my mom, she dead."

"I'm sorry," I stepped closer to the canvas and inhaled the stale smell of oil paint, "That's a terrible feeling." And I thought of Mitch, and how I didn't have time for him like I should have when he was alive, and my heart sank a little.

Grayson turned to me. "So did you decide what you're going to do for the show?" My face must have given away my feelings about it, that I wasn't at all prepared, because he added, "I feel like you're going to have an actual meltdown about this whole thing. Maybe you can do an installation and just call it *I make art*, and it can be you standing there just looking terrified."

"That's not a bad idea, honestly. I'm kind of fucked right now. The grotesques I've been working on are going to be shown in a different gallery, some show that Demyan set up. I honestly have no idea what to do. It's too late to make something for the grad show."

"I'm confident you'll figure it out. Are you hungry? Want to come to my place for dinner?"

"Jesus, is it already dinner time? I walked over to the window, it was black outside. I grabbed my jacket from his desk and slid into it. I checked my phone and saw a text from Francesco: "Just got back from Sicily, want to drop something to you at the studio. Are you there?" it read.

"Yes," I quickly typed, "but I'm leaving soon with Grayson."

"Be there in one minute."

"I'll meet you downstairs," I told Grayson, who was cleaning his brushes. I ran down the drafty stairwell and into the main area of the studio where some of my peers were quietly sketching or painting. Kuhle came wandering past me with the top half of her body covered in ceramic dust, like a ghost. "Hey babe," I smiled, "What are you up to?"

She laughed, "Oh, you know just getting things finished up. I'm doing some sculptures and working on a traditional dance. You?"

"You're dancing now, too? I'm waiting for Francesco to drop something off."

"I'd love to wait with you and say hello to that sweet man of yours but I've got to go water my face."

"Huh?"

"My face sculpture. I'm growing a plant sculpture that looks like my face. Tell Fran I said hi." She tap-danced away, disappearing at the end of the hall. Then she popped back around the corner. "I might sleep at your place tonight," she called and disappeared again.

Francesco came into the studio building in his black peacoat, the same one I'd met him in. He smiled and held up a lime-green box just a little bigger than a Rubik's Cube. He'd been in Sicily for a week and I'd missed him, but refused to really show it. It took a lot of self-control for me to remain stoic instead of leaping onto him and dry-humping his leg.

"Hi!" he said.

"Hi!" I gave him a hug. "How was Sicily?"

"It was work so not fun, I guess." He handed me the box. "But I brought this back for you. Some typical *dolci*."

I opened it. Little squares of chocolate, rose and pistachio sweets that I'd never seen before. The box smelled like cinnamon, flowers, and heaven.

"This is so nice. Thank you!" I tried to gauge the right amount of smile and enthusiasm, and leaned in and gave him a kiss. I didn't know how to show appreciation even though I felt gratitude. Part of me never felt like I deserved gifts, and there wasn't a lot of unbridled enthusiasm in my home growing up.

"I'm going to eat with Grayson. Wanna come?"

"No, I'm going home to shower and unpack. I'll call you tomorrow," he said. He paused for a minute and looked around. "Can I see your studio space? I still haven't seen it." I panicked. Showing him the deformed sketches in my studio would probably be pretty disappointing. I'd go from "cool artsy girlfriend" to "sad girl who seemingly learned art in prison as part of therapy."

"There's nothing really in there right now, plus I have to leave with Grayson…"

112

"Oh, okay." He seemed slightly suspicious and a little disappointed. "That's okay. Well, I'll call you tomorrow?"

I nodded and gave him a hug before he left. I opened the box and shoved one of the pistachio candies in my mouth. My throat instantly began to itch and feel restricted. Grayson came hopping down the stairs.

"Ready?" he asked.

I made a garbage disposal noise trying to itch my throat.

"Ew, what is that?"

"My throat itches. I ate pistachio."

"And?" he cocked his head to the side.

"And I'm allergic. It's itchy!"

"Are you going to die? Why would you eat it knowing that you're allergic?"

"I won't die, I do it all the time," I said.

"How have you made it this far in life?" He followed behind me. "Seriously."

In Grayson's apartment, we tossed our wet jackets on a chair. It had been raining for weeks and with the humidity I felt permanently pruned. His two-bedroom place was a mish-mash of vintage items from the fifties, sixties, and seventies. Grayson put on a pot of water for pasta as I slid into a chair at the table. He handed me a glass of wine and sat down across from me.

"Sooo, how are things?" Grayson raised his glass to mine. "Do you want to talk about your projects?"

"Ugh," I groaned.

"Mmkay, how are things with Francesco?" He got up to add pasta to the water.

I took a sip of wine. "Good, fine. He's great. He's sweet and I really love being around him plus it doesn't hurt that the sex is, uh, amazing."

"I'd put the sex on him," Grayson added.

"I know you would," I winked, "he's great but, I don't know. I'm not going to live in Italy forever. At some point, we have to break up and school is over in just a few weeks. Jesus, saying that out loud is awful. I'm not ready to go back home. *Non lo voglio.* But, it's not like we're going to get married so what are the other options?"

"I feel like he would marry you right this minute though. Like I've said before, you just have this thing. Who isn't in love with you? I mean, other than Leonardo. He hates you. It's possible that I'm in love with you. Is it possible to be in love with someone and not want to sleep with them at all, ever? If you don't want to go home, don't. Come with me, we'll move to Mars." He added salt to the water pot and began making tomato sauce.

"I don't want to go back to New York," he continued, "but Italy is full of *actual* insane people so I'm not sure what I'm going to do. *Che ne so io.*" He shrugged. "I don't-a know, either."

"You're not in love with me, Grayson, you don't even like women. Also, yes, let's move to Mars."

"That's true. But I definitely kind of love you."

"Well, I kind of love you, too."

The very thought of going back to Salt Lake made me a little queasy and sent a ripple of anxiety down my sternum like someone had pulled the nerves that ran down my abdomen taut and slid a violin bow over them. What was waiting for me in Salt Lake? I'd last seen my brother alive there; my dad and I were at least speaking now but he spent all of his time with his new family, the upgraded version, Family 2.0. My mom had all but turned inward since my brother died and she didn't call or write. It's like his death had sucked the last remaining maternal bits from her body and all she could do was focus on how to get through every day without falling apart. As much as I wanted to move home to be there for her, I couldn't because blocking out my own grief took all the extra emotional energy I had.

My friends were back home and I missed them, though in the past year while I'd been in Italy half of them had left Utah, and a bunch got married and had kids. A few still went to all the same bars, drank all the same cocktails, had all the same baggage and angst. Which had me wondering, did we have anything in common anymore? I had a handful of friends that I still talked with, although sporadically. I did miss them. Everyone always says that living abroad is a transformative experience because it is. But nobody tells you that the changes are unpredictable. I felt enriched with new experiences, skills, relationships, art, and culture, but other times diluted, like parts of me were going away to make room for the new things. Even the word "home" was becoming a vague word with multiple meanings. Where I grew up felt like "home," but so did my apartment with Amy, my nights with Francesco, the long walks with Grayson, the coffee dates with Violetta, and dancing with Kuhle and Jenny. Things that I'd loved, places with significant memories, friends, were scattered throughout Italy and Salt Lake, and I felt scattered with them. As the school year sped towards the end, I found myself at another crossroads, just like that night in the strip club or sprawled out on my mom's guest room floor. What's next? I wanted to stay in Italy, where I was happy, truly happy, maybe for the first time ever.

Grayson put a plate of pasta in front of me and refilled my wine.

"So you don't want to go back to New York?" I asked him.

"No. The city makes me want to curl up in a ball and rock myself. Thinking about it, it makes me want to cry."

"Yeah," I said and took a deep breath. "I know what you mean."

11

Mourning in Solidarity

The energy in the studio changed as we entered March. It had become somber and tense as the weeks pushed on and our countdown to the end of school, the end of Italy, came closer. Like an angry hive, my classmates were in constant, buzzing motion. Amy sprinted to her cubicle going two hundred miles per hour to get the last of her jewelry pieces hammered out and soldered; Jenny kept her head down, avoiding eye contact while prying cylinders from ceramic molds; Violetta stitched a long white gown so large a Cadillac could have worn it.

"I'm going to hang it from the rafters," she said, reaching into her bag and handing me a piece of chocolate. I scribbled endless ideas in my journal.

Grayson stood in front of me. "But-a Misty, a-why you do dis?" he imitated Leonardo, glitter stuck to his fingers and a little in his hair. When the light hit just right his head looked like a disco ball. Leonardo blurred passed us, like a windmill.

"You don't understand," he fretted to no one in particular. "This show needs to be perfect!" Apart from guidance, it seemed that his job was to motivate by radiating anxiety.

"He does realize this is an art school, not *medical* school, right?" I said. "If we fuck up, nobody will be maimed or die. I could honestly just frame a tampon and call it a day if I wanted to." I thought about it. "Aaaah..."

Grayson looked disgusted. "Please, don't."

I met Demyan in front of a toaster-size painting of worms in dirt done by a fellow student, Ali. Demyan was also now the major professor for Kuhle, Violetta, and Ali, and had set up a separate show for us. We were going to get coffee together to talk about our work and plan out the space in the gallery. We met pretty regularly, either as a group or one-on-one, although I avoided being alone with him whenever possible. Last week we'd scream-whispered in a café after he'd given some harsh advice and I told him that I really disliked working with him sometimes and questioned whether or not I should find a major professor who wasn't an ass. He'd yelled, "Oh, you're not going anywhere, don't be ridiculous. You know, you piss me off so bad sometimes I want to toss you out of that fucking window there." But most of the time the meetings were mild; he'd smile with the enthusiasm of an Anne Rice villain and ask, "What are all of you working on right now?"

At coffee, we brainstormed ideas on how to improve and he offered advice on what to tweak, if he liked them, or tell us where to shove the ideas if he didn't.

Demyan sipped his espresso and turned to me. "I think you should take some of your grotesque sketches and turn them into small framed digital photographs. How you evolve the work or present it is as important as or more important than the actual work itself."

"I don't actually know how to use Photoshop," I said.

He glared at me. "Then when we get back to the studio I'll have to show you." I looked across the table to Violetta, who was drinking tea and quietly observing the interplay.

Kuhle sat up tall. "I'm still practicing for my dance performance."

"I'd like to see it later," he told her.

She smiled and nodded.

Back at the studio Demyan marched me to the computer room and spent an hour walking me through steps on how to "transform" some of my paintings. In other words, take something that sucked and change it so that it looked like it sucked *on purpose.*

"No, no, that's ridiculous, you want it to have a raw quality," he said, bending over the computer and resizing my paintings from huge to microscopic. It was a great idea, but my loan money was quickly running out so I couldn't opt for an idea that would require me to buy frames since I could barely afford wine at that point. He grabbed my hand and moved it so he could show me something. With his face next to mine, I could hear him breathing and feel the heat radiating off of his body. My paintings were crude and messy. They were not "technically good" as Demyan put it, but they were "interesting." In the same way, I imagined, that a man wearing a tank top to proudly display his shoulder hair could be interesting. My artist statement for the grotesque pieces read that I wanted to "question beauty standards," but really I just liked the way it looked when pretty women made ugly faces. But I had finally learned how to bullshit my projects, unlike my earlier days, and it was glorious.

"There, done." He stood up suddenly. "I have a class to teach."

"Thank you," I said, standing up to shake his hand. He turned to face me and stepped forward, glancing down at my hand. He didn't take it.

"You're welcome." He lingered for a long moment, staring at my mouth again and the tension in the room made the air thick. Then, as

118

always, he quickly turned and left. Kuhle, who'd been at another computer on the other side of the room, turned in her seat.

"Oh shame, he can't help himself," she laughed, gesturing to her crotch. "He wants to cut that cake."

I rolled my eyes. "I'll see you later at my place," I said on the way out. "Grayson's coming over, too."

"Later, darling," she called.

* * *

In my bedroom I rubbed my eyes hard, "I feel like I'm going to throw up," I groaned and fell back on the bed next to Grayson.

Rape, rape, rape. I knew that rape had been used as a war tactic for centuries but what I didn't know was that up until the Yugoslavian war in the '90s, about the time that *Ace Ventura* opened in the theaters, it wasn't considered a war crime. I didn't know that it was still happening in the Congo right then, while I sat on my bed in Florence. Twelve-year-old girls, elderly women, every age in between, were torn in pieces, brutally raped, left for dead or deformed; pawns in a war they didn't agree to. I couldn't get the images of battered women and unspeakable violence out of my mind: their broken vaginas and spirits seared into my brain like a goddamn laser had embedded it there. Kuhle continued to read more from a link I'd been sent from a professor.

I'd received an email asking if I'd be interested in showing something at *The Vagina Monologues* show in Florence. They were looking for "local" artists to create work around what was happening in the Congo to draw attention to the cause. Grayson stared at the ceiling. He hadn't said anything for a while.

Kuhle whirled around from the computer. "I don't know. I really don't know. I just want to mourn. For all of the women, for humanity. For all of it." She shook her head. "Shame, why can't we love ourselves? Where's the self-respect, eh?"

"How fucking *depressing*." I reached for my wine glass.

"What if we made a video installation mourning humanity?" Kuhle suggested, her face lighting up.

"For *The Vagina Monologues*?" I asked. "I like that, let's do it."

After some research, we came up with the idea to carry out the mourning ceremonies of our ancestors.

"I'll do Xosa and you do Persian," Kuhle said.

"Perfect," I said, *before* I'd taken the next step, which would have been to actually research the ceremony before agreeing to it. I turned to Grayson who was still staring at my ceiling in shock.

"What do you think?" I asked.

"I like," he remained fixated on the ceiling, "but I want to be put back in the womb."

I Googled "Traditional mourning ceremonies Persian," at the studio the following day. Google responded with, "You're fucked, asshole." Apparently, my ancestors were *intense mourners*. Traditional mourning called for bathing and then tapping your forehead against a *machete*.

Kuhle bounced into the studio. "Heeey, there you are! You ready for this?" she asked, swinging a metal wash bucket, one of the ones that people apparently lost their peasant toddlers in, hence the phrase, "Don't throw your baby out with the bath water."

Kuhle's Xhosa mourning tradition also involved bathing. She set the video camera up on a tripod in a small back room and aimed it at the wash bucket we'd set against a blank white wall. She filled the metal basin with warm water from the sink, stripped down to her birthday suit and stepped inside, where she stood, shivering. She wet her washcloth and scrubbed her skin as if she were desperately trying to remove cooties. Then she stepped outside of the bucket, reached down to the ground and found a cordless hair shaver. The shaver buzzed in her hand like a thousand hives; she looked directly into the camera and sobbed as she ran it from her forehead to the crown of her head. Small clouds of black hair floated to the floor. Tears streamed down her face for both the women in the Congo and also because "black hair grows slow as fuck."

Then it was my turn. I slowly peeled my clothes off, reluctant to get naked in the ice box that was our studio. I threw my clothes in a pile and walked on my tiptoes to the wash bucket. Kuhle had refilled it so at least the water was warm when I stepped inside, which immediately triggered the need to pee. I had my silver hunting knife in my hand, the one I used to cut canvas and possibly to defend myself from potential lunatics or, in this case, to mourn the world like my historically hardcore brethren. I scrubbed my skin with a rag, stepped outside of the tub, knelt down, and whacked myself with the hunting knife, right on my widow's peak, hard enough to cause little blood beads to form on the surface but not hard enough to do significant damage. I was not happy to chop my widow's peak into alfalfa sprigs but I figured it was the least I could do for people who were dealing with a lot worse.

Later that night when Francesco came over to my apartment, I opened the door with my bangs all chopped to shit. He stared at the red lines on my forehead for a second then shook his head. "I seriously don't even want to know."

Years later, my mom stumbled across the DVD of our installation in a box of my things. She called me, crying, to ask if I'd been kidnapped and forced to whack my head by some deranged man. I sighed, "Yes, Mom, then they let me and Kuhle go, completely unscathed, and we never mentioned it to anyone. After, they gave us the DVD as a souvenir."

My mom rolled her eyes. "Well, how am I s'posed to know?"

They showed our video in the foyer of the theater where they performed *The Vagina Monologues*. From the back of the room, Kuhle and I watched people watch us mourn and we were proud.

In The Raw

12

Arrivederci

Jenny and I stopped for a coffee on our way to the gallery to set up for *the* show, the end-all of our year abroad.

"I don't want to go back to Salt Lake," I said, dumping three packets of sugar into my cappuccino and attracting some judgy side-eye from an Italian woman at the table next to us.

"I don't want to go back, either," Jenny said. "How will I live without all this craziness?" She looked towards the street where two old men were squabbling about something in front of the window.

I put my elbows on the table and felt naughty. This would never be allowed at home where my mom would jab you with a fork for reaching across the table or putting your elbows on it.

"So, let's stay. I've been thinking about starting a design business and selling shirts with some of my designs. We could do it together and use the serigraphy studio? Let's stay and make shit to sell."

Jenny smiled. "Yeah! Let's do it, buddy! But are you serious?"

"Yeah, I really can't go home yet. It feels way too soon."

We both had tickets to go back home in June, me to Salt Lake and she to North Carolina because in order to get the student visa you have to buy a round-trip ticket. It's supposed to discourage people like us from overstaying our welcome. So it made the most sense for us to go home for the summer and come back to Florence in the fall, and that's what we agreed on.

"Looks like you can't get rid of us that easily, *Italy*," Jenny laughed.

Once we'd worked out the details, I texted Francesco: "Jen and I just decided to come back to Italy in September. To live. How do you feel about that?"

He responded immediately, something that rarely happened when he was at work. "Seriously? No way!" he wrote. "That would make me so happy you can't even believe."

Later that afternoon, at the gallery hosting our end-of-year show in Florence's hip, artistic Oltrarno district, I made my way to a far corner to claim some wall space. My legs were heavy like I was wading through sand. Even though Jen and I were staying until June and coming back after the summer, Grayson would be gone. Violetta, Amy, and Kuhle, all gone. We'd scatter to different states and continents, and who knew if we'd ever see each other again.

I stared at the wall, then dumped the contents of my bag out onto the floor: sketchbooks banged open, pages torn from my journals floated to the ground, and porn I'd printed out for my vagina paintings fanned out across the polished cement. Grayson had joked that week that I should "just hang up a bunch of stuff from sketchbooks and be done with it" and I thought, why the hell not? I pulled out a book that I'd bound in book-making class and set it on a chair, next to my pile of trash. I called it my *Lady Garden Party* book because inside were pictures of some of my classmates in the school's courtyard in their Sunday best, acting like they were crashing *Alice in*

Wonderland's tea party. The women threw back their heads and laughed, tea spilled down their arms and, because none of them were wearing underwear, vaginas were all over the place. It went well with my accidental theme for the year: pussy power.

I aimlessly wandered around the gallery for a minute to say hi to Jen while she arranged her sculptures, watch Violetta hang her giant dress, briefly help Kuhle set up the video player for our joint *Mourning in Solidarity* video project, and admire Grayson's glitter paintings. Then I dragged myself back to my corner of the gallery, where I grabbed pieces of paper from my pile of crap at random and sloppily taped them into a doorway-size collage on the wall. I titled my work *Das Gift*, which meant *The Poison* in German. I stepped back to get a better view and realized that during my year of art school, I had basically produced a teenager's spank bank.

While admiring my decoupage wall of smut, I remembered that I'd invited Francesco to the show that night. What if he didn't "get" the genius behind sticking random porn to a wall? He was as straight-laced as it gets; an engineer who wore shawl-neck, cable-knit sweaters, and boat shoes, and looked like at any moment he might sail away on his yacht. Would Francesco still like me if he saw what I did all day at school? Did I care? Of course, I cared, but it bothered me that I did because I shouldn't. It made sense to dump him when/if he got all judgmental because it would hurt less to reject him first.

When the gallery doors opened I was in the back corner with Violetta, admiring her cocktail dress and amazing cleavage. We'd all gone home to change and Violetta had pulled out all the stops.

"Violetta, you look hot, I'd totally go down on you," I joked. She laughed. Professors trickled in, then students, and eventually the general public. The school's benefactor, a painter, entered dressed in splendor and over-the-top elegance like a Baroque vampire. He paused briefly in front

126

of my installation and I cringed thinking, Why can't I paint trees like a normal fucking person? He leaned on his cane, inhaled, and moved on to the next piece of work, probably feeling a little frustrated that idiots like me were a by-product of his legacy.

I was in the middle of telling Jen how worried I was about Francesco coming when a young blonde girl, one of the women I'd interviewed for my orgasm video, the one who described an orgasm as "wet," briskly approached us.

She stopped in front of me, unusually close.

"I fucking love you," she said. "Your work is amazing and you're hot, holy shit, you're so hot." Then she grabbed my head and kissed me, fast and hard, flicking her tongue against my tonsils. And then she pivoted and walked away, leaving me stunned and speechless.

"What the hell was that?" Jenny asked.

"I–I don't know," I said.

"That happens to her a lot," Grayson added from behind us. "She has really strong pheromones."

I smelled my arm and shrugged.

Francesco glided into the gallery a few hours later, after most of us were somewhere between buzzed (everyone else) and drunk (me). As soon as I saw him my stomach knotted and I immediately regretted my decision to invite him. He'd brought his colleagues and his ex-girlfriend's best friend with him. They seemed like the kind of guys who would faint if they saw a vulva in direct light, and any moment they were going to walk over to my wall and get a full view of my not-so-private privates, and later I'd have to shake their hands and be like, "What did you think of my labia?" *Holy Jesus no.* I hid behind a crowd of students in the opposite corner with a plastic cup of wine clenched in my hand and mouthed to Violetta, "He fucking brought friends!"

Francesco made his way around the room and stopped in front of my work. His colleague picked up the *Lady Garden* book from the chair. Francesco leaned into my wall of torn-up vomit. I tried to duck into the bathroom but the door was locked. Then he saw me. I eyed the exit but I knew there would be no decent explanation for randomly sprinting outside and down the street.

Instead, I did what I often do in times of humiliation: I tried to own it. I walked up to him, grabbed his head, said, "You're so hot," and planted one on him, just like that woman had done to me ten minutes prior.

"Thank you," he laughed. Then I firmly and aggressively shook hands with his friends and held my breath while I waited for a reaction.

"I love your stuff," Francesco said. "It's really interesting and your video with Kuhle is really bold and emotional."

"Thanks," I leaned in and whispered, "I'm really sorry your friends saw my uhm, *everything*."

"It's art," he whispered back. "Sometimes people are naked in art. They'll live, I'm sure." He winked.

After the show, we made our way towards Angie's in Via dei Neri, where Jenny, Violetta, Grayson, Amy, Kuhle and I danced with cocktails in hand. Vodka ran down my arm and dripped onto the floor. I was relieved that I hadn't been laughed out of the gallery and grateful that I got to spend a year doing things that I loved; to have met these people and learned so much from my very weird and brilliant teachers. I wanted to hold on to these fleeting moments, grab them and staple them to the ground, but I couldn't so instead I focused on the music.

We swayed to the band La Roux and Violetta sighed. "I'm going to miss this," she said. I mentally responded that it wasn't over, in a sort of "I'll keep you all in my basement" kind of way. Grayson spun on the dance floor, waggled his shoulders, threw back his head. How had I ever lived in a world without him and his twirling, OCD perfection, and glitter-covered everything? He was my goddamn unicorn.

One by one, everyone left that week. Grayson and I walked down to the Arno and sat on a bench to soak up some sun and share a baguette and mozzarella with a bottle of wine. Italians in large sunglasses and scarves swaggered along the sidewalk; a few with gelato cones, a few with cigarettes, a couple with both. Tourists paused to snap photos of the Ponte Vecchio and the Italians themselves. I looked at Grayson while he talked about his most recent Grindr date with some dull Italian man who lived at home with his overprotective parents. I already missed him.

"Why you look at me like that?" Grayson asked, in his fake Italian accent.

"I don't know. I mean, I'm going to miss you."

"Don't say that. You make-a me sad. But seriously, Peanut, we'll still talk, it's not going to be a big deal. No-a reason to-a be--a sad-a. What are you going to do in life now though, who will you go on to terrify? Also I feel like Leonardo might have an actual meltdown after our class. Something tells me he'll never be the same." He laughed.

"He's going to throw a fucking party now that me and my 'fire' have left."

"I feel like every time he talked to you he probably went home and curled up in his wife's lap."

"I'm going to miss him. Surprisingly. I'm going to miss everyone. Could we import Priscilla? Would she like New York?"

"I don't think she could handle it. She'd be too overwhelmed and just implode."

Grayson handed me the bottle of wine. I took a sip and we looked off into the distance and were silent for a long while.

"Love you Peanut," Grayson said, without looking at me.

"Me too." I concentrated on a male pigeon trying to woo a female nearby so I wouldn't cry.

* * *

Later that afternoon, Kuhle and I had a late lunch at Demyan's house just outside of the city. We walked into his living room and came eye-to-eye with a large naked portrait of him. There he was in all of his fleshy glory, flat on his back with a penis the size of a sixth grader's arm flopped up onto the smooth skin of his stomach.

"Is that fully erect?" Kuhle whispered to me.

"Partially," he said behind us, making us both jump. We exchanged wide-eyed shock.

Demyan fed us pasta marinara in his garden. We drank too much wine and scrambled to the top of an olive tree to get a better view of Tuscany while he watched from the ground and begged us not to kill ourselves. From up there, we could see all of Florence, the medieval towers, terracotta roofs and the top of the Duomo next to my home. Later, he returned us to our apartment and bid us farewell with a big hug and a kiss on the cheek.

Kuhle and I went straight from lunch to dinner and met Amy and Francesco downstairs from my apartment at a little tourist restaurant in Piazza del Duomo for some pizza. When we got a little loud after our third bottle of wine, an American man next to us turned and spat, "Could you please watch your language! I'm with my family!" Kuhle, the sweetest person on earth, slowly stood up, a storm brewing across her face as she glared down at the man.

"With all due respect"—she mimicked his accent—"fuck you, Colonel Sanders. What is it with you entitled white men walking around telling everyone else how to behave? I grew up during apartheid, and I am sick and tired of being told how to behave in public by people *like you*. The world doesn't revolve around your family! And your adult children will actually live if they hear bad words."

She calmly sat back down and fluffed her pink skirt. Stunned, we sat there for a minute before slowly raising our wine glasses to Kuhle.

"*Moondawaka!*" Francesco added, nodding to reference Colonel Sanders, his glass still held high. This was a Xhosa word Kuhle had taught him that meant something like "asshole."

The next morning, I said goodbye to Kuhle as we waited for the cab to take her to the airport for her flight to South Africa. We hugged and I kissed her cheek and she said, "We'll speak soon, Angel Muffin."

Amy left a few days later. We hugged tightly and Amy's eyes glistened. "Don't do that!" I said and bit my cheek. Violetta and I had one last dinner together before she returned to San Francisco, toasting "to the end of freedom." We hugged in the piazza next to the cathedral, and I watched her walk away, her hips rocking her purple dress until she was out of sight.

I moved my things upstairs to Jenny's place and said goodbye to my gorgeous apartment, plum comforter and massive living room where Amy and I had spent so much time on the couch talking. I tried not to think about all of the changes that were happening. In fact, I'd stopped thinking at all. I'd narrowed my focus entirely down to Francesco and the things I needed to do to move to Italy long-term. Growing up, I'd gone to eleven different schools, made and lost friends, and frequently lost touch with my dad. When my brother died, I moved. People in life came and went. No time to dwell: I coped by staying in constant motion.

But it was clear that somewhere below the surface the end of school and everyone leaving was a big deal, otherwise, I wouldn't be so desperate to hold on. Italy gave me a fresh start, far from the grief I felt after losing my brother, far from my dad's expectations or my friends. I wanted to cling to the coattails of all that possibility, of a new life, for as long as possible.

13
Plan B

I had two weeks left in Italy. You'd think that I'd have spent the time frolicking in vineyards and stuffing my face with lasagna, but I had something more important to do—ensure I had a reason to come back. I talked with the owner of a serigraphy school, and she agreed to let me print shirts in her studio. Both Jen and I had hand-drawn a few designs, and I'd hired a seamstress to make shirt patterns for us. We planned to do it all: have the shirts manufactured in Prato, hand-print them, and then sell them in high-end boutiques. I was sitting down at my desk researching business plans when I got an email from Francesco.

"I have to go to Sicily for work," he wrote, "we could turn it into a vacation. Want to come for a few days?"

A trip together? That seemed *really* serious, like *marriage* serious, because why would you go on vacation with a partner instead of a friend unless you planned to spend your life with them?

"Are you *sure* you want to spend four entire days with me?" I wrote back. Francesco and I didn't spend a lot of time alone together because we always had friends with us to act as a sort of buffer. He worked long hours as an engineer, traveled often, and on the weekends we were always with Jen, which I orchestrated and preferred. We were only alone in my bedroom late at night or on the occasional dinner date. How long into that trip until he realized he'd made a horrible mistake? Sometimes I felt like I'd tricked Francesco into liking me and wondered how long until the ruse was up. It just didn't make sense that someone who loved Coldplay as much as he did would be into someone who loved Bikini Kill as much as me.

"You're leaving Italy in two weeks for the entire summer. I want to spend as much time with you as possible," he responded.

"Okay. Sure." I wrote, against my better judgment. Did I even have a swimming suit?

We landed in Palermo on a Thursday morning, jumped into a black Mercedes rental (paid for by Francesco's company) and sped off into organized chaos. It was humid, and the lush green vegetation hinted that you might be on an island, but the city was all stone and jammed with tiny cars and the whole place reverberated with a cacophony of screeching tires and honking horns. Heaps of water bottles and plastic bags lined the roads and sidewalks. Where were the garbage cans? A man in front of us leaned out of his window and shook a fist at the traffic congestion in front of him, screaming wildly. A woman and her toddler sprinted for their lives through a busy intersection and literally dived for the sidewalk when a three-wheeled truck came barreling towards them. A strange fragrance of rose water and car exhaust wafted into the car.

"It's crazy here, isn't it?" Francesco smiled.

"Jesus," was all I could say.

At a stop light, a Senegalese street vendor came up to our car and poked his head right into Francesco's window. "Ciao!" he said, a huge smile on his face and a twinkle of grit in his eye. Did we want our windows cleaned? How about a box of tissues? A cat-ear headband that lit up? Francesco shook his head and the man moved onto the car behind us. It was strange, all of this traffic and garbage and screaming in the middle of ancient buildings. I loved it. Sicily had an energy that was uniquely wild.

In our dated art deco hotel, I showered while Francesco went over our itinerary on the bed. We were going to spend the weekend in Scopello lounging on a beach or two.

"Is there anything you want to do?" he yelled to me in the bathroom.

"Cocktails!" I called out.

I sprayed some rose perfume on my neck and watched him labor over the papers through a crack in the bathroom door. My life had taken such a weird turn. In another life, in Salt Lake City, it's as though I'd walked around in a fog of hurt. But now I was vacationing in Sicily with my hot boyfriend in a country I loved, and it was like I'd started over. My brain flooded with so much dopamine that nothing mattered—not the mistakes I'd made in the past, the grief that crept up on me when I was alone, the fear of failure or my future.

Francesco spotted me peeking at him. "What are you doing?" he asked.

I pushed the door open all the way and ran and jumped on him. He wrestled on top of me, brushed the hair out of my face and kissed me on the forehead.

"Let's go eat, *amore*," he said.

Downstairs in the restaurant, Francesco finished the last bite of tiramisu. I swirled my wine glass and watched a group of waiters joke together on a nearby wall. You'd never see that in the States, wait staff allowed to mess around at work in plain sight.

"I'm happy you came," said Francesco.

"Me too." I touched his hand on the table.

"I don't want you to leave," he said with a wince. He was so open with his emotions, just telling me how he felt and what he wanted all the time.

It was different from what I was used to with American guys and their Anglo-Saxon stoicism.

"Yeah but it's only three months. And there's Skype, and we'll talk every day." I wasn't worried about going back home, in fact, I just wanted to get it over with. Get home, get my shit done, and come back. I was too excited for sorrow.

"That's true. Don't forget about me," he laughed uneasily. And a part of me wondered if I could. Was that even a good thing? That's how you lose yourself, right there, by needing too much.

At a coffee shop the next day, I sat alone on the patio and scribbled observations into my journal while Francesco finished a few things at work across the street, in a building that looked like a prison because his company took government contracts that required a security clearance. I wrote about the widows in black who walked arm-in-arm together, the delicious chocolate *cornetto* I'd had for breakfast, and my feelings towards Francesco. My very *conflicted* feelings. This was not like any other relationship I'd ever been in. Unlike the people in my life who'd come and gone over the years, I knew he'd never leave. He felt so *permanent*. So, stable. And that was frightening because it would be so easy to get used to it; let my guard down, allow myself to have expectations. But letting go also meant opening myself to being blindsided. And I was afraid of losing myself. It happens, people get a serious partner and poof—it's like they've had a lobotomy and their entire life gets sidelined for a bit of sex and brunch. Fuck that. I didn't want that. And like most things in life, the things you're the most resistant to are the things you're most susceptible to, and somewhere deep down I knew it.

While I wrote in my notebook, two elderly Sicilians came and sat next to me and began arguing passionately about something. I kept my head down so they wouldn't speak to me. My Italian was terrible and the Sicilian dialect is practically another language that not even other Italians can understand. For example, "to work" in Italian is *lavorare* but in Sicilian dialect it's *travagghiari*, which comes from French.

At around noon, Francesco scooped me up from the café and took me to a local bakery for lunch where we ordered *arancini*, a delicious baseball-sized rice and mozzarella mixture, breaded and fried, from a local bakery. We ate it at the counter, like everyone else, and I suddenly understood what we were missing in the US: proximity. We walked through Palermo together for hours, saw the Palazzo dei Normanni, and learned about the Arabic influence in Sicily from a local barista named Paolo. We did the usual things that lovers do—held hands, kissed at stop lights, and took photos together in front of empty storefronts. We ambled around the city until the sun set, casting an orange glow over the gray stone buildings.

In a pizzeria near our hotel, we sat for dinner under painfully bright lights that beamed down on every table like we were plants in a greenhouse. The walls were a tyrannically vibrant orange and a warm gentle breeze blew in from the open patio. Francesco ordered us two margherita pizzas and two glasses of local Sicilian wine, a Nero d'Avola. We sipped the wine and Francesco asked again,

"But are you really going to come back?"

"No," I shook my head, "I'm actually already married to a pharmacist named Doug. I have nine children and a chicken coop waiting for me back home."

Francesco chuckled. "Oh? What are your chickens' names?" he asked.

"There are two hens, named Paula and Abdul."

"Huh?"

"Like the singer." I started dancing in my seat and singing, "He's a cold-hearted snake, oooh, look into my eeeeyes. No?"

He laughed but his eyes were more pensive than usual, so I detailed my plans for him once again: I'd go home to Salt Lake City for three months, get a job, save money, get a visa, and return in the fall. Nothing to stress about. He smiled crookedly and seemed to believe me.

A stray puppy walked timidly into the restaurant, a boxer mix no more than six months old. The puppy cautiously moved from table to table, his ribs poking out, his tail between his legs, sniffing for food. Every table ignored him. My heart sank and I started to gather my plate up to give it to him when he finally made it over to us. He pushed his little nose against my leg and I put my hand on his bony little head. Out of nowhere, a troll-faced waitress holding a fat baby ran up and kicked the puppy.

"Get out of here!" she yelled in Italian. Without thinking, I flew out of my seat like a fucking speed-skater.

"If you touch that dog again, I swear to God I will fucking drop-kick you, you psychotic bitch!" I screamed in her face. My hands were shaking, my face burned and adrenaline surged through my gut. Then I burst into tears, snatched my pizza and the bottle of wine from the table and stormed out of the restaurant.

The dog cowered at the patio entrance and I called him to follow me a little way down the block. He trotted behind me. Francesco had watched the entire scene in horror, his eyes bugging as though two everlasting gobstoppers had been jammed into his skull. He ran after me.

"*Amore*! Amore? What was that?" he asked when he caught up with me.

I turned to him and struggled to catch my breath. "Yeah, sorry," I sniffed, "I-I-I really lo-o-ve dogs." I set my entire pizza on the sidewalk for the puppy, who eagerly gobbled it up. "It's not h-i-i-s fault he's homeless and hungry. It's some asshole's fault. Someone loved him for a while, then they threw him away and he's staa-rrr-viiiiing." I vomited feelings all over Francesco and cried in front of him for the first time ever.

"I want to take him home," I declared, wiping my eyes.

Francesco touched my chin. "Amore, we can't take him home. We don't have a way to transport him. Unfortunately, there are stray dogs all over the south of Italy. We can't take them all."

"Why?" I asked defiantly.

The puppy finished the pizza and trotted away, with a little pep in his step. I hoped he'd be able to get a good night's sleep somewhere safe on a full belly. Then I turned back to Francesco, embarrassed.

He smiled. "Well, let's go get you a drink, yeah? You're upset and need a cocktail." I nodded, my lip still quivering. He grabbed my hand and led me sniffling down the street, all the way to the pub.

Inside, Francesco held my hand on top of the bar and looked at me lovingly but I was pretty sure he was thinking, *What the fuck did I get myself into?*

"So, you really like dogs, huh?" he asked.

"Yeah, all animals, really," I said, "but especially dogs."

I ordered a greyhound and chugged it, while he studied me attentively with an adoring grin.

"What?" I asked.

"Nothing, it's just that the more I get to know you, the—"

"More I terrify you?"

"No," he smiled, "the more I like you. I didn't know you had this passion for the dogs. I really thought you might attack that woman."

I rubbed my temple and thought, yeah, me too.

The next morning, we said goodbye to Palermo and zoomed towards the Sicilian coast in our rental car. Once we were out of the city, the landscape changed dramatically and the congested traffic, smog, and noise were replaced by the fresh smell of salted air blowing in from the rocky beaches and the soothing sound of the tide. Francesco blasted "A far l'amore comincia tu" by Raffaella Carrà and we sang along with the windows rolled down. My long hair stuck to my face and flew in my mouth; it was difficult to look sexy while eating your own head.

We did a lot that weekend. We stayed in Scopello, in a room rented out by an elderly lady and her five Maltese dogs (which seemed suicidal the way they ran into traffic constantly as though they were begging the cars to kill them). We saw Burri's famous land art project in the city of Gibellina because even after art school the universe kept rubbing my face in Burri and his penis art. And at Lo Zingaro nature reserve in Scopello, we walked along a ridge overlooking vast fields full of flowers.

"So," Francesco waggled his eyebrows, "do you want to get a dog?"

"I do love them," I said.

"I've never had a pet," he continued, "because my mom hates animals."

"Weird."

My shirt-dress blew up in the wind. I should have been gazing out at the green brush and the seaside but I was too distracted by trying to cover myself so all of the German tourists (in their amazing socks-with-sandals ensembles) didn't see my ass.

"Yeah, I've always liked animals a lot. Vegetarian, remember?"

He laughed. "Yes, I remember. And pigs are not plants. I'm learning so many-a tings."

We reached a cliff that shot out over the turquoise water. Francesco pulled me into him for a kiss.

"I love you," he said pressing his forehead against mine like a scene from every rom-com ever. Then, he slowly dropped to one knee and my stomach knotted. He looked up at me with his sincere brown eyes. "Will you marry me?"

The German tourists nearby stopped to watch and I squealed, "Yes! Just please get up!" while I fought with my dress more. We hugged and kissed with the wind whirling around us like we belonged on the cover of a grocery-store romance novel. I was happy but wondered if he really meant it. Did it really count if he didn't have a ring? Did I even care about a ring? We'd only been dating for six months; it seemed too soon for proposals and yet it somehow felt right.

At our bed and breakfast, we had he-just-asked-me-to-marry-him-sex and Francesco literally said, "I put a baby in you!" and he actually tried to put a baby in me. Really. We had been irresponsibly doing the whole "pull out" thing but this time he didn't pull out. I furiously shoved him off of me and paced around the room naked, yelling at him.

"We aren't ready to make a baby! Are you fucking *insane*? You can't just hijack someone's womb, even if you want to marry them. A baby is not a tomato; you don't just go around planting seeds you fuckin' farmer. You, you fucking baby farmer!"

"But I love you. We're going to get married, no?" He looked like a toddler that had just been scolded for pinching the family dog.

"Yes. Maybe? I don't know! I love you. But I will castrate you if you do that again. *Capisci?* You can't trap me into marriage through my vagina! God that's so *weird*!"

"Okay." He hung his head. "I'm sorry. I guess I wasn't really thinking it through. I just love you and want to be with you and a baby would be so—"

"Stupid. A baby would be so stupid," I snapped. "Get up. We're going to the hospital." We drove silently to a nearby hospital to get the morning-after pill.

The hospital was empty, the halls were dark and unlit, puddles of water gathered on the cement floor, and it smelled strongly of urine. It reminded me of a hospital in any dystopian story where the world has gone to total shit. When we finally found an administrator we were directed to take a seat at a desk in a small exam room. Four doctors came in and sat at a table across from us, giving the impression that we were about to be interviewed. A small man with male pattern baldness began. "*Cosa possiamo fare per Lei?*"

Francesco translated the conversation for me. "He wants to know what we're here for." I nodded. He spoke to them for a minute in Italian and then the doctors looked at each other.

"You want the morning-after pill?" asked a woman with long black hair pulled tightly into a low ponytail.

Francesco said yes.

Then a younger man who fumbled with his stethoscope asked, "Why?"

The woman leaned forward. "How-a old-a are-a you-a?" she asked me.

I had no idea why that would be relevant. Did they think I was too young to have sex? "I'm twenty-eight," I responded.

The woman shook her head, disgusted, and rambled off in Italian for a very long time, waving her hands with her face twisted into a scowl. I didn't need to speak Italian well to know that Francesco was being lectured.

"She said that twenty-eight is old enough to have a baby," Francesco announced.

I glared at her, then turned and smiled threateningly at Francesco. "Did she?" I said to him. "Well, if I'm pregnant, tell her I'll be shipping the baby to this panel of assholes and you can explain to them why they'll be raising our orphan."

I headed for the door while Francesco politely thanked them for absolutely nothing.

Luckily, the next morning I jerked awake with horrible, life-ending cramps, the same ones I'd had every month since Junior High. Often, the pain would get so bad I'd throw up, and I'd even fainted a few times in high school. Lying in bed, my legs contracted and twisted against the crisp sheets and my feet went numb.

I thrashed around and whimpered. "Just put the fucking pillow over my face and kill me! KILL ME!" I moaned.

Francesco bolted upright and stared at me, wide-eyed. Then he flew out of bed and began shoving his legs into his pants.

"What are you doing?" I groaned. He ran out of the room shouting, "I'll fix it!" before slamming the door behind him. His footsteps thundered down the hall and disappeared. Ten minutes later, he burst into the room, gasping, waving orange juice, ibuprofen, and a thermometer in my face. He fumbled to unwrap the thermometer and then tried to plunge it into my mouth; I turned my head and he jabbed me in the cheek. I was lying there dying and he was repeatedly ramming a thermometer into my face. He tried to shove it in my mouth again but this time I blocked it with my hand.

"What the fuck are you doing?" I clutched my lower abdomen.

"Your-a temperature!"

"My *what*! For cramps? Did you not have a maturation program in Italy?"

He looked down at me, baffled. "Huh?" I snatched the ibuprofen out of his other hand, threw three pills into my mouth, and passed out.

It was dark when I woke up except for a strange light that bounced along the walls. I rolled over. Francesco was sitting next to me and behind him, I could see our little hotel table. The last time I saw it, it was brown and empty, but he'd decorated it with a white tablecloth and a candelabra. There were dinner plates, a bottle of wine and two wine glasses.

"What's this?" I sat up feeling like I'd just woken from a coma and probably looked that way too.

"You are hungry? You need to eat-a." He leaned down and kissed my sweaty forehead.

Francesco helped me up from the bed, wrapped a robe around me, and led me to the table. I had this feeling of awe like I'd just stumbled across a real live centaur in the forest.

"You scared me today!" he said as he poured the wine in a glistening crimson stream into the glasses.

"Ugh, yeah, sorry about that. Cramps are the fucking worst. I'm really sorry we lost an entire day today."

"Your body tried to kill you," he said.

"Tell me about it."

He held up his wine glass. "I'm sorry I was stupid yesterday. That was not okay at all. I love you so much. To you."

I held up my glass. "And thank God for that thermometer. Seriously, I might have died without it."

"Asshole."

I cackled.

"Listen, so," he tapped his fingers rhythmically on the table to some beat in his head, "I spoke with my family while you were sleeping and my parents and my sister really want to meet you."

My throat tightened. "Hmm, I really think it's kind of soon, don't you?"

"It would-a be nice if you met them."

I couldn't imagine a world in which his Bible teacher mother and retired police officer father would like me.

"But what if they hate me?"

"Babe," he smiled, "it's impossible to hate you."

It was not the first or last time that Francesco was *painfully* wrong about something.

14

Eat Drink & Die

We'd only been back from Sicily for an hour when Francesco began to wear me down about meeting his parents.

"Please meet them!" he begged while I emptied the contents of my luggage into the laundry basket in my tiny temporary room in Jenny's apartment. "They'd love to meet you. My sister loves tattoos! Please!"

"Wouldn't it be cool if we could talk to dogs?" I said.

"Come on! It will be great! You can see where I was born!"

"Was it in your parents' bathtub?"

He narrowed his eyes. "No, *asshole*. A hospital like everyone else."

"Well, that's not interesting then."

"Please?"

"Can't. My cat is sick and he might die," I said.

He laid out a pair of skinny navy-blue slacks and a blue polka-dot shirt for the next morning and yelled over his shoulder, "You don't even have a cat!"

"Oh my God! No! Is he already dead?"

Francesco sat down on the spare twin bed.

"Look, if you won't come to meet my parents, at least come to Cumino before you go back to the US and meet a few of my friends. They're having a party this weekend. And, if we have time, maybe we will have lunch with my parents." An Italian party could be fun. I got really close to his face and looked directly into his eyes, an aggressive negotiation tactic I learned from my dad as a teenager.

"Can Jen come?" I asked.

"Of course she can-a come!"

I didn't share Francesco's enthusiasm. As far as I was concerned, no good could come from me spending time with his family. None. For one, we'd only been dating for six months and sure, he'd proposed, but that seemed like a grand gesture at best. I appreciated it, but I wasn't about to start planning our honeymoon. Also, I'd already lumped his family into "Group B."

When I was eight years old, I was playing on the sidewalk with a little blonde neighbor girl. Her pigtails had been smoothed into place and curled into ringlets, while my thigh-length brown hair grew out of my skull like a weed and cascaded over half of my body. We were examining potato bugs and laughing when her mom came out of the house and approached us.

"Where do you live?" she asked me.

I pointed down the street. "That one on the corner."

"Which ward do you belong to?" she asked.

"Ward?" I looked up, confused.

"Church. Is your family LDS?"

"We don't go to church."

"I see," she said. She reached down and grabbed her daughter's hand and led her into the house.

Growing up in Utah was like growing up in that one Dr. Seuss book about the Star-Belly Sneetches. In the book, there are Sneetches with stars, and Sneetches without, and the ones without are treated like shit and banned from everything worth doing. In Utah, the Star-Belly Sneetches belonged to a specific church club and everyone else was basically a starless heathen who didn't get invited to birthday parties in kindergarten. While parents in our area went to worship Jesus on Sundays (dressed like they'd just stepped out of *Little House on the Prairie*), my mom went to the bar (dressed like my hero, Dolly Parton).

I learned early on to lump people into groups. Group A would give me a chance, mostly because they were outcasts like me, and Group B were bigoted assholes who did not like people like me and were a waste of time. The irony of this sort of reactionary categorization is that it essentially made me a bigoted asshole, too.

Francesco told me that his parents were super traditional, and so as far as my upbringing went, that meant that they already didn't like me. Don't get me wrong, I loved to visit tradition, get dressed up in it, but it wasn't a space I could occupy for too long. In my experience, "traditional" often came with the bad kind of "isms" and "phobias," group-think, some weird thing to do with modesty, and being all "Rraaaar, men are beeest, yay patriarchy!" (I love men but having a penis doesn't make you *that* special).

At least, that's what I'd witnessed growing up. In fact, my dad's traditional streak was the reason we fought so much. We viewed the world so, so, differently. For example, he believed that tank tops were a crime against decency and I've been topless on a number of European beaches because weee! My dad also believes anything that any Persian tells him, including every old wives' tale ever. He believes that if you're tired you should put black tea in your eyes, and if someone is having a stroke you can bring them back to life by violently tugging on their ears and jabbing a needle into their fingertips, whereas I believe you should never carry out "life-saving medical tactics" you find in a chain email from your Persian cousins. I imagined that things would be exactly the same with Francesco's parents, only worse: they would expect me to show up and win them over in a language I didn't even know. The *assholes*.

My Italian skills were limited to present and past tense, and livestock. Basically, I could have a very simple conversation about Old McDonald's farm but I couldn't express my opinions on social problems or even recount my day without sounding like a drunk toddler. If I couldn't fully express myself, what the fuck was the point of talking? I was the opposite of Jenny, who could get by with a ten-word vocabulary in any language. She was likable, plain and simple, and could go on for hours about the weather. Truly, I've heard her. I envied anyone who could talk about impersonal things like snow or cake at length because I'd never been good at it.

Once at a cocktail party, I told a stranger that my earliest memory was of sitting on the floor in a housing project eating my mom's birth-control pills when I was one. "Do you think I'm sterile now?" I asked. I only realized after she got really quiet that I'd said something "off."

I told Francesco my concerns but his eyes glazed over and he described a scenario very different from the one I imagined. He envisioned me as a sort of Disney princess, all but gliding into their apartment in a ball gown, covered in songbirds, enchanting as hell. My God, I thought, is that how he sees me? According to him, I'd walk in and my scent alone would convince them to love me as much as he did. I saw the opposite, the reality; I saw the horror on their faces as he announced me as his one true love, a mess of a woman he'd dragged home, paint-stained, tattooed, and wild-haired. I knew I was right and I was afraid. I loved Francesco and I wanted them to like me, desperately, but they wouldn't.

On a Friday afternoon in July, the three of us left Florence for Cumino in Francesco's Fiat Punto. For the first hour, Jenny and I talked about our flights back to the US the following week. She couldn't wait to see her dogs and friends. I couldn't wait for my brothers and sisters, and Mexican food. The next three hours, Jenny read a book and I looked out the window at the green pastures splattered with sunflowers and the occasional medieval town perched on passing hilltops. Tiny cars whizzed past us at one hundred miles per hour, weaving through traffic like they were in *Mario Kart*.

A family with a German license plate sped up on my side of the car to pass us. Their blonde hair and pale complexions reminded me of my brother, Mitch. When I was five, I used to hold him on the couch, his head resting in the crook of my knee. I'd tell him stories while gently stroking his blonde curls. I wasn't looking forward to going back to Salt Lake and being surrounded by the memories of him and the unrelenting regret. I inhaled deeply, sucking the sadness down into my core, where it belonged.

We passed Rome and I thought of Grayson and spring break.

"We'll be there in about forty-five minutes," Francesco said.

I welcomed the distraction; my sadness swapped places with anxiety. We were close to Cumino, close to Francesco's parents' apartment, where we'd be staying.

"But it's fine," Francesco had reassured me, "we'll hardly see them. They're never home." I fixed my eyes on the dashboard and took a few measured breaths. What am I going to do if they don't like me? I really wanted his parents to like me. If they didn't, and they had plenty of reasons not to—my general weirdness for one—he probably wouldn't like me anymore either. Jesus, I wondered, when did I start thinking like this? I didn't like it.

"Babe, what's this look on your face? You don't look very good."

"I'm okay," I lied.

He eyed me suspiciously and put his hand on my leg reassuringly.

At nightfall, we pulled into the parking lot that belonged to a cluster of pastel-yellow apartments that stood out against the dark sky. Francesco parked his car in front of one of them. He pointed to a balcony with pink pajamas drying on the line.

"That's where I grew up," he said. I pictured little Francesco running around this parking lot with his friends. He must have been adorable.

Jenny leaned forward. "Don't worry, friend! It's going to be fine." But I caught her flashing a concerned look in Francesco's direction in the rearview mirror.

Francesco's parents swung open the front door. The first thing I noticed was that they were both tiny, inches shorter than the rest of us, like the size of an American eight-year-old. The dad was older than my parents, maybe in his sixties, but his wife was about ten years younger than him. They were in casual business attire like they'd just got home from the office, but it was hours past dinnertime. The dad had a cloud of white hair that seemed to float on his head and a matching white mustache as though he'd enjoyed the seventies way too much to ever let go. The mother wore her dark brown hair in a sleek chin-length bob, one side tucked behind her ear.

"*Buonasera*," they said. I let out an inaudible "buonasera," like air escaping from a leaking bike tire. Francesco leaned down to kiss his parents. It was bizarre how the dad looked so serious and the mom stood with her hands clasped together, composed and polite like they'd never met Francesco before. They introduced themselves to Jen and me in Italian as Amalea and Marcello, and gestured for us to come in.

In the foyer of their apartment, the four of us faced each other awkwardly and silently.

The white tiles were so clean they glowed, an automatic Glade freshener puffed a chemical fragrance at us, the one that's supposed to smell like laundry but really just smells like bleach laced with peonies. Amalea examined me the way I'd seen so many people do in cafés or restaurants or in the street. She started with my feet and then slowly scanned up to my face where she lingered with her eyes narrowed skeptically. The mood was notably somber as though someone had just died and we were there to give our condolences. When she spoke to Francesco, I understood less than usual.

"Sorry, she's speaking dialect," Francesco explained. "Do you guys want something to drink or eat?"

"*No, grazie,*" I replied.

She nodded and showed Jenny and me to where we'd be sleeping. The bedroom must have belonged to Francesco's elder sister; there were dolls on a shelf and pink accents on the picture frames and pillows. Francesco went to the next room over. We put our bags on the bed and looked around for a minute.

"So, here we are," Jenny said.

"I need a drink," I said, laying back on the bed.

"Me too!"

Francesco popped his head into our room.

"Let's get out of here. Grab your stuff. Come on!"

He ordered us around like we were making a break from prison. Ever since we walked in the door, I'd noticed that he seemed jumpy and agitated, like the opposite of his sweet, composed self. Maybe the long drive had worn on him?

In a small square, young people were drinking cocktails on a large patio. It looked a lot different than Florence or Rome. Instead of medieval or Renaissance architecture, the buildings in Cumino were newish, from last century, and it felt a little like Utah, as if we were about to have a drink at a strip mall. The piazza was surrounded by two bars, a Calzedonia swimsuit store, and a playground.

"Why's the architecture so different?" I asked.

"Heavy bombing during the Second World War," Francesco said hurriedly, like he had no time to answer my silly questions.

A group of Francesco's friends jumped up from a table some ways away and ran over to us.

"I'm Lorenzo," one man said in Italian. His eyebrows had been plucked into two perfect Nike swoosh logos, and his forehead was glowy and smooth like a polished stone. He put an arm around Francesco and lifted his chin, almost possessively. I liked how Italian men weren't afraid to touch their friends, unlike a lot of American guys who were paranoid about what people might think. We sat at a table and ordered a round of Campari spritzers from the waitress. Francesco was in his natural habitat, where he grew up, and I didn't like it. There was something drastically different about him—the way he sat, and talked, even his movements—and I felt like I didn't even know this person. He'd never been so distant or cold towards me. Usually, when we went out he stayed right next to me, proudly, almost pouring himself over me in this obnoxious way that kind of drove me crazy, but here he wouldn't even look at me, almost like he wanted to downplay our relationship. He spoke dialect with his friends and ignored me.

"Where are you from?" a guy asked me and Jen in very broken English.

"Salt Lake City," I answered.

"North Carolina," Jenny said.

"Where?" he asked.

"Kind of near New York?" Jenny said.

"OH! NEW YORK!" he yelled, super excited.

"I guess I'm kind of near Las Vegas?"

"WHOA! LAS VEGAS!" he yelled excitedly again.

He went back to speaking dialect with the rest of the group, and I was like, okay, fuck this, so Jenny and I talked amongst ourselves in English for the remainder of the night.

We woke up to a banging in the kitchen and the smell of tomato sauce. It was late, almost ten o'clock. Francesco came into our room and told us to get ready, lunch would be served soon.

"How ready?" I asked.

"Shower, hair, makeup, very ready," he said. He closed the door and I rolled over to Jenny and groaned, "Here we goooo."

"We have to do our hair to eat at home?" she asked.

"Apparently, *very ready.*"

In the dining room, Francesco's dad, Marcello, had a fistful of bread in one hand and cheese in the other. He ate heartily and watched the television, which was so loud I could feel the sound vibrating in my spine. Jenny and I took a seat next to him but he was totally oblivious to both us and his wife, who shuffled to and from the kitchen twenty-five times. Sweat glistened on her upper lip and her biceps pulsed under the weight of the plates she carried.

Francesco came into the room and sat next to me. He poured wine for the table and said a few things to his dad, who nodded but didn't look away from the TV. Amalea had changed into slacks and a shirt and sat at the table, her cheeks flushed. She smoothed her bob into place and looked around the table.

"*Mangia!*" she said, ordering us to eat.

We all raised our glasses. "*Salute!*" Clink, clink. The wine was delicious.

"My father made this wine," Francesco said.

"It's really good!" Jen responded.

We dug into the appetizers (*antipasti*), some *frutti di mare* (seafood, mostly calamari), fresh olives, and *verdure sott'olio* (vegetables in oil).

I smiled at the father. *"Buona!"*

He laughed. Had I said it wrong? Francesco sat unusually tall in his seat, rigid as if he'd just graduated from the Marines. He spoke with his parents in dialect and occasionally spoke Italian to me but I struggled to understand him.

"What did you say, babe?" I asked.

"Speak Italian!" he barked.

"But I don't know how to say it in Italian," I whispered to him. "Should I just not speak if I don't know how to say it?"

He glared at me and shook his head, clearly annoyed.

Frankly, he was being a complete asshole. I considered standing up and leaving, or throwing my wine in his face, or breaking up with him then and there, but eventually just settled on quiet resentment.

After the first course of pasta and a second course of rosemary chicken, potatoes, and oil-roasted peppers, I'd calmed down a little and tried again. I wanted to tell Amalea, "This food is delicious, you're a wonderful cook," in Italian but it came out as, "You make food, good. Food is good. Very nice," like a Neanderthal.

"What?" She looked around the table to see if anyone else could have possibly understood the jumbled nonsense coming out of my mouth.

"Food nice?" I repeated with less confidence, a whisper, really.

She turned to Francesco and said something. He translated my compliment for her.

Amalea turned back to me and said in very clear Italian that I actually understood, "Grazie. You know," she shook her head in disapproval, "you need to learn Italian."

Lunch lasted a tortuous *two hours*. I cut my food slowly, chewed quietly, and willed myself to disappear. I felt like I'd been dragged into a situation I didn't want to be in, put on display and then chastised for being an outsider—basically my entire childhood as a non-Mormon in Utah public schools. I felt like that same little girl again, the one who got it all wrong. Francesco and his parents had a lively conversation about something or another, Jenny chimed in on occasion using the few words she knew and everyone laughed. How did she do that?

After dessert, I jumped up to collect the plates, hoping for redemption, but his mother yanked the dirty dishes out of my hands and scolded me. The father shook his head, and Francesco said flatly, "Guests don't help clean up here."

"Oh. I'm sorry," I said to her in broken Italian. She sighed loudly, threw up her hands and walked into the kitchen.

The car ride back to Florence was quiet but you could feel the tension in the air, the same way you can somehow feel fog. You move and the particles around you feel heavier. Jenny read her book again, I watched the blur of vineyards pass by, Fedez rapped on the radio. When Francesco stopped to get gas I turned to Jenny.

"Am I insane or was that weird and they hated my guts?"

"Um, I mean, I don't think they *hated* you. But to be honest it was definitely weird. It kind of seemed like they weren't excited to meet you. I don't know, friend. I'm sure it will get better."

Back in my bedroom in Florence, I tore off my clothes and wiggled into a tank top for bed. I waited for Francesco to say something about the weekend but he didn't. In fact, he'd barely said a word since we'd left, almost as if he were in shock. Finally, I'd had enough.

"So, your parents really didn't want to meet me, did they?"

"Yes, they did."

"Don't lie to me."

"They wanted to meet you."

"So why were they so put off then?" I asked. "I didn't even get a *chance* to say something weird. Did I do something wrong culturally that I'm unaware of? Did I violate a custom?"

"It wasn't a cultural thing," Francesco responded. "You could have tried to actually talk more instead of just sitting there in silence."

"What are you talking about? You told me not to speak English and I don't speak Italian! What did you think? That I'd get to their house and magically become fluent by breathing in their air? *That's not how language works!* And you were being so cold and such a dick."

Francesco lowered his head and took it all in. Then he sat down and put his arm around me. "I'm sorry. I know. I wasn't being very helpful. I was just so nervous and I wanted them to like you so bad that I was frustrated that it wasn't going as well as I'd hoped."

"But why? They liked Jenny a little, which makes sense because she's super outgoing and has really nice teeth and—"

"No, babe, they were warmer to Jen because I'm not dating her. Surprisingly, you didn't do anything weird. If anything, I was a *dickhead*, as you said. And-a, well, my mom, she's an Italian mother. She's nervous because this relationship is important for me and she doesn't like that."

"And that's bad because I'm weird?"

Francesco took a deep breath as though he was about to tell me something he didn't want to say out loud.

"They have no idea how weird you are, yet," he said with a smile. I stared at him with growing concern.

"No, babe," he hesitated, "it's uh, they don't like that you're American."

I fell back on the bed.

"Seriously? Did our road trip time-travel back to the 1800s? Also, I'm only partially *American*. I'm also brownish with a Middle Eastern daddy." I held up my arm towards the ceiling for inspection.

Francesco lay down next to me. "Yeah, I don't think that the Muslim thing helps with Catholic parents."

I rolled over to face him. "And my mom used to strip."

He grinned. "I know."

"And I make nude art."

"Yeah, I've seen it," he said, raising his eyebrows playfully.

"So really this is more humane for everyone because if they started out liking me they'd just be really disappointed later when I gave them a reason not to like me. I guess it's a little less personal this way?"

"Nah, come on. They're going to love you eventually. You're great!" He laughed. "They just think all Americans are terrible wives and bad mothers because they watch a lot of TV."

"That's true," I said, "we do hate babies, all of them because babies are assholes. And you know what? I doubt my dad will be excited about you, either. I mean, he watches a lot of TV, and you know, *Jersey Shore*."

"Alright, point taken, it's unfair, I know," Francesco said. "And I love my parents but it doesn't matter if they have problems for this. But you know what does matter?" He put his hand on the side of my face and looked into my eyes.

"What?"

"I love you." He kissed me on the forehead and ran his hand through my hair but I hadn't brushed it in a few days so his fingers got stuck.

I pulled his hand free, ripping out a handful of hair in the process.

"Brush your goddamn hair!" he laughed.

"Nope," I said.

Unconcealed

15

The Wild West: Back in 'Merica

July 2010

Francesco looked like he might cry at the airport. He hugged me. I hardened like a corpse, patted his back (like we were college bros), pulled away and jazz-hand waved goodbye. I'd always prided myself on a certain level of emotional restraint (less so when it comes to rage) but Francesco was the opposite of me and seemed to freely display his full range of emotions anywhere and everywhere, from grocery store aisles to intersections and airports. He stared at me, visibly heartbroken like he'd never see me again.

"*Ti amo*," he whispered. I should have reassured him and, I don't know, been a person, but I couldn't stop thinking that we were in a Telemundo series, or an episode of *Days of Our Lives*, in one of those scenes where a character reveals something like, "The man you love died a decade ago and I'm actually his twin but, by God Barbara, I love you! I love you! Can't you see?" I struggled not to smirk.

"*Anch'io*," I told him, but cheerfully, the way someone might admire nice weather. I looked around the crowd to see if anyone had been watching us and of course they were, they always were, and it embarrassed me. I'd regularly witnessed all forms of public affection while in Italy, from aggressive hand-holding to "let's make a baby in this square" dry-humping. I still hated it. I didn't see the point in liking people publically; I mean, why did everyone need to know we liked each other? There was also a part of me that worried I'd somehow damage our chemistry if I had a face full of mucus and running mascara when I said goodbye. As though I'd sear that image into his head and it would be the only thing he saw when he thought of me for the rest of eternity. So, he poured his heart out and I stood there like a mannequin person.

Francesco forced a weak smile. "Call me when you land, okay?"

"You won't even notice I'm gone!"

I picked up my bag and followed the moving line. His eyes followed me until I turned the corner and disappeared.

From the air, Florence shrank into brown-and-green specks and I missed Francesco already. Three months seemed like forever. I used the last of my phone credit to text my parents my arrival time. I hadn't seen them in months and I had mixed feelings about it. I was excited to go home, to see loved ones, to spend time with my brothers and sister and my friends, but also nervous. I'd changed a lot in the past year. I resented the very idea of being slammed by everyone's myriad expectations of me and all the baggage that went along with it. Everyone back at home would expect a version of me that just didn't exist anymore and it irritated me. Who was I? Not totally new, because I don't think that anyone can completely abandon who they are, but I wasn't the "same old me" anymore either. Going home would be complicated and a little uncomfortable. The best way to describe how I felt as I crossed the Atlantic towards Salt Lake City was this: it felt like being touched too soon after an orgasm.

I landed in the early evening and found my younger brother Dakota waiting for me in his white Honda Civic. I gave him a hug and kissed him on the cheek then stood back to admire him for a minute, his solid muscular frame and kind eyes. Man, I'd missed him.

"Mom didn't want to drive 'cause it's gettin' dark," he said as he lifted my four enormous bags into the trunk and backseat.

"Jesus sis," he laughed, "are these bags full of Italians?" I punched him in the arm and we wrestled for a second before we finally jumped into the car. We sped north to my mom's house in Ogden, past smokestacks and the mines that smelled like rotten eggs, past suburban neighborhoods with matching floor plans and identical siding. For the first time, I had a strong opinion on urban planning: these hodgepodge cities were so fucking *ugly*, and who thought it was a good idea to just stick stores and neighborhoods like patchwork across the landscape? The urban sprawl wasn't only hideous, it was an offensive use of space, unlike Italy where care went into aesthetics. In a green, mountainous state, what asshole approved gray fiberglass siding?

"So you're going to see Mom's new house for the first time?" Dakota asked.

"Yeah. How's Mom by the way?"

"Honestly? Not great. She still cries all the time," he paused for a moment, "and drinks pretty much every day now. But, I don't know." He shrugged.

"How are you?" I asked, patting his leg.

"Good, I guess. Probably better if you hadn't run off," he said, laughing nervously. He pretended to be joking but I knew he wasn't. It was selfish of me to leave—I knew that he knew that, but I'd done it anyway. I didn't feel like I'd had a choice if I wanted to be okay, and I needed to be okay so I could eventually be there for Dakota.

I cleared my throat. "I'm sorry, honey. I just had to get away. If you weren't a senior in high school I could have dragged you with me."

"I'm just kidding anyway," he smiled.

"I am sorry," I said, wholeheartedly. He nodded as if to say thank you.

We pulled up to a small, red-brick rambler.

"This is it, sis," Dakota said, "it's cute, huh? Anyway, I'll come over for breakfast tomorrow. I have to get home." I hugged him, pressing my face into his thick neck and inhaling that strange teenage boy mix of grit and too much cologne.

"Love you," I said.

"Love you, too."

I walked in the front door with my bags. My mom and her boyfriend, Brian, were holding beer cans in the kitchen and the house smelled like food, strawberry potpourri, and cigarette smoke, my mom's personal perfume. As always, she'd decorated every room thematically. The kitchen had been done up in red with cartoon French chefs, the living room green with bears.

"Misty!" My mom called out and stood up straight. I set my luggage down and ran and jumped on her. She smiled a big toothy smile and hugged me with teary eyes. It caught me off-guard because she's always hated being touched and often recoiled from affection as if hugs wielded tiny knives. It hadn't even occurred to me that she might have missed me. I hugged Brian, a tall, kind man with tanned skin from long days laboring under the sun and happy eyes that twinkled in spite of his obvious hardships.

"Sit down at the table," my mom said. "I made a tater-tot casserole."

I hesitantly lowered myself into a chair. After a year in Italy eating handmade pasta and sauce from local tomatoes, I wasn't sure how my stomach would react to tater tots, cream of mushroom soup from a can and two pounds of bulk cheddar cheese.

She set a heaping plate down in front of me and I shoveled it in with abandon like I hadn't eaten for weeks. Apparently, I subconsciously missed my mom's personal brand of cooking: all from a box, can, or freezer, preservative-filled, processed, and *delicious*.

"How was your flight?" she asked.

"Good. I'm going back after the summer," I said, shoveling more food into my face.

"Wait, what?" She froze. "Why?"

"To start a design company and to be with my super cute boyfriend. You'll have to come visit!" I beamed at her.

"How long would it take me to drive there?" she asked, sliding one of her long Misty cigarettes out of their blue-and-white box.

"In your hovercraft? You can't drive over the ocean, Mom."

"There's no way to drive there? Well, how the hell am I s'posed to know? I dropped out of school when I got pregnant with you."

"I know. And thanks for having me and all that."

My mom smiled with all of her teeth. I'd never seen her smile so much. I missed our banter. This is what it was like with my mom when she was happy, I teased her and she giggled. When I was little, she'd put on the A-track and dance with me in the living room to "Islands in the Stream" with Dolly Parton and Kenny Rogers. When I was a teenager, young and insensitive, I'd scream, "SHE LET ME OUT OF THE BASEMENT! OH BLESSED DAY," at her in the grocery store until she'd grab me and cover my mouth, laughing hysterically. I loved seeing her like this, giggling, happy, but it was rare. When I left, she hadn't smiled in months and at the time I worried she might never smile again. I worried that none of us would.

"Let me show you the house!" Mom said as soon as I finished eating. She was proud of herself that she'd bought the house on her own, working long shifts as a CNA in hospice care, and that she and Brian had remodeled it themselves, too. He walked around with us, pointing out what he'd added, the new cabinets that he'd built, the floor tiles that they'd installed with their own hands. He put his arm around my mom and pulled her close.

"I think we did pretty good," he said with pride.

"We did, baby," Mom beamed up at him. This was all new to me, seeing my mom be so nice to a man. My mom fought with my last stepdad weekly for their entire fifteen years of marriage. The husband before that? The same. "Fuck you, you mother fucker," was the soundtrack of my childhood, and now she was calling this dude *baby*. I loved it.

I excused myself to go to bed. While peeing, I realized there was no bidet and groaned in disappointment. Gone were the days of a twenty-four-seven, sparkling clean "down there." I collapsed on the bed in the guest room, jutted my leg out into the emptiness and missed Francesco's body next to mine. I wondered what he was doing. I grabbed my phone and sent him an email. "I'm at my mom's house. This is so weird. I miss you. I'll call you soon."

After a week of catching up with my mom, I begrudgingly hopped on the train to Salt Lake to visit my dad. I re-read *Slaughterhouse Five* as stations blurred by and commuters got on and off, and paused occasionally to wonder which version of my dad I'd get that day: cold and indifferent, or warm and charming. Love, it seemed, was conditional and dependent on whether or not you were disappointing him.

The train pulled into the final stop. My dad wasn't there yet so I waited in the parking lot with my bags. I worried I might get murdered, even though it was two in the afternoon. The station was in the middle of nowhere and a few sketchy men hovered around the stop like flies around a BBQ. I heard loud music from afar. A gray sedan screeched around the corner, Lady Gaga blasting "Mo-Mo-Mo-Mo" from the speakers. When the car came closer I could see the familiar paper car-dealer plate glued crookedly onto the back window with superglue. My dad. He slammed on the breaks and squealed to a stop in front of me and yelled, "Get in baby!"

I hopped into the car and leaned over to give him a hug and a kiss.

"Love you baby, glad you're home baby," he said dryly.

We made small talk about the weather on the way to Starbucks and I grappled with my feelings. I loved my dad, I'd missed him, but I knew that everything I wanted to talk about was off-limits. I couldn't talk about school or Europe, or my boyfriend because it would start a fight. Did I want to fight? Did I care? He wanted to ignore that I'd gone to grad school altogether and seemed to be pretending like I'd been on holiday somewhere respectable, like Dana Point in California. Nothing had happened and I was already pissed. I wanted him to be a normal dad like those I'd seen on TV, the kind who compliment you and support you and who don't feel the compulsive need to endlessly criticize and punish you for *perfectly reasonable* life choices like going to grad school.

I sat across from him in Starbucks and took a sip of my soy latte. It tasted like pisswater compared to the tar-like thickness of the espresso in Italy. My dad sat back in his chair, crossed his legs and puffed out his chest, stretching his tight blue v-neck so the world could see his large pecs and biceps. He picked up his coffee and held it with his pinky extended.

"What's your plan now? Are you going to get a job?" Ah, here we go. He wasn't wasting any time launching into it.

"Yes, I'm going to find a writing job or something remote and—"

"Writing isn't a job, baby," Dad said casually, pursing his lips to sip his coffee but in a dramatic way like he was giving his cup a kiss. *Sllllluuuuurp. Smack.*

"That's your opinion, *Dad*," I said like I were twelve again.

He narrowed his eyes. "It's not my ope-pin-eeyon, it's the reality."

"I'm not here to fight with you," I responded. "I'm going to get another copywriting job so I can work remotely and move back to Italy. Oh, and try to contain your enthusiasm, but I have an Italian boyfriend." I threw that one in just to bother him.

He examined me for a moment, deciding whether or not he had the energy to freak out, and scowled, "What are you doing with your life? These kinds of relationships don't work, him from Italy and you from here. You'll never understand each other."

I glanced down at my pale olive-toned hand, thought of my mom, my stepmom, my sister's mom, the lengthy list of blue-eyed, blonde babes my dad had made babies with.

"You've only been in multicultural relationships, Dad. Your current wife is a Germanic American. All of your kids are mixed."

"That's just my opinion that it's too hard and you're vay-sting your time. Baby."

An elderly man came into the café. He walked slowly, using a cane for support. My dad saw him and cheerfully yelled, "Oh! You're so *cute*! Here for some coffee, buddy? God loves you boy!" The elderly man jumped and nearly fell over. This type of buoyant outburst was normal for my dad. In public, he entertained himself by being explosively social, from a grocery store line to the airport. He loved to talk, loved to get to know people, and his enthusiasm was often contagious even when it was bizarre. He didn't say, "God loves you," because he's religious. He's not religious at all. In his own words, "Religious people are not to be trusted." Instead, I think that "God loves you" roughly translates to a form of thank-you, or "I like you" in my dad's Farsi dialect, or at least that's what I've always assumed. In Farsi, I'm sure it sounds lovely and normal, but in English, he sounds like an evangelist.

"Oh! I nearly killed that poor old man! He's so-eh cute!" Dad chuckled to me. I gave him a disapproving shake of my head.

"You're nuts, " I said with a sigh.

The old man had been a welcome distraction, a way to end our conversation before things got too heated. Dad pursed his lips to take another loud slurp of his coffee. I thought, *this* is the guy giving *me* relationship advice? Still, he'd planted a tiny seed of doubt. What if he was right? But what if he wasn't? I loved Francesco and he seemed to get me, to love me in spite of myself. Someone needed to, if not my own dad. Besides, I could handle difficult, I told myself.

Couldn't I?

16

Overthinking It

Summer 2010

I sat in a wicker chair on the patio in my mom's backyard, thinking about what a good idea it would be to have a hotel made entirely for dogs. You'd check them in, and then they'd have the run of a one-hundred-floor sky rise. I imagined them pissing all over the ballroom in that weird competitive way that dogs do, where one dog pees in a spot and then every dog that comes across that space is compelled to do it too. There would be a line that never ended to lay claim to that one specific, precious spot until they all went crazy.

My imagination was an old friend, one that sometimes kept me occupied in times of boredom or stress, and other times haunted me. In elementary school, I told a friend of mine once how I'd figured out a way to locate unicorns; another time I'd daydreamed about a circus being led behind my brother's father's barn, and for years I believed that what I'd imagined had happened. In kindergarten, during a period that my mom refers to as "your night-terror phase," every night I was plagued by bloody, murderous, haunting nightmares.

My daydreaming typically signaled that I had way too much time on my hands. I'd been back in Utah for three weeks and had already checked off everything I needed to do to get back to Italy. I'd found a job as a copywriter for a tech startup, a remote position just as I'd wanted. I'd filled out all of my paperwork to apply for a new visa for Italy and sent it off, and I'd registered House of Ossimori, Jen's and my design company, as a partnership. Now, I just had to save up a few thousand dollars to fly back, which I was earning by working super early in the morning, which left me with nothing to do but watch bad daytime TV and wait. And wait. And having too much spare time was *dangerous* because I used it to sit around and think—or worse, to ruminate until I drove myself insane.

I missed things and people. I missed Florence. I missed Amy, Violetta, Grayson, Kuhle, and everyone else, too. I missed Demyan barging into the studio to suggest I stop sucking and do better. I missed Priscilla's wide-eyed enthusiasm. I missed walking along the Arno River with pistachio gelato. I missed the smell of charcoal in the morning while I drank a cappuccino in front of one of my sketches. I went through pictures of my year in Italy, of Grayson and me eating *gnocchi alla sorrentina* in Sorrento, of Kuhle twerking in my room, of Jenny laughing at one of her own jokes. I pestered Grayson, Jenny and Violetta like a clingy ex, and called them frequently to catch up but regardless of how often we chatted, I felt like there was a hole inside of me that I just couldn't fill.

In Italy, to say "I miss you," you say, *"mi manchi,"* which means "you're missing from me." That's how I felt. All of these things were missing from me. How had I gone from feeling so full, to so empty, so quickly? A black hole had opened up and with it, darkness crept in.

In the hallway between my mom's bedroom and her sewing room hangs a hand-drawn picture of my brother, Mitch, that I had to see every time I went to the bathroom. It was a gift from me, the Christmas after he died. In it, he's smiling, teeth perfect, eyes twinkling, and it's how I wanted to remember him. But it brought up other things, too, like my guilt. Why did I tease him? Why did I think I was so fucking cool, anyway? The reason, logically, is that he was an annoying little shit, and like all younger siblings in the world, he irritated me to no end. But when people die, we saint them. We forget their wrongs and forgive their mistakes almost as if to justify our grief because you can't mourn, or miss, or love the imperfect, it seems. It's a disservice, really, what we do to the dead, smashing them into two-dimensional versions of themselves and by comparison turning ourselves into monsters.

Once I felt bad enough about Mitch and had successfully beat myself down, I turned my focus onto Francesco. Why was he really with me, anyway? Didn't he have any better options in Italy? If not, why? He was stupid, he was blind, he was broken if he didn't see just how broken I was, how cruel I could be to the people I loved. I started to distance myself from him. Two weeks passed and we didn't talk at all, and I felt totally fine about never seeing him again.

I leaned over the kitchen counter to grab my coffee cup. Mom was cleaning the counters for the second time that day, really laboring on the already spotless sink, while I yammered on about the difference between food in Italy and food in the US. My phone buzzed with a text from Francesco.

"Can you please call me? I need to talk to you. Are you avoiding me?" I rolled my eyes and groaned.

"What's wrong?" Mom asked.

"Nothing, Francesco wants to talk."

"Well how mean of him," she teased.

I wrote Francesco back: "I can chat online now or Skype in one hour after my mom leaves."

"Now," he responded instantly.

I grabbed my computer and went outside to the back porch, blood rushing into my face, my heart kicking up the pace, ready to fight for no reason. What's the big deal? So what if I'd been a little distant, he didn't need to be so goddamn *needy* and demanding, I told myself (out loud, because I spent hours a day having conversations with myself).

Francesco popped up on chat.

"Is everything okay? I haven't talked to you in days and days," he wrote.

"I've been busy," I jabbed into my computer.

"I know but it doesn't take a lot of time to send a short email or to Skype for a minute."

"It does take time, *Francesco*. Time I don't have because I'm trying to get back to Italy. Jesus."

I was lying. I mean, it *was* slightly less convenient to Skype or email instead of texting, but I had plenty of time. Time to push him away and build up walls because I couldn't make sense of us or the world. He was too nice and liked me too much and couldn't possibly be a good catch because of it. It's a thing we do when we get comfortable with difficulty, when we're taught to value scarcity: diamonds, gold, men who aren't that interested, women who won't commit, parents who aren't there. Love and acceptance never came easy to me and I was used to it. But as I grew older, the various types of rejection—my dad's absence when I was young, being an outsider in an all-Mormon neighborhood as a kid, my mom's toxic marriages—had compounded in my brain and evolved me into someone who never felt welcome, though if you'd asked me then I'd have said I'd been completely unaffected by any of it. But it did affect me; it warped my sense of reality, eroded the part of me that made me feel valuable to people. So, at times like this, I couldn't trust Francesco.

"I understand you're busy," he wrote, "but you've just disappeared."

"I'm honestly just really busy doing paperwork and all of that." I wasn't. I'd spent the entire day before sitting in my mom's backyard under the patio, staring at the garage as though I'd never seen one before.

"When you move back here, I was thinking maybe me, you, and Jenny could live together?"

I panicked a little. Live together? Had he lost his fucking mind? I felt suffocated. Why couldn't he just leave me alone?

"No," I wrote, "you need to slow down and give me space."

"Slow down? Why? I love you. I want to marry you. Are you playing games with me? I don't understand."

"Games?" Again with the goddamn games.

"Sometimes Italian women pretend to love many men at the same time to get gifts or attention. Are you just pretending for this?"

I laughed maniacally, startling my mom who was coaxing her fifty-pound cat, Snowball, off of the kitchen table inside. But then I pictured Francesco in his room, sad in front of his laptop, confused, wondering if I liked him or not, and suddenly I felt terrible for being so cold and snapped out of my blind rage.

"Listen, I hardly ever shave my legs," I pounded on the keyboard. "Don't you think I might be a little too *lazy* to pretend to like you for attention?"

"True, haha," he wrote back, "Well, I want to marry you so I don't think that moving in together is such a big deal. I found a four-bedroom apartment so you could still have your own office or room, and rent would be very cheap for us. Three hundred euro each per month."

Three hundred euro was half of what I expected to pay living with just Jenny. And Francesco did sleep at my house almost every night anyway. He'd be at work all day while I worked from home, so I'd have plenty of space. It terrified me to be that dependent or close to someone, but maybe?

I texted Jenny to see what she thought and she instantly wrote back. "Hey friend, I love Franny. I'm down. And that is way cheaper."

"Alright," I wrote Francesco, "we can move in together. Now, will you please just calm the fuck down?"

"Really? Oh, you make me so happy, *amore*! I'll take care of everything. Oh, one last thing," he added. "I want to come to the US with Greco in August. We're going to San Francisco, LA, and Las Vegas but I thought maybe you could come to Vegas and then we can come to Salt Lake to meet your parents?"

I swallowed hard. Meet my parents? Oh, God. What if my dad went on his rant about the shadow government or my mom's love of wooden woodland creatures freaked him out? What if we went out and one of my friends drank too much and got into a fistfight because some handsy bro groped her on the dance floor? This wasn't uncommon. As a poor kid, I was scrappy and made scrappy friends. But Francesco wasn't used to it and I didn't want him to be. In my mind, he'd come, be horrified, and never speak to me again. And if that's what he wanted, then *fine*.

"Okay," I said bitterly, as though he were consciously making the choice to end our relationship by coming. "If that's what you want."

In August, Francesco and Greco flew to Los Angeles where my best friend, Dani, picked them up to show them a night out in LA. She'd been curious to meet Francesco ever since I told her about him, and jumped at the chance to spend a night interrogating him. It was a test, in a way, to see if my oldest friend liked the man I'd fallen madly in love with. I wanted her approval too because I knew it might help me to stop pushing him away. She wasn't the kind of friend who'd tell me, "Oh, he's great and I love him for you," unless she really meant it.

Dani texted me at 10 p.m., "Your boyfriend is nice and super cute and I really like him. But he hates ramen and is afraid of strip clubs. Are you dating a prude? Or a fun-hater?"

"Which strip club?" I asked.

"A good one and the dudes wouldn't even go in."

The next morning, Francesco called me, utterly confused and a little nervous. After the pleasantries, I asked him how his night had gone with Dani.

"Your friend is really nice but she tried to take us to a strip club! But I didn't go in, *amore!*"

"Why?" I asked.

"Huh?" I could hear the confusion in his voice.

"Why didn't you go in?" I asked again.

"I tink she took me there to see if I would go in so you could break up with me."

I exploded into a giggle fit on the phone, the kind that makes the eyes tear up and causes gurgling sounds in your throat because you've closed your mouth trying to hold it all in.

"Oh, Jesus, babe. Seriously, stop it with the paranoia; there are no ulterior motives here. She took you to a strip club because they're fun. I've been a million times, half of them with Dani. I suspected she'd take you."

"Really? Well, I didn't know! I thought it was a test!"

What happened to you, Francesco? I wondered. Or was this a cultural thing? I prayed it wasn't a cultural thing because I couldn't handle a long-term relationship with someone who read into *every single thing*. Like me. I didn't want to be in a relationship with me. How exhausting.

"You didn't like the ramen?" I asked.

"I couldn't eat it. I didn't know how to use the sticks," he sighed.

Being Italian, neither Francesco nor Greco was familiar with chopsticks. But they didn't want to be rude either, so they sipped the broth with the little ladle spoon, poked at their noodles a bit and left the restaurant starving.

"Why the hell wouldn't you tell anyone?"

"I didn't want to seem rude."

"Nobody's going to think you're rude for being foreign and not knowing stuff. Wow, I just realized I'm going to see you *really* soon. Jenny flies into Salt Lake next week, then we'll drive to Vegas to meet you."

"I can't wait!" he said.

I hung up the phone and invited my mom and Brian to come to Vegas with Jen and me for the weekend. They liked to gamble and drink, and if Mom had enough drinks she liked to dance, too. Plus, it would be a good opportunity for her to really meet Francesco and get to know him.

"Why not?" Mom said, "I've never been!"

Brian leaned down and wrapped his arms around her, "We're going to Vegas, woman!" Then he looked up and asked, "Should we drive separately in my truck?"

I nodded. "Yeah, because Jen and I need to bring Francesco and Greco back to Salt Lake after."

"Cool! Sounds good," he said, then started twirling my mom around, singing, "Viiiiiiva Laaaas Vegas!" Then I joined in, linking arms with her and skipping around, "Viiiiva, viiiiivaaaa Laaas Veeeeegas!" My mom blushed and playfully smacked Brian's arm.

"You two drive me nuts," she giggled.

17

Curb Appeal

At the Paris in Vegas, I spotted Greco and Francesco in the lobby while we were checking in. It was as though they'd just stepped out of an Italian film, bronzed and beautiful in tight t-shirts and skinny jeans. Francesco spoke Italian and laughed as he handed his passport to the receptionist, while Greco nodded, pulled his shirt sleeves down over his large biceps, and ran his hand through his thick black hair. A group of blonde women standing behind Francesco and Greco was trying to flirt with them.

Jenny stepped out of line to call for them but I grabbed her arm.

"Wait, don't call them yet, Jen!" I pleaded.

She stared at me like I'd lost my goddamn mind.

"It's your boyfriend?"

I shook my head. "I just... not yet," I said, suddenly scared to death, sweating like I'd spent the afternoon on a chain gang in the Mojave Desert. But Francesco had already spotted us and was sprinting in our direction. He hugged me tightly and spun me around. I hung in his embrace, like a sack of dead kittens, and flatly introduced him to my mom and Brian, who were so wrapped up in being adorable together that they hadn't even noticed he was there. Jenny and Greco hugged, and Jenny yelled, "Welcome to Vegas, ya'll!"

When I realized that I'd be sharing my room with Francesco, not Jenny, I felt a little betrayed by no one in particular. I reluctantly went up to the hotel room with Francesco to put our bags down and get ready. He was a knockout, all tan, his espresso hair short and messy. I mean, it was so handsome it was gross. He stared at me in the elevator like a famished animal while I focused on the buttons and pushed a few extra to stall. This was someone I loved, who I'd thought about every day, and yet I was so nervous to see him that I wanted to end the relationship and scurry back to Utah where I could live out my days under a rock.

"Are you okay?" Francesco asked when we stepped into the hotel room.

"Uhm, yeah, I don't know. I'm kind of weirded out to see you but I'm not sure why."

He looked disappointed. "I'll be right back," I said. I grabbed my bag and headed into the bathroom. After a shower, I found him sitting on the bed staring at the floor, his shoulders slouched forward.

"What's wrong?" I asked.

"You don't seem like you want me here," he answered woefully.

"I do! I just—I don't know."

I flopped down next to him. And I didn't know. My feelings didn't make any sense to me. I loved him and missed him but partially resented him for being there. Francesco looked up and I leaned in to kiss him, then he grabbed me and flipped me backward onto the bed. I laughed a shrill, unattractive laugh. After a quick romp, I felt a little better, a little more relaxed and connected but still not completely myself around him.

We met Jenny and Greco in the casino downstairs and wandered outside into the baking Nevada heat on a painful stroll over to Caesars Palace to meet my mom. She and Brian were playing slot machines in an eclectic row of humans, young and old, rich and poor, optimistic and dejected. A couple in matching purple sweat suits played robotically— insert a coin, pull arm, smoke cigarette, repeat. When they saw us, Mom and Brian jumped up from their seats and stretched their legs.

"Wanna walk around?" Mom asked.

I nodded.

We paused in front of the famous fountain in Caesars Palace for my mom to take a picture. A group of college kids stumbled through, reeking of liquor and abandon. Francesco tapped me on the shoulder.

"What's going on?" he asked. I turned around.

Brian was down on one knee, a dainty ring pinched between his fingers. My mom's face turned raspberry-red and the corners of her mouth turned up into a broad and joyous pageant smile.

"I guess he's proposing," I said to Francesco. He looked confused.

My mom enthusiastically nodded and we cheered. We hugged her and Brian and dragged them over to the bar for some champagne. I explained our proposal tradition to Greco and Francesco. Greco perked up, "Ah! Like in the movies!"

Jenny laughed out loud and held up her champagne glass. "To getting hitched like in the movies!" Mom and Brian took a short break from breathing in each other's carbon dioxide and listening intensely to each other speak and announced their plans to get married in Vegas, that night. I drummed my fingers on the bar; yeah, it made sense. Why not?

"Well," my mom said, standing up, "we better get back to our room to get ready for a wedding!" They ran off across the ornate marble floors, holding hands.

Francesco scanned my face for a reaction but I didn't have one. Coming from a family where his parents had always been married, the entire event must have seemed so strange to him. But my mom had me at eighteen, so she was still trying to find herself while I was learning to tie my shoes. Her relationships had been a roller coaster for both of us: people came, they went, and I was a quiet observer through it all. It never really occurred to me to have opinions about my mom's decisions, and after everything she'd been through with my brother's death, I was all for anything that made her smile. At that time, she could have taken up black tar heroin and I would have been like, fuck yeah, whatever Mom. Plus, Brian was a good man, and I liked him more than anyone she'd ever dated before. He didn't scream, hadn't been to prison for assault, and didn't spend all of his time at home silently drawing dragons. So, to use my mom's expression, more power to her.

"Let's go check out the other hotels," I said. Francesco, Jenny, Greco and I pounded the last few drops of our champagne and headed towards a good time.

We shared a crepe in the Paris, my favorite hotel, gambled a little to take advantage of the watered-down but free cocktails, suffered the unforgiving sun (it was summer in an artificial city and consistently 9,000 degrees) then ducked into the MGM Grand for another snack and a refreshing vodka soda. After living in Italy for a year, where a vodka soda is basically a glass of Stoli with two ice cubes and a splash of soda, it took a lot to get me drunk. We'd been casually drinking all day and I barely felt a thing.

At dusk, when the topless dancers began to appear on bar tops in the casinos, I called my mom to see if she wanted to get dinner before her wedding.

"Uhm," she giggled, "we're at the courthouse GETTING MARRIED NOW!" My jaw dropped.

"Wait, you're getting married without me there, while I'm literally on the same block?" I asked.

"Yes, but it's like my third wedding so it's fine," she said playfully dismissive. "Everywhere else was booked and this place said they could only do it right when we came in, so we decided to do it now. Oh! Getting married, gotta go!" She hung up.

I turned to Francesco and Jenny. "So, apparently my mom is already married." Saying it out loud hurt a little and I was embarrassed. I knew that it wasn't personal, my mom can be impulsive, but who gets married without inviting her daughter who is literally less than five minutes away? My mom, that's who.

Jenny burst out laughing, "Wow, that's crazy. That's totally something that would happen to you. Well, let's go get dinner then. You okay, friend?"

I nodded. "Yeah, I'm fine. Classic Mom, yeah? Let's eat. Then, let's take a shitload of shots and ride that terrifying roller coaster on top of the hotel."

"Yes!" Francesco shot his fist up in the air.

"Vegas is probably a good place to die," Greco said with the hint of a smile.

Since Greco and Francesco wouldn't go into the strip club with Dani, I thought it would be fun to take them myself. We found a place off of the strip, a place "where the locals go," according to a blackjack dealer. The lights were dim, the music loud, and I walked in like I owned the place, my head held high, cash in my fist. Jenny smiled politely to the strippers we passed, while Greco and Francesco looked painfully out of place and uncomfortable as we took a seat around a table. I waved my hand to the cocktail waitress to order a few drinks.

"I'll do boob shots for ten bucks too, honey," she added. She was a veteran of the industry, in her late sixties at least, tan and very Vegas with her big teased hair and glitter shadow. Her attitude kind of reminded me of my grandma, that kind-but-tough, "I've seen shit and I will cut you," tone in her voice. I liked her.

"Yes, I need to buy two of those immediately for these two dudes right here."

I handed her the cash, and she winked at me and stuffed a shot deep into her cleavage. Her boobs were epically large, each one the size of a German Shepherd puppy and being a woman, my first thought was, *Pretty!* followed by, *She must have the strongest core*. She grabbed Greco's head and stuffed it into her chest. He flailed his arms around as though he were being drowned in her fleshy sea. When he came up for air, the shot glass was successfully wedged between his teeth. Down the tequila went. Next, Francesco. He turned bright red as she straddled his lap and prepared the shot. After it was over, I ordered him three more.

A stripper named Fierce took the stage and crawled to the top of the pole and slid all the way down into the splits.

"Oh my God, that's so cool!" Jenny said.

Then she started twerking and her tampon string wandered out of her thong. I thought about running over to tell her, but realized the guy in the front row, who had his face less than two inches from her vagina, seemed to be really into it. I figured she'd probably bank on Mr. Eager Beaver as is, so why mess with her hustle? I threw a handful of bills onto the stage as we left.

The next day, I left a dozen messages on my mom's phone ranging from, "Hey Mom, we need to leave soon, just wanted to say bye," to "If you've been kidnapped, I'll find you!" It was our last day in Vegas and I really wanted to see her because she'd barely had a chance to say more than a few sentences to Francesco. I wanted my parents to know him. It was important to me as much as it was unusual. Neither of my parents had met most of the guys I'd dated because what was the point? But Francesco mattered. I planned on moving back to Italy where I would live with him, and there was this small, weird place inside of me that just knew that despite my current mixed feelings, we were going to get married. I knew this because even when I pushed him away, I still couldn't imagine my life without him. On the fifth call, she answered.

"Mom, where are you?"

She laughed. "Honeymooning with my baby!"

"Well, that's adorable. Congrats again. But the whole point of you coming here was to get to know Francesco and you haven't even talked to him. Don't you want to get to know him a little before I go back to Europe and, like, *live* with him?" She was quiet for a second.

"I DID too talk to him, Misty. And you're not dumb, so if you think he's good then that's all that matters." My mom was the most defensive when she felt bad about something.

I sighed loudly. "Okay. Well, I've gotta go. I love you and will see you back in Utah." I hung up and chucked my phone on the bed, frustrated.

Someone knocked on the door. I thought it was Francesco finally bringing back our coffee because he'd been gone forever. I flung open the door and my mom stood there, all chipper and glowing.

"*Mooooom!*" I groaned and turned to sit down on the desk chair.

"Hi, baby. Let's go find Francesco and hang out." She sashayed into the room all covered in wedding happiness.

"I appreciate that but we have like thirty minutes before we leave. I'm really happy that you got married, I mean Brian is great, but this was really important to me."

She paced around a little, stopped, put her hands on her hips.

"Okay. I get that. We still have plenty of time. Let's go find him. Don't be mad at your mamma. I gave birth to you." She hugged me but it wasn't a consoling hug because even at 5'6" I tower over her like an Amazon woman, so she was basically just suffocating in my boobs.

Back in Utah, Francesco, Greco, and Jenny admired cowboy boots in a western store in Park City while I paced the sidewalk trying to call my dad for the tenth time. No answer. I texted my sister Chloe to try and track him down. More likely than not, she'd know if he were out of town or simply ignoring me. I suspected that he might do this when Francesco came to town, and he knew Francesco was here because I'd casually told my stepmom on the phone the week before.

"He's ignoring you on purpose because he doesn't want to meet your boyfriend." Chloe wrote back. She wasn't being mean, just honest.

"Goddamnit!? Are you serious?" I responded.

"Are you surprised?"

"No."

My dad hated it when any of us, his four daughters, interacted with boys. Not in their teens, twenties, thirties, or sixties. Not ever. It was *weird*. When we were teenagers, he didn't even like us talking with male shop assistants and I always assumed it was because he was terrified of us having sex. Apparently, it was way better to have a vagina packed with dust than dicks. And why? My guess, he believed some antiquated and biased bullshit where chaste women are "good" women. Or maybe he worried that we'd get pregnant. But these ideas didn't seem to apply to boys and in my opinion, it's a lot scarier for a boy to have sex than a girl. A boy can spread his seed all over the damn place, make loads of unwanted babies as far as the eye can see. Girls? Put her on birth control and you're good to go. Chloe's theory is that when my dad was young, spry and dating (around the time he knocked up my mom), he wasn't a very stand-up dude. So deep down, he just wanted to protect us from guys like him. My theory at the time of dating Francesco was that he didn't believe anyone of worth could possibly be interested in me so he decided to hate Francesco before he ever met.

Francesco glided out of the cowboy store, beaming. "I need a pair of cowboy boots! So-a COOL! Did you get ahold of your dad so we can meet him?"

"I can't get ahold of him. But it's fine."

"Oh, ok," he said, disappointed.

"Sorry," I said. But deep down I was relieved. I loved Francesco but I was afraid that at any minute he would realize I was a fraud, a failure, and he'd be disappointed.

For most of his trip to Utah, I'd been on edge, irritable, and defensive. But my insecurity peaked at a friend's club the night before he left. I couldn't stand the thought of him there, watching me laugh and dance to Depeche Mode with my old friends, *judging* me.

I'd had a solid five or six cocktails and my brain functionality floated somewhere between "Weee!" and "Who needs pants?" Francesco and I were dancing, against my will mostly, and he could tell that I didn't want to be around him.

"Why are you being like this again?" he asked.

"I have no idea what you're talking about," I said. But I knew that I was being distant again and also knew it wasn't nice to roll your eyes when the boyfriend you love tries to dance with you at a dance club. Our argument quickly escalated into a heated fight.

"You're a terrible fucking person!" I shouted.

I heard the words and knew they weren't true. A little voice whispered for me to come down off the ledge, to take a deep breath. I ignored my voice of reason; worse, I practically throat-punched her.

"What the fuck is wrong with you?" Francesco shouted back. "You're acting insane!" He'd apparently had enough of my general ice-queen demeanor.

"I am fucking *done* with you," I yelled with a shocking amount of conviction, for absolutely no reason. In no way did our small disagreement merit that kind of reaction but I couldn't stop myself because I'd lost my goddamn mind. Blinded by insecurity, fueled with rage, I wanted him gone.

"LEAVE!" I pushed him away from me.

"Stop it! What is wrong with you?" He grabbed my arms and shook me, à la every fifties movie ever made, and every argument I'd ever seen on the streets of Florence. I pulled away from him and stormed outside. He followed. I dramatically rushed up to Dani, who had flown in from New York where she was now living to see me and was outside talking with old friends.

"I want him gone. We are done!"

She stared at me. "I'm pretty sure that you're just being an asshole and you're pushing him away for no reason," she said.

"I have reasons!" I scoffed. "He shook me!"

She shrugged. "Violently?"

"I don't know?" I crossed my arms.

"I wasn't trying to be mean!" Francesco pleaded to Dani.

"I like you a lot Francesco," Dani said, "but, sorry babe." And she walked over to my car, popped the trunk, and took his luggage out. Nicki, one of my other friends who'd been standing there, helped Dani drag the bags to the sidewalk, shaking her head disapprovingly at Francesco.

Francesco tried to grab my arm. "Just please talk to me!" but Nicki stepped in front of him.

"Don't do that chimpanzee thing," she said. "Get your stuff, call a cab, and go to a hotel."

Francesco nodded slowly, as the reality of what was happening sunk in. My friends and I yanked open the car doors and sped away. I left Francesco, Greco, and a pile of their luggage on a curb in front of a crowded nightclub in an area full of meth addicts. Jenny pleaded with me to turn around, but I was too far gone.

* * *

When I woke up the next morning, everything came flooding back to me. I groaned and sat up.

"Oh my God, what the fuck did I do?"

Dani opened her eyes and turned towards me.

"Did you just remember that you left your boyfriend on the street last night?"

"Fuuuuuuuuuuuck." My heart pounded in my chest, RE-GRET, RE-GRET, RE-GRET.

My brain raced with thoughts. "I'm a monster" was followed by a mental clamoring for justification: he shook me (valid, because WTF?), he yelled at me (less valid), he wanted to dance with me and it was way annoying (not valid at all), he breathed oxygen, also annoying (also not even remotely valid or sane).

I looked at the time. They'd already left for Italy, so even if I knew how to fix what I'd done there was no way to do it. In my drunken haze, I'd never been more sure of anything. But sober, I could see how things had really gone down and I felt deeply ashamed.

Days went by and I didn't hear from Francesco and part of me wondered if I'd hear from him ever again. He didn't respond to any of my 10,567 apologies via email or text, even though I'd tried everything from "I'm an asshole, what's wrong with me?" to "You know, this is really your fault." We were over. Really. I moped around my mom's house in my pajamas for days, replaying what had happened over and over again, examining every angle, in search of a way to absolve myself or a way out. I'd messed up.

I assumed that I'd been deleted and blocked from everything in his life because that's what I'd do if I were him. So I was surprised when I got on Skype a week later and saw him online. I jumped up from my mom's kitchen table and paced the dining room; what could I say? I fell back into my seat.

"Hey," I typed. I put my hands over my eyes, I couldn't look at the screen. I heard a "ping." I slowly moved my hands away and held my breath.

"Hey," he responded.

"I'm so sorry! I'm so sorry! Really. I don't know what happened."

"You're such a jerk," he wrote.

"Yeah, definitely overreacted just a little bit."

"A LITTLE? You left me on a curb in front of a club at 2 a.m., in the ghetto."

"Well, when you put it like that. But I totally knew you'd be okay."

"I just don't understand why you were so mad at me."

"I don't know what was going on. I wanted you here but I didn't at the same time."

"I know. I don't understand. I thought you loved me."

"I do love you! I do! In fact, I think that's why I was pushing you away. I don't know how to be in love."

I'd never seen a healthy relationship in real life. And I liked being independent, being alone, because deep down I think I knew I was the kind of person who'd love too much. My being was made up of razor wire wrapped around a fucking rainbow unicorn cupcake.

"But you trust your friends," Francesco wrote. "You don't seem to push them away."

"Yeah."

"Why can't I be one of your best friends? That's what I want."

Such a simple sentence and yet it was mind-blowing. Friend? Him? It had never occurred to me that he could be my friend, too.

"Oh! I like that. Do you still want to be my boyfriend, though? Like both?" I winced.

"I love you. Of course, I do. But I'm still mad at you because seriously, who just-a leaves someone on a curb?"

"I have excellent follow-through."

":/"

"And also I'm a real dickweed sometimes."

"I couldn't have said it better myself," he added.

18

My Very Own Puddle

September 2010

I walked into my mom's house and dropped my gym bag next to the door. I'd been going to the gym every morning with my friend's mom to help pass the time. I had a ticket back to Italy in just four weeks and being in limbo was driving me crazy. Plus, a decent gym in Florence could cost three times what I paid in Utah, pricey for a country that pays most employees pocket change.

There were white orchids on my mom's table in a cloud of her cigarette smoke. Mom came out of the bathroom and danced forward when she saw me.

"Honey! These came for you! I bet they're from Francesco! Open it!"

I opened the card. It read:

Practice keeping this alive. Good luck!
Yours, Francesco.

"He's so cute!" she said, clapping her hands excitedly.

Francesco called right then and I was like, Jesus, does he have the house bugged?

"Babe! Are you home?" he asked.

"Uh-huh. Just got home now."

"Did you get the orchids? I ordered them on the phone, from Italy! It was amazing! It took two seconds and the woman working didn't give me a two-hour lecture about what she thought I should buy instead."

"Wow, that *is* cool," I laughed. "I love them, thank you! They're so cute. I've named it Bianca."

"Happy Birthday, amore!"

It was September 2nd, 2010, my birthday. I'd just turned twenty-nine. One year ago today, I was stepping off a plane in Florence and falling directly on my ass in front of my new apartment. Now, I was getting orchids for my birthday from my sweet Italian boyfriend and preparing to go back to Italy to live with him. So many changes in a year.

I apologized to Bianca for the unfortunate death that was surely waiting for her, because no matter how hard I tried, it seemed I could not keep plants alive.

"You want your birthday gift now or later?" Francesco asked.

I touched Bianca's petals. "I thought this was my gift. This is plenty, babe."

"No, come on. Now or later. Tell me."

"Um, now? Now!" I hopped up and down.

"Okay! Okay, the surprise is this," he paused for dramatic emphasis. "I got you a puddle!"

"Hmm, what's a puddle?" I asked.

"A puddle!"

"Like when dirty water collects on a sidewalk?"

"Huh?"

"For hopping in?"

I heard typing. "Wait, I get online. I think you don't understand."

I opened my laptop and pulled up an email from Francesco. I flopped down into the kitchen chair and opened the attached image. The photo slowly loaded and revealed, one centimeter at a time, a little fluff ball the size of a russet potato. A puppy. A poodle puppy.

"Honey?" My nose practically touched the computer screen.

"Yes!" He burst with excitement.

"Did you buy me a poodle for my birthday? A baby dog?"

"Yes!"

"A baby one?"

"Yes!"

My entire body went flush. "Honey, nooooo."

"No? Why?"

I took a deep breath. "Don't you think that's maybe too much for us right now? I mean, a dog is a *huge* responsibility, a twenty-year commitment. If you're not an asshole it's as much work as a toddler. I mean, think of how dumb a toddler is and picture that for eighteen years."

He paused for a moment to consider it. I opened more pictures of the puppy. He was so cute, big brown eyes, his little fuzzy head cocked to the side. He'd already perfected the look that would get him free snacks and hugs for eternity.

"No! *Dai!* Come on! It's a dog. They're like a plant. You feed it and water it and it's fine. And I already paid for him, they no give back the money. And you said you loved dogs and wanted one!"

"Oh God! Yeah, but not right now. Like I want a dog *eventually* but not now."

"It will be okay, I promise," he said. I had doubts. I'd fostered dogs in college, volunteered with rescue groups and had tons of pets as a kid (many that tragically died for strange or inexplicable reasons like cannibalism, but that's another story). Francesco had never had a pet. Ever.

He continued, "So what will you call him?"

"Did you get him from a puppy mill?" I asked.

"No, a friend!"

Francesco's friend owned Sheena, a bitch of a poodle who'd accidentally gotten knocked up by their neighbor's poodle. He showed me a picture of her, a chubby beast with a glittery pink scrunchie on her forehead and, I assumed, a neon switchblade tucked into her leg fur.

"That puppy is adorable! But he looks like a little shit," I said. And despite all logic, I fell in love with his little face. Damnit.

"How about Oliver?" I suggested. "Like Oliver Twist."

"I like it! Yeah, Oliver," he said.

I nervously shifted in my seat and wondered what I'd gotten myself into. Part of me was excited, the other part not so much.

"So, in only a month I'll be coming back to Italy—"

"I know! I can't wait!"

"And I'll be living with you, roommates, and our infant poodle."

"Right."

"Uh-huh."

"Oh. Are you freaking out?" Francesco asked.

"Yeah, for sure. I'm *terrified*. Aren't you?" I asked.

"No," he said with absolute conviction, "you're everything that I want. This is everything that I want." He was so sure of himself, so sure of us, that his conviction was contagious.

"Yeah," I inhaled deeply.

Uncovered

19

Ferret Shit in the Middle of Nowhere

October 2010

My fingers were cold and tingly. Ever since we got in the car at the Florence airport, Francesco had held my hand in a death grip and wouldn't let go.

"Are you actually trying to mangle my hand or are you worried that if you let go I'll leap from the car and run back to the US?" I asked.

"Oh, shit, sorry," he loosened his hold, "I just want to touch you." He looked at me the way Gary Oldman looked at Winona Ryder in Bram Stoker's *Dracula*: a little bit ravenous, and like I was the only person on earth who mattered. It made me feel special in a way but also suffocated. Who can live up to that much pressure?

We were driving to our new apartment, the one we were going to live *together*. I tried to focus on the landscape, roads I'd walked on a hundred times; all familiar but completely new like I was revisiting a dream. The world around me became distorted through jetlag and absence. It took everything I had to keep my dry, scratchy eyes open.

Francesco took a sharp right turn that sent me into the door. "Ouch. Asshat," I mumbled.

"There's the sweet girlfriend I know," Francesco grinned.

He cleared his throat. "So, our new apartment is in the Statuto neighborhood," he announced. "It's not in the center where you lived before. It's where all of the Florentines live. I hope you don't hate it," he added.

"I'm sure it's great, babe," I said, partly because I was too tired to care. He could have driven me to a murder shed and I would have groggily accepted my new accommodation. The idea of moving in together warranted only one legitimate response, a visceral scream of, "*It's all moving too fast!*" which would have been totally rude considering how excited he seemed about the whole thing. And I didn't have the energy to scream.

"*Eccolo,*" Francesco said, parking the car in front of a nondescript apartment building. There were no businesses, cafés or humans in sight. Gone were the bustling crowds of tourists, of students gossiping, of Florentines commuting. The understated empty streets of my new home whispered solitude.

"Where are the people, babe? Has this area been quarantined or something?"

He rolled his eyes. "No amore, this is a family area. It's more quiet and peaceful." I translated this as "boring and uninhabitable," and my guts were hit with a heavy dose of loneliness. *You're alone! You're alone! You're alone!* my brain looped like a hit record. While in school, I'd felt really at home in Florence so why did I suddenly feel so different now?

I wrote it off as exhaustion and first-day jitters which seemed to work, and my muscles relaxed again and my mind went back into hibernation mode.

Francesco grabbed my luggage and I followed him into a building. He placed me into a cage-like elevator no larger than a refrigerator. As the doors closed, he turned and ran up the three flights of terracotta stairs while my tiny baby elevator inched upwards. The doors opened to Francesco panting. Jenny and Alice, a tall beauty we'd met at art school who was now also our roommate, came out of the apartment and hugged me.

"You're here!" Alice beamed. She grabbed one of my bags and dragged it inside the apartment.

"Check out the place," Jenny said, gesturing around the narrow living room, barely wide enough for the burnt-orange, vintage mid-century couch and walnut credenza. The plaster walls were slightly cracked, the terracotta floor tiles crumbled into themselves, and it smelled. It *really* smelled.

"What the fuck is that stench?" I asked, looking around.

"Yeah, it's bad," Alice scrunched up her face. "Apparently before we moved in, three Italian sisters lived here with like ten ferrets. They were *nasty twats*. This place was disgusting. You're lucky we got here a few days before you. We've been cleaning nonstop."

"It smells like a pet shop," Jenny said, pretending to puke.

"Wow, a ferret-hoarding family of filthy Italian triplets," I said. "Is it weird that I'd like to meet them? Just for like a minute, because they sound both horrifying and fascinating."

"Francesco has been really stressed out about this place," Jenny shot a look towards the bedroom where Francesco had dragged my luggage. "He wanted it to be perfect for you but it was really gross and it's still pretty nasty."

"Aww, Francesco loves you. It's so *weird*." Alice added.

"Thanks for cleaning, guys. Seriously. Sorry I wasn't here to help."

I wandered around the apartment. We had a cute little kitchen that reminded me of my first-ever apartment in Florence with Kuhle and Amy, which had the same little kitchen balcony. The bathroom was nearly the size of a football field with a glowing bidet. I smiled at it and whispered, "Old friend, I've missed you. Scrub-a-dub-dub, crotch in the tub." I put my toiletry bag in the bathroom, took a steaming-hot shower, and brushed my dirty mouth. Then I dragged myself into my new room and flopped down on the thin Ikea mattress and threadbare sheets that came with the place, which had no doubt been broken in by a dozen other bodies and apparently a lot of weasels.

Francesco sat down next to me.

"Do you like the apartment, babe?"

"Yeah. Thank you so much for finding this and setting it all up."

He leaned over and kissed my head. Jenny and Alice wandered in and lay down on the bed too. Jenny yawned and stared at the ceiling. Alice was mad at her boyfriend, an Italian Fascist she'd met while we were in school.

"I mean, I'm a brown Canadian Jew, so it's impossible for us not to fight about his political beliefs," she said. I drifted off to sleep, lulled by their chatter.

The next morning, I awoke to an empty apartment and the sound of drilling. The neighbors were doing construction and because the walls were made of cement, remodeling sounded like the surrounding world was crumbling. I padded into the bathroom, then the kitchen. Francesco was at work doing engineer things, Jenny was interning at a jewelry studio, and Alice was in language school to learn Italian. For the past year, I'd lived with roommates, spent all day surrounded by friends or schoolmates and then spent all summer with my mom and dad. Being alone all day was a completely foreign concept, and I was as excited as I was nervous about it.

I made coffee and opened my laptop to write marketing copy for a freelance contract I had with a small company in SLC. I worked, I absorbed the silence, and by the afternoon felt painfully lonely. That entire first week I did the same thing every day: wake up, work, drink ten thousand espresso shots, and work more. I tried to get out a little, to go for walks, but I was disoriented by the new neighborhood so I mostly stayed home. Which was a terrible idea because I have always dealt with my particular brand of crazy by being forever in motion. Sitting, thinking, obsessing, has never boded well for me. By the end of the week, though, I'd had enough.

On Thursday, I went to the only bar in our area for a cappuccino. I brought my computer with me so I could at least be around people a little bit. The bar was full of locals, mostly housewives, and when it was my turn I stepped up to the barista.

"*Dimmi,*" the barista said. My brain turned off completely. I stared at her like a deer in a headlight trance.

"OH! MADONNA!" She rolled her eyes and made fun of me to the other baristas. The other patrons stared at me, one whispered "*Americana*" to another. My face flushed pink, my armpits practically rained, and I bolted from the café like I was being chased by a bear. I walked as fast as I could to my apartment and once I got inside, took a few deep breaths and realized that this time, I wasn't surrounded by the understanding camaraderie of students or Italians who were used to foreigners and our idiotic inability to communicate. This time, things were going to be different.

When Francesco came home, he assured me that my experience was just a fluke, a woman who'd had a bad day, "Or maybe she is just a mean person," he said soothingly. I nodded in agreement and went back the next day, only to repeat the exact same thing. I spoke incorrectly, the barista got annoyed trying to understand me, and I left feeling utterly stupid and like a lesser person. I thought about my dad and how he must have felt moving to the United States without speaking the language. People don't realize how debasing it is when you lack the ability to communicate, to defend yourself, to say, "what's your fucking problem, twat?" I felt vulnerable in a way that I hadn't since I was a kid, different and unwelcome, and just like that, social anxiety that I thought I'd outgrown came back with a vengeance.

As the weeks went by, I started to feel anxious whenever I had to interact with locals alone. Slowly, I spent more of my time huddled in my musty ferret-pheromone office sketching out new designs for our shirt company or writing for work. Francesco felt terrible and tried to be supportive by telling me that I wouldn't be lonely for long because soon my new puppy, Oliver, would be there to keep me company.

I was still hesitant about getting Oliver. Dogs are like fuzzy human toddlers. They're helpless—they need to be fed, exercised, cuddled, and taught for a ridiculously long time because instead of moving out at eighteen they're just dependent forever until they tragically die from some weird cancer or by swallowing a stuffed animal the size of their own head. They need a lot of patience and love, and I wasn't sure I was in a good place mentally for that. Plus, I loved animals so much that it hurt way too much when something happened to them, and something always happened. As a kid, two of my dogs were hit by a car and one was tragically "put down" because my mom had her taken to the pound. We lost a lot of pets to a needle, anytime they got sick or if they were "too difficult." Truly, it's a miracle that my mom didn't drown me in a bucket the second I entered puberty.

On the third weekend in October 2010, after I'd been back in Italy for a very dull couple of weeks, Francesco drove to Cumino to pick up Oliver, who was ten weeks old at the time. I stayed home with Jenny and Alice claiming I needed to work on some designs, but really I just wanted to avoid his parents. Pacing around our apartment, in a foreign country, in suburbia, totally mute, where I now lived with my boyfriend and soon an infant dog, I tried to breathe my anxiety away. This seemed bad.

Around 5 p.m. on Sunday, Jenny and I went to the city center to stroll around for a while. At six Francesco called to tell me he was in Florence with Oliver.

"I'll swing by and pick you guys up," he said.

Francesco parked his Fiat on Via Nazionale where we were having coffee, next to the other fifteen Fiats packed in like sardines, and jumped out smiling. He reached into a little crate in the front seat and pulled out Oliver, who weighed about three pounds and looked like a stuffed teddy bear that had been fluffed on the tumble cycle of an industrial dryer. He was perfect, so cute, and so, so tired. He yawned and I ran over and snatched him out of Francesco's hand, holding him in the air like Simba from *The Lion King* to examine him. He looked down at me with his dark brown eyes, breathed sweet little puffs of puppy breath in my face, and I fell deeply in puppy love. I was hopelessly hooked. I would love him more than anything else on earth. My attachment was so instantaneous and deep that you'd think I'd given birth to him.

Jenny rubbed her hands through Oliver's fur. "Oh, he's so soft!" she said. We fussed over Oliver but he seemed completely unimpressed with us.

Back at our apartment Alice and Jenny played with Oliver on my bed. I lay back and Oliver tottered towards me.

"Hi little sweetie," I cooed at him.

He crawled up on my shoulder and began clumsily humping me. I screamed and Francesco pulled the little pervert off of me. We dissolved into a fit of laughter.

At bedtime, I put Oliver in his little bed next to ours. Then I pulled off my shirt and leaned in to kiss Francesco but was startled by ear-piercing screams from the floor. Oliver yelped, howled, and cried so hard that I worried he would pass out. I'd had dogs all of my life and had never heard anything like it.

"We have to ignore him," I told Francesco. "It's really sad but if we bring him onto the bed he'll learn that if he cries then he gets what he wants." Thirty, forty, fifty minutes went by and he still cried. And cried. Too loud for his tiny body, so loud that it sounded like we were murdering him.

I covered my ears. "How can something so small make so much noise? It's like he has an amplifier in his throat."

"Babe, I have to work tomorrow," Francesco pleaded. So finally, I reached down and pulled him onto the bed. He teetered over to Francesco's head and flopped down into his hair, where he slept for the rest of the night. I woke up every twenty minutes, terrified that Francesco might accidentally roll on top of Oliver and squish him to death.

The next night the exact same thing happened. Once again, I caved in and brought Oliver onto the bed. After he fell asleep, Francesco leaned over and kissed me and I pulled him on top of me. We were having very quiet, virtually motionless sex to avoid waking the dog when I felt a soft, fuzzy thing latch onto my foot. Francesco was fuzzy but not that fuzzy. I peered around Francesco and there was Oliver, humping my toes.

"Ack! No!" I threw Francesco off of me and gently moved Oliver. "No, no!" I said to him, firmly placing him back on the other side of the bed.

Francesco and I went back to business but after a few minutes, I felt something warm and wet on my right ankle. I pushed Francesco off again and this time, there was Oliver standing over my leg and peeing on it. *Peeing on my leg.*

"Ew, Oliver! You asshole!" I picked him up, pee shooting everywhere like a tiny broken hose. I ran for his puppy pad, pee still spraying everywhere, but when I sat him down on the pad he stopped peeing, sat down, and looked up at me like, "Hi! What's up?"

Francesco screamed from the bed in Italian, something about pee being everywhere followed by a string of swear words in dialect.

We changed our sheets and hopped in the shower. Oliver cried outside of the bathroom door so loud and shrieky that I had to leap out of the shower and let him in before the neighbors woke up and came over to throat-punch us. He seemed content with that and sat on the bathroom rug. I stepped back into the shower. Francesco and I soaped each other up and began kissing again, and things were heating up when my foot bumped into something fuzzy. I spun around and there was Oliver, in the shower with us, soaking wet, his little eyes clenched tightly closed as the water pounded him in the face, his little tail wagging despite it all.

"ACK! Oh *shit!*" I grabbed him out of the water as fast as I could and held him to my chest, "How did you get in here, you little psycho?" I said incredulously. We looked at the shower door and sure enough, he'd slid it open just enough to fit his little body through it.

"What the fuck is wrong with this dog?" Francesco asked, with genuine concern.

"I think you picked the dog version of me," I said, staring down at Oliver as he blinked up at me through beaded eyelashes with an undeniable sense of satisfaction.

20

Sì o No? A Proposal

I spent all morning cleaning and sweeping our apartment after I discovered that Oliver had been busy collecting suicide objects from around the house and burying them in his bed. Under his cushion, I found pieces of glass from broken mugs and plates, one razor blade, a steak knife, and terracotta pebbles.

"He's either saving up to murder us all or he's going to off himself." I texted Francesco. While I swept, Oliver bounced into every room cheerfully as though something exciting was about to happen and he couldn't wait. He was the same on walks, showing endless enthusiasm for all things mundane like rocks, bushes, and every person that had ever lived. Every so often, though, he'd leave the room where I was cleaning and head for my bedroom to battle Mirror Puppy. He'd growl and bark and eventually, I'd go in and tell him, "That's you in the goddamn mirror, Oliver! That's your reflection!" Then I'd shoo him out, go back to cleaning, and the entire cycle would start all over again. I complained under my breath that I had better things to do than mitigate his imaginary battles but the truth is I welcomed the distraction. Lately, the outside world felt unsafe so I preferred to be at home, just me and Oliver, where nothing could hurt us.

My newly developing agoraphobia was baffling. Just a year ago, I'd moved across the Atlantic to live alone in a foreign country and now I felt nervous anytime I was solo.

Looking back years later, it seems so obvious to me what happened: I was suddenly responsible for a tiny little creature I adored and since losing my brother I didn't trust myself to care for him. After all, everything that I loved left or died.

I sat down in my office to research plague masks for one of my shirt designs and saw an email from Violetta.

Hey babe! I can't wait to see you this month for Befanica (Befana+Christmas+Hanukkah). It's already been six months, which is way too long! So, hypothetically speaking, what kind of ring would you want if Francesco were to propose?

I read and re-read the email. Propose? Why was Francesco talking with Violetta about engagement rings? It's not like he would *really* ask me to marry him. Francesco loved to propose to me and had done it a million times. In addition to proposing in Sicily, he'd asked me to marry him every time he'd had a few cocktails since I'd moved in with him. He proposed on his knees in the street and even went so far as to beg a police officer to do the honors—"Please marry us, I love her!"—while tourists merrily Instagrammed the whole thing.

The officer replied, "I can't." Francesco pointed frantically to his own hat. The officer shook his head. "No, not even if you're wearing a sailor's cap."

I'd watched so many of his Italian friends purr lofty things to women who they hadn't even liked. Blatant lies of, "I love you, my life, my love, my flame, my everything! Such beauty! Such beauty! Oh! I'm dying." You're dying and I'm puking in my mouth, I thought. I still had a hard time believing that anyone would be crazy enough to actually marry me. Especially Francesco, who had been lucky enough to witness me in all of my unhinged glory.

Francesco and I were opposites in every way. It was bizarre to me that we got along at all. I'm like a mix of rock and roll and homeless, and he literally dresses like the mean, rich, preppy douchebags from *Cruel Intentions*. He loves movies where everyone dies in the end and I like indie movies like *The Secretary*, a movie about a woman who gets out of a mental institution and enters into an S&M relationship with her controlling boss. Francesco closes the curtains before getting naked and I took pictures of my vajayjay, painted it, and hung it in a gallery. And, even more extreme than our differences as adults, were those of our upbringing. It's like we were raised on different planets. He went to church and got good grades, and I toddled around bars while my mom dry-humped strangers for cash. So, given all of that, I had a hard time believing that any proposal would manifest anytime soon. Still, a small part of me wondered, and I didn't hate the idea of marrying Francesco. It felt weird but it also felt right.

Violetta arrived in Florence right before Christmas. She was on holiday, staying mostly with our other friend Aleksander in the city center. I hadn't seen her since school ended and I felt complete again, having her back in Italy.

I told her about the loneliness and my fear of leaving the apartment over coffee.

"Misty, I'm worried about you," she said. "That's not healthy to be alone so much. Can't you move back to the center?"

"No, we signed a year's lease for the ferret cave."

"Oy veh." She laughed and shook her head. "But, isn't it nice to stay in Italy? I miss it so much."

I felt a pang of guilt for my complaints. I was living in Italy, a dream destination, arguably one of the most beautiful countries in the world; I should have been on cloud nine.

"I wanted to get back here so bad but honestly without all of you here it's so empty. It's not the same. I'm not on vacation but I'm not here with a real purpose either. I feel like I'm floating."

"Then why are you staying?"

"I don't know. I guess because I loved it so much before, and I'm holding onto that. And I want to be with Francesco."

When things were good, Italy gave me what I needed at that time. I felt secure with Francesco. I was an artist and a writer. Back home I was an unloved daughter, a mourning sister, a floundering twenty-something.

She nodded thoughtfully, rubbing my arm. It was so good to have her back.

"Now," she said, brightening, "tell me more about your designs and shirts! Are you making art?"

I shrugged. I painted a little but mostly stuck to drawing. I explained that Jenny and I were saving money to manufacture our own shirts in Prato, where a large number of Italy's textiles are made, but it was difficult with the language barrier (we didn't speak enough Italian or any Chinese) and bureaucracy.

"An LLC is about ten thousand dollars here," I explained, "because they apparently hate small business." We had registered the company in the US but couldn't sell in Italy with that license. We had designed over a dozen shirts and made an agreement with Seri Studio, a serigraphy school that partnered with our school, and where I'd taken serigraphy classes. And now we just had to save, promote and print.

Violetta and I was momentarily distracted by two lovers next to us. An Italian man with an Italian woman seated side by side, kissing deeply. He tangled his hands in her curly hair to cup her skull.

"It's like they're both goblets trying to drink wine from each other's face," I said.

Violetta giggled, "Oh, Italy."

* * *

On an uncharacteristically sunny, albeit freezing, winter's day, Francesco and I took Violetta on a day trip with Jenny and Oliver to see the Cinque Terre, a cluster of fishing villages off the western coast, a few hours by car from Florence. I spent most of the drive trapped in my head, trying to figure out what I wanted out of life for the next few years, while Jenny sang along with some Italian song on the radio, Oliver napped on his back with his legs straight up in the air, and Francesco and Violetta talked about nerdy engineering things.

"We're here," Francesco announced. "Let's find a place to get a coffee or a hot chocolate?" We parked the car and followed a winding dirt road down to a little village that consisted of a handful of restaurants, a couple of bars and a dozen tourist shops all next to the sea. I wondered if anyone actually lived there. And if so, how severe was the gossip in a place where everyone certainly knew everyone else's deep dark secrets?

We snapped a group photo on a cliff with the sound of waves crashing below us. In the picture it's cold but bright and our eyes are all shielded from the sun by giant Jackie O sunglasses. We're smiling. The scenery gives the impression of warmth, of the carelessness of the wind, sand, and water, but it was so cold we were all dressed like polar bears in hooded coats and mittens.

The town was small in size, but big in personality. The buildings seemed to squat down compared to the typical twelve-floor buildings of Florence, but these were more vivid. Every café, gift shop, restaurant, and apartment building had been painted a different color—vibrant oranges, blues, purples—and from space I imagined the city would look like an enormous gay pride flag. We paused briefly for Oliver to pee and watched Italian children play tag on the cobblestones of the slanted street as we strolled along in our moon boots in search of some hot chocolate (or at least Italy's version, which is more like a hateful, bitter pudding).

We found a café. It was deserted except for a few locals, mostly old men drinking grappa, and a mom encouraging her toddler to take another bite of his ice cream. "*Dai, tesoro*," she begged.

Francesco leaned over to kiss me. He stared at me for a long time with a dopey smile on his face that just made me ooze with love for him. Then I remembered the talk of a proposal and wondered if it was coming.

"We should get going," Francesco declared, wiggling his hand in the air. "I can't feel my hands anymore."

I felt silly on the car ride home. Why did I think he might propose then? Violetta had been in Florence for a week and there had been no talk of rings or proposals, so it clearly wasn't going to happen. Which was *fine*, totally fine. Except that I was disappointed, and puzzled by my own disappointment. A year ago, the thought of marriage would have had me sprinting for the hills yet there I was, bummed out that my boyfriend hadn't popped the question. Maybe it was because I felt so alone and wanted some reassurance that he was better than other guys. Maybe I wanted to believe that what we had was, in fact, exceptional and that I wasn't letting myself get bogged down in a run-of-the-mill relationship. Or maybe it's because deep down I needed the permanence. Our brain has a clever way of tricking us into getting what we need, especially the things we won't admit to.

"Goodnight!" The four of us—Violetta, Jenny, me and Francesco—yelled to each other in the living room before dashing to our respective bedrooms. Our apartment was forty degrees and the only way to warm up was to jump under the covers in full pajamas and a robe. Alice was in Canada for Christmas, so Violetta was staying in her room. Francesco and I jumped into bed and I tried to thaw my toes on his leg but he kept shrieking, "Please God no!" and recoiling from me. Our apartment typically stayed five degrees colder than outside, the cement walls acting as a sort of icebox, absorbing the frost and holding it there in a chilly embrace.

Francesco and I huddled under the comforter. Oliver had frantically climbed in between us and fallen asleep with his head on the pillow. He spooned Francesco, stretching out his lanky legs to put his growing paws on his shoulders, his fuzzy dog back against my bare chest. He snored a little puppy snore from an exhausting day of taking in new smells and covering the world in puppy piss. Francesco started to doze off.

"So," I began, "What if we were walking and a bus ran me over? What if I couldn't have sex with you anymore because it shattered my pelvis? Just so you know, I'd totally let you sleep with a licensed sex worker. So, keep that in mind before you start exploring your options."

"What the hell are you talking about? Why would I want a bitch?"

"I didn't say that the woman would be *mean*, just that she would be a professional sex worker. You'd need sex at some point. Better a professional than some secretary from your work. But the sex worker would have to be working consensually and in charge of her own business and not be stolen or anything. Sex work is awesome but also human trafficking is a real thing. Oh my God, can you imagine how bad you'd feel if you slept with a sex slave? Now I'm sad."

"Huh? 'Bitch' is the same as 'prostitute' in Italian. What are you talking about? I'm confused."

"Well, that seems mean. 'Sex worker' is a lot more respectful, dude. And I'm just being practical. I'm *planning*. You'll thank me later."

"Ugh, please just stop talking and go to sleep."

"Fine!" I cuddled into his side for warmth.

I woke up on Francesco's chest to a melodic tap on the back of my hand. The room glowed with the soft hue of lamplight and I struggled to orient myself. Why was the lamp on? A little blue Tiffany's box sat next to the lamp on the nightstand. Huh? Francesco squeezed my hand and I looked down to see a dainty, shiny ring on my ring finger. It was a delicate, white-gold band with tiny, round-cut, glimmering stones. It took me a minute to register what was happening. I just lay there, looking at his face, half in shadow, half illuminated. He looked down at me, his eyes bouncing from my eyes to the ring nervously.

"Um, *sì, o no?*" he whispered.

I pushed myself up onto one elbow to get closer to Francesco's face. I held my hand up to examine the tiny little stones sparkling in the lamplight. I couldn't help but smile.

"Sì," I turned to him, "definitely sì."

"Oh thank God," he exhaled.

"You really proposed," I said.

He leaned down and pulled me up on top of him for a long kiss.

I pulled back and looked into his face. "Is this because I said you could have consensual sex with a sex worker if I'm ever maimed?"

He smirked. "Yes."

"I thought so. *Ti amo,*" I said.

"Me too," he said, kissing my forehead.

We turned off the light and snuggled down into each other because otherwise we would have died from hypothermia. I lay in bed for a long time experiencing a strange onset of mixed emotions. I was elated, the man I loved had just asked me if I'd spend the rest of my life with him. But this terrified me. I wondered if I'd be a good life partner or not. I imagined myself in ten years driving a minivan to a soccer game, using words like "gee golly" or "gosh," pleading with one of my nine toddlers in the back to stop jamming paper clips up her nose as I cruised down a wide street in suburban America. Then I imagined myself in the Italian version of that scenario where I walked twenty paces behind Francesco, smoking three cigarettes at a time while my mother-in-law lectured me about how to properly polish my husband's balls. Francesco had one baby strapped to his back, and pushed another in the stroller, carefully navigating the road while somehow managing to stare at every woman's ass on the block.

I'd never liked the idea of packaged identities, that being someone's wife or mom meant specific things to people and that they'd relentlessly try to make you fit into that mold until you succumbed or died. And then I thought about our families. Lying in the dark, listening to Francesco and Oliver snore, I realized we were going to have to tell our parents. Fuck.

21

Not a Romantic Comedy

December 2010

Francesco and I sat across from each other in a café around the corner from our apartment. I sipped a cappuccino, Francesco slurped his espresso and Oliver obnoxiously pawed at the table next to us, putting his muddy black feet all over anyone within reach. He'd learned that he could demand attention from anyone nearby, and we'd learned that if we told him "No," some elderly Italian woman would epically lose her shit and demand that we let him do whatever he wanted. The life of a puppy in Florence is a hard one.

I wore gloves to keep my hands warm but every so often I'd move my hand and feel my new ring pressing into my finger, a reminder that we needed to make some phone calls. Francesco kissed my forehead and smiled at me as though he'd just found out I only had three days to live. After coffee, we walked to the park to do "lovers" things, like we were trying to imitate a love story movie trailer. We gazed into each other's eyes in a gross "I'm gaga for you" way while we strolled along the path, Francesco took pictures of me playing on the monkey bars of the playground, Oliver flung himself into piles of muddy leaves. We bashfully laughed and laughed.

Back at our apartment, I stretched out on the bed and fondled my cell phone. I reluctantly called my dad (better to get the hard part over quickly, just rip off the Band-Aid). Embarrassed by my own excitement, I tried to remain calm. My dad answered flatly.

"Hello." He was still mad that I'd moved back to Italy "to ruin my life."

"How are you?" I asked.

"Good."

"The kids?" I asked, referring to my two youngest siblings.

"Good."

"Great. So, Dad, I have some exciting news! My boyfriend just proposed! I'm engaged!"

The line went dead. He'd hung up on me. I was not surprised. I scowled at the phone for a minute and then called my mom.

"Oh! That's great! Congrats honey!" my mom said, distracted. "So, guess what? Your little brother Dakota is going to have a baby!"

"He's eighteen!" I yelled.

"Yeah, but he'll be fine. I did it at eighteen and you turned out fine! I'm going to be a grandma!"

I wondered how she defined "fine."

"And he's going to keep it?" I asked.

"Of course he's going to keep it. Don't be negative, he's really excited."

"Isn't his girlfriend sixteen? Mom, teenagers have the emotional intelligence of rocks. What about the emotional health of their kid?" Then my voice croaked and I started to cry.

"This is dumb," I sniffled.

"Oh, Misty," she said, annoyed, "they'll be fine. Don't freak out. I'm pretty excited! I'm gonna be a grandma!"

"Hooray," I mumbled through worried tears.

I hung up and couldn't stop thinking about my brother. My mom was so young when she had me and tried so hard to raise me to the best of her abilities, but it was hard, for both of us. I needed some levity, so I called Dani in LA.

"Hello!" she answered. Traffic roared in the background.

"I'm engaged!" I said.

"Wow! That's great." Silence for a moment. "Oh, fuck you, buddy! Sorry, not you. Anyway, that's great but I mean, are you *sure*? You're not *really* the marrying type. I mean, if you're sure then that's great. Is he forcing you? Oh, fuck off you asshole! Not you. What I mean is, congrats! If that's what you want."

If anything, I could always count on Dani's honesty. Was I being a cliché, running away from a million things at home, attaching myself like a tick to something to give me life because I was truly broken inside? Or was I doing that thing where I wanted to settle down because it's what I thought I needed to do? A "because society told me to" marriage, the place where many a strong women go to illogically doubt themselves for no apparent reason, wondering "what if," until they grow old and die. Panic.

"Do you think it's insane?" I asked.

"No babe, I really like Francesco. I just never thought you'd get married. You guys haven't been together for that long. I don't know, I can't picture you as someone's wife, you know? I've gotta go but let's talk more about this soon. I love yoooou!" Then she hung up without saying goodbye as always.

Francesco hadn't made any phone calls because he said he had to "have that conversation in person." Francesco never called people unless it was to quickly ask his mom how to cook lasagna or what to use to remove a stain. When he had questions about products or services, he dragged me down to the store to ask in person. Did the electronic store have a certain brand of printer? Let's drive down to ask. Question about our phone plan? Drive to the store to ask. I often wondered why he even owned a phone. So, it made sense that he'd tell his family in person, which I assumed would be the next time we went to Cumino. It wasn't.

About a month after he proposed we went to Cumino to visit his parents. The days passed awkwardly as they still hadn't warmed up to me and Francesco never brought up the subject of our engagement. On Sunday, when we were packing our things to return to Florence, I realized that he wasn't going to tell them. There was a chance he had a good reason for not telling them; my Italian was still fairly bad so it was entirely possible I'd missed something big. I'd also noticed that Italians could be really superstitious, always throwing salt over their shoulders and talking about curses, so maybe he needed to deliver the news while wearing white, sitting under a cross and eating an apple.

On our drive home, I decided not to ask him about it but then two hours later it just kind of flew out of my mouth because I'd been obsessively thinking about it.

"Why didn't you tell them?" I blurted out.

"It didn't seem right to tell them without my sister there. I should tell everyone at once," he answered.

"You were being distant and rude *again*."

"I know. They're just, I don't know. You don't understand how my parents are. I can't be myself there."

"Well, frankly, you can't be an asshole either."

"I know. Please just be patient, I'm working on it."

* * *

In the blink of an eye, six months passed and we'd gone from an ice-cold winter into a sweltering hot summer. Oliver had mastered potty training, thanks in part to the T-bone steak Francesco used to train him, and he'd also learned "down," "off," and "stay," though he still wailed and yelped when we tried to leave him alone, even for a short time. Jenny was also dating a Florentine who was a self-described neo-Fascist, which I learned was a growing thing in Italy, and Jenny and I were close to printing our first batch of t-shirts for House of Ossimori.

A lot had happened in those six months, except one thing stayed the same: Francesco still hadn't told anyone that we were getting married. I'd taken to running my hand through my hair in slow motion in a pathetic attempt to angle my finger just so to catch someone's attention—one of his friends, his parents, anyone. But Francesco told me that engagement rings weren't necessarily a thing in Lazio, the region he's from, so most likely anyone who saw my ring just assumed I'd picked it up for five euro at the nearby H&M to go with my outfit. The silence made the engagement feel fake, almost like it had never really happened, and weeks went by where I totally forgot that he'd ever proposed. Other weeks, we'd argue over it. During one particularly dramatic argument, I took the ring off and threw it at him, screaming, "If you're so embarrassed by me, why did you ask me to marry you? Go! Seriously! Find some Italian woman who is super stoked about ironing your sheets for the rest of your life! I bet she won't even make fun of your accent!"

I huffed around for a minute before Francesco hugged me, slipped the ring back on my finger and said, "I proposed to you because I love you. Nobody is like you. I want to spend-a my-a life with you!" and after his Academy Award-winning performance he followed up with even more bullshit promises: "I'll tell people if it's important to you. I just don't care about telling stupid people my business." I had a growing hunch that this

216

translated to "I don't think my parents will approve so I'm going to keep it a secret until I have no other options." Maybe he hoped that if he just had more time his parents might finally warm up to me. Who knows, with an extra year or two maybe he'd manage to successfully groom me into a sloppy Monica Bellucci, someone his parents could understand and relate to.

I knew that Francesco loved me but I started to feel like he was embarrassed by me. Why wouldn't he be? Try as I may, I spoke "crazy lady with a shopping cart on the street" Italian. And no amount of studying could fix my "resting bitch face," or my inability to lie or filter the things that popped into my head. Though I came to Italy with self-esteem to spare, it didn't take much for me to believe that something was wrong with me. I'd never felt good enough, not even for myself.

* * *

I was in Cumino with Francesco, in the main square. The sun was just barely setting in the early evening so the group of us were still drinking spritzers with wine and Campari. Francesco joked with Lorenzo, one of his best friends from Cumino, who never quite took to me because sometimes I "upset" Francesco. And it's true, sometimes I did upset Francesco but sometimes Francesco upset me. So, as far as I was concerned, we were even. I spoke with one of Francesco's friends who spoke English, a perfectly groomed man who didn't have even a single hair out of place.

"How are you?" he asked. "Getting along fine with Francesco's family?" He said it mischievously, with a smug expression that hinted he knew something that I didn't.

"I don't know," I shrugged, "I'm not sure they like me."

"Oh, they don't," he smiled. "Amalea told everyone in the town how much she doesn't like you. She really doesn't like you." He smiled even more broadly. This baffled me. Who says something like that with a shit-eating grin?

I gulped down my half-full cocktail.

"I thought so. I don't know. But maybe she is just the kind of mom that doesn't like anyone? Did she like his ex-girlfriend?" I asked, bracing myself for bad news.

"Oh yes," he said, matter-of-factly. "You're much prettier than she was but I think she was nicer. She was always smiling."

"Oh," was all I could get out. I looked over at Francesco who raised his glass to me with a huge grin plastered on his face because he was out of earshot and had no idea what we were talking about.

The next morning, I tiptoed into the office where Francesco slept and sat down on the bed. He gave me a big hug. Then I told him everything his friend had said the night before.

"So not only does she hate me, she's telling everyone that she hates me. Please, just be honest with me, what am I doing wrong?"

Francesco lowered his head. "You're not Italian."

"I can't FIX THAT," I stage-whispered. I searched his face. He *knew* his parents didn't like me and that's why he wouldn't tell them about our engagement. And that's why he suddenly wanted to come to Cumino so fucking much: he was buying time for me to win them over.

"*This* is why you won't tell them! Jesus, I'm so *stupid*. How did I not know? I mean, I had suspected it but I didn't *really* believe it."

"Please just keep trying, honey. It's going to be okay," he said, caressing my face. This stung because I felt like he was setting me up for failure, and as much as I wanted to not take the rejection personally, I did. He sat up and said, "Let's go into the kitchen and get coffee."

I froze, my heart sped up and I had to fight the urge to crawl under his sofa bed. How could I face his mom? I am the *worst* liar in the world. Sure, I could go out there and say, "Good morning," but there's no way my face would cooperate with my mouth and I knew I'd just be scowling at her.

"I don't want to go out there!" I shrieked.

Francesco stared at me. "You have to. If you don't they'll be mad."

"And? They already don't like me. Haven't you heard? How am I supposed to trot out there and chat about the weather when your mom is basically telling everyone that you're dating the human equivalent of a *barbwire face tattoo?*"

Francesco pulled me to my feet. "Babe, come on. I know it sucks but what can I do? It's my mom. You have to just try. If we avoid them, it will only make things worse."

I nodded and, against my better judgment, dragged myself into the guest room to get dressed so I could tap-dance into the kitchen like everything was totally A-okay. Tap, tap, tap! I just didn't know a better alternative. Would it fix things for Francesco to get into a huge fight with her? Would she suddenly like me more if he told her that we knew how she felt? No. So until I could think of a better plan, I begrudgingly took Francesco's suggestion. Or tried. All through breakfast I basically sat across from his mom wearing the confusing grin of a murderous clown.

For months, we played a game: Francesco and I would go to Cumino, I'd be fake as fuck while his parents were endlessly bewildered by me and my way of existing in the world. It reminded me of the way two Republicans are confused when they mate and somehow produce a Democrat. And the more I talked, the worse things got.

"Are you Catholic?" Amalea asked.

"No, me no have religion." I fumbled in Italian.

219

"WHAT IS SHE SAYING?!" Amalea said with wild eyes. Francesco rapidly explained that I wasn't religious and a heated argument quickly ensued about my lack of moral education. Oliver ran and dove under the couch and I wished I could join him.

Eventually, I completely withdrew and started to feel anxious about having to talk with them because every word somehow escalated things.

One evening we'd just finished eating dinner and I was guzzling my glass of wine when Marcello turned to me abruptly.

"You need to learn how to cook, you need to learn to set the table. Get us coffee and grappa."

"Pardon? Can't Francesco bring you coffee and grappa?" I asked.

"Francesco doesn't need to do it because he's a man. This is how it is in Italy; if you're going to live here, you have to be Italian." He sat up straight with his hands up like a referee calling a goal. I turned to Francesco and spoke in English.

"Dude, please tell me how to respond here or what to do because I'm at a loss right now and this is some crazy shit."

Marcello looked around. "What is she saying? She's speaking Japanese!"

"Babe, please just do whatever to make them happy," Francesco said. It was dehumanizing that they expected me to serve them specifically because I had a vagina.

I slowly got up and spat in English, "Cool, I guess I'll just jump in my fucking time machine and take it back to the 1950s. I'll be right back to wait on you, Your Heinous," I curtsied dramatically and walked over to the stove to make them coffee.

"WHAT IS SHE SAYING?" Marcello yelled.

I turned back around and glared at Francesco. "But know that you're going to pay for this when we get home," I said threateningly.

"WHAT!?" Marcello yelled, again.

Francesco was like the shadow version of himself in Cumino. Instead of the witty, sensitive nerd I fell in love with, Cumino Francesco resembled a caveman. Sometimes I almost expected his knuckles to start dragging on the ground, for him to shake his dick at me and roar, "LOOK! LOOK! I'm a maaaaaan." He was nothing like the person I shared an apartment and a poodle with. In Florence he did almost all of the cooking, often while wearing an apron and dancing to flamenco music. In Cumino, he morphed into all of the things that he believed a small-village man was supposed to be and what he thought his parents wanted. I wasn't attracted to Cumino Francesco. Five minutes with him and my lady part practically sewed itself shut and went on strike, and I had to resist the urge to stab him in the balls with a dull fork. It was maddening. But I understood that it was hard for him, too. I mean, we all occasionally revert back to who we were expected to be as a child. And no matter how much we tell ourselves we don't need it, we all, deep down, want our parents' approval. Still, I knew things couldn't carry on like that forever.

22

And Then Someone Brandishes a Saucepan at You

July 2011

Jenny and I lay on the bed in her room and I counted the many, many ways that this weekend could go wrong. Francesco was in Cumino, supposedly telling his parents the big news. I stayed behind to whine to my roommates and forcefully love Oliver against his will.

"What if he doesn't really tell them we're engaged like he promised?" I asked her. She sighed and twisted her long hair into a bun on top of her head then let it fall loose again before responding. "For his sake I really hope he does." I pondered what it would mean if he didn't. Would it be over? The thought of it being over made me feel sick and I hoped that he'd muster the courage to finally tell them.

To help the weekend go by faster, I took Oliver to the park on Saturday morning. He ran around on his lanky teenage legs and peed on every blade of grass, every flower, and every leaf. I chased him, I giggled, he happy-barked, and then I looked up and caught a middle-aged pervert standing there with his pants around his ankles, masturbating furiously to me and Oliver playing. I grabbed Oliver like a football and speed-walked towards the park exit, eyeing the dirty weirdo as I made my way to safety. On Sunday, I lay around my room all day and read a book, and not long after I finished the last page, Francesco came home.

He plopped down on the bed next to me and patted Oliver on the head. I prepared myself for the worst and refrained from being excited to see him, making an effort to seem totally okay in case things were absolutely not okay.

"How did it go?" I finally asked. My voice was weaker than I wanted it to be, noticeably disappointed.

"Everything was fine!" he said, brightly. "They weren't even surprised!"

I eyed him suspiciously, it was too good to be true.

"Really? When can we start planning then?" I asked as a challenge more than as an earnest question. I wasn't really in a rush to get married but I didn't want to be duped either.

"Let's go to Cumino together next week, we'll talk about it then," Francesco answered.

"Okay," I acquiesced. But I was thinking, *something is wrong with this*. It couldn't have been so easy.

On the car ride down to Cumino, I felt uneasy. It didn't make sense that his family would have an oh-cool-bro attitude about him getting married to someone that the entire world knew they hated. Sure that there had been a misunderstanding, I tried to give Francesco a pep talk about what to say when we arrived, to clear the air.

"Are you sure they knew you were marrying *me*?"

"Yes, babe," Francesco said, exasperated.

"To me? And they were like, 'Oh, great!'"

"Yeah, it was fine," he said.

"Well, when we get there, just be confident," I said. "We're totally in this together and it's going to be great!" And I totally meant it, until we pulled up in front of their apartment.

When his mom and dad opened the front door, I completely changed my tune and was like, ah, hell, fucking no! *Help!* The minute Francesco and I were alone together in the foyer, I grabbed him.

"Maybe all of this is wrong! This is a bad idea. Let's just wait until they die! They're *old*! Let's elope! I can't do this to you! I'm ruining your life! I really need a glass of wine. They're going to ax-murder me! I'M NOT GOOD ENOUGH FOR YOU!" I cried.

Francesco stared at me bewildered, like I'd just declared myself as Athena and plunked a hubcap on my head.

"Calm down! What's wrong with you?" Francesco asked. "Nobody is going to ax-murder you. They'll-a be fine! Let's just have dinner and-a we can talk about-a wedding stuff."

I nodded and tried to contain myself.

His mom had dinner on the table in the kitchen for us, an array of cheeses, olives, and salami, with a basket of bread, white wine, and some kind of pizza with broccoli and sardines. I poured the wine first because without it I might have screamed, "ABANDON SHIP!" Right before running out of the apartment never to be seen again.

Francesco asked his mother about his niece, Emma, and they laughed about how at three years old she could already speak dialect. His mother always beamed when she spoke of her. Then Francesco said, "Bippity boppity boop, *matrimonio*, bippity."

She tensed up like she'd just accidentally farted, her face went hard, she looked at us both for a moment—me, then him, then me again. I showed her my ring. She looked at my hand like I was wearing a dead baby and visibly choked on the words one is supposed to say, such as "How lovely," or whatever. She turned her back to us and started to clean the stove with raw, unbridled force as if her goal were to strip metal. She turned abruptly.

"When?" she asked.

"Maybe two years or three we make a wedding," I whispered in my best Italian.

She shook her head, "I don't know why you're rushing all of this. What is the point in getting married so soon?"

She tossed the sponge onto the counter and wiped her hands on her apron. She wasn't entirely wrong, I mean, the engagement had been really fast. Even I thought it was fast. But I had no intentions of getting married in less than two years and we'd already been together for two years. That wasn't crazy, right?

It didn't take that long for the fight to escalate.

"Why couldn't you find an Italian girl?" Amalea demanded. I stiffened a little and thought, Jesus, can she not see that I'm right here? Did I blend into the fucking wallpaper? Francesco mumbled something about not wanting an Italian woman and she leaped up from the table, slammed a cupboard and threw up her hands, and made this weird "eh eh eh" noise like a dolphin, which means something like, "And what now?" and "You're an idiot!" in Italian.

Francesco spoke quietly. "Mamma, come on…" She walked to the other end of the kitchen, her face all twitchy from stress. "Oh *Dio!*" she sighed, then she crossed herself and murmured something towards the ceiling like she did. She banged the pots and pans into place and wrung her hands while facing me, so I concentrated extra hard on the wall, tracing a crack in the plaster. "Well, I don't know," she said in Italian, "I don't know."

Francesco looked at her with his mouth half-open, like he'd hoped that words would come out in his defense but was bewildered that they didn't. He shut down anytime there was a conflict with his parents, and it made me wonder what happened in his childhood to make him so scared.

The fight raged on for a while and finally, when I saw an opportunity, I snuck off to the balcony to get some fresh air and put some distance between me and the screams to God. But one can only watch laundry ripple in the wind for so long, plus I'd had too much wine, and needed to pee. This meant that I had to leave the safety of the balcony and venture back into the kitchen, where the fighting had intensified from panicked hollering to machine gun-like outbursts.

I stepped inside and slid the door shut quietly behind me, and Francesco's and Amalea's eyes darted over to me and then back to each other.

She waved her hands, "Where will your children live?"

Whoa, whoa, what children? What conversation had I just walked into?

I stepped forward and chimed in like a hillbilly in very bad Italian, "We don't make together not for a long, long time the babies."

Francesco let out a loud sigh, audibly exhausted. "Mamma, our children will live in an apartment with us?"

An indigo vein popped into visibility on Amalea's forehead and she shook her head emphatically.

"You have to buy an apartment before you get married! Where will the children live? WHERE?! Your children will be homeless! They'll live on the street!" Her voice was panic-stricken, speaking Italian so quickly I could barely follow it.

As far as I was concerned, there wouldn't be any humans walking out of my womb anytime soon, so we had plenty of time to worry about housing.

"No!" she continued, "You can't get married until we buy you an apartment! Then after we can discuss these plans for *marriage*."

Wearing Only a Smile

23

Live Sex Show

August 2011

I sat on the floor of our new, hobbit-sized apartment, slowly unpacking a corkscrew, percolator, and a gnocchi board. Jenny was out with her boyfriend, and Francesco was at work. Alice had moved back to Canada saying that she couldn't take Italy's shit anymore. So Francesco, Jenny and I decided to move to the city center. It was summer in Florence, marked by one-hundred-degree days and eighty percent humidity. The Tuscan sun hammered down on the stone buildings and turned the entire city into an incinerator. We were lucky to have found an apartment with air conditioning, even if the bread-loaf-sized contraption only worked in the living room and dripped water down the far left wall, causing the paint to peel in long, thin sheets. In our last apartment, I took four cold showers every day to ward off heat exhaustion and sat on cold washcloths while I wrote marketing ads, with literal swamp ass, for hours. A shitty air conditioner was a huge improvement.

Outside, teenagers chased each other, a wife yelled at her husband to "use his head," and bike bells dinged. I welcomed the noise of the city center, the diversity, and the chaos of locals and two hundred tour groups in matching baseball caps. A far cry from our previous neighborhood of Statuto, where I'd started to lose my mind from the silence and creeping loneliness. Our new apartment was on Via San Gallo, a block from our favorite Irish pub, Finnegans, and three blocks from Piazza del Duomo, where I'd lived during grad school with Amy.

"It's about time you moved back to civilization," my friend Josh, an artist from Texas, said one day while bent over a work table in the printing studio where Jen and I were printing shirts, "you were turning into a RenFair expat." RenFair expats, or Renaissance Fair expats, according to Josh were an elusive, antisocial, quirky/angry group of expats sprinkled throughout the city. They are strange creatures often spotted sitting alone in cafés, obsessively posting pictures of their cats on Facebook, talking in code about their day-to-day life, with hollow skin, claws; crazy. It was true, replace "cats" with Oliver, and I was a few months shy of that.

I finished unpacking a box of pictures, many that I'd taken while in school: Grayson and I hugging at a museum, Amy and me in our first apartment. Things had changed since then. Living abroad wasn't all sunshine and rainbows. I turned to Oliver, "You know Oli, I used to be happy-ish and fun." He raised his head to see if I had anything useful to say, realized I didn't and went back to sleep. I smiled. I hoped that in our new place I'd maybe start to feel at home again. Things were shitty, sure, but I desperately wanted to make it work because Italy was supposed to be my refuge. It was supposed to be paradise. It was supposed to be better than at home.

Tired of pulling things out of boxes I begrudgingly pushed through; I had no choice but to finish. Francesco's parents were coming to Florence the next day to stay with us, our first weekend at our new place. I'd planned to go full-on Stepford that weekend, to wake up early and start making lunch so by the time they arrived at noon the food would be ready.

I got up at 6 a.m. and made ravioli *from scratch* with the help of YouTube. Flour and eggs, mix, roll out, put dollops of spinach and ricotta filling on the bumpy pasta sheets. Put on the top. Wet edges. Push it down and together. Cut. Set aside on a wooden board that has been dusted with flour. Then I made the marinara sauce with San Marzano tomatoes. One sprig of basil. Boil on high, decrease heat, simmer for hours until the smell permeates all the fabric in the house, including your favorite dresses. I cut up antipasti. I made coffee. I drank coffee and cried a little out of sheer frustration because who the fuck was I becoming and why was I going to all the trouble?

Francesco sighed. The doorbell rang. I dried my eyes with my shirt sleeve and bit my lip.

Francesco took my hand and whispered, "It's going to be okay."

Amalea and Marcello entered our tiny apartment. They set their stuff down like they owned the place and slowly scanned the kitchen and living room.

"*Benvenuti,*" I forced a smile and kissed both of them.

Amalea turned to Francesco, "It's too small." she said, disdainfully.

"Yeah, it's very small," Francesco told them in Italian. "Are you hungry?"

I boiled water for the ravioli and stirred the marinara sauce with sweaty palms. Anxiety surfaced and resurfaced the way vomit eases up into your throat after too many vodkas and a car ride.

Amalea came over to examine the stove and the gurgling, boiling contents upon it. She raised her eyebrows smugly, made some joke I didn't understand but she found hilarious, and then took her seat at the table with Francesco and his father. They talked amongst themselves.

"What shit is she making?" Marcello asked Francesco in Italian.

I hoped that my lunch wouldn't give them more fodder to use against me because I wasn't sure how much criticism I could take. I served everyone at the table while Francesco sat there like a prince to the left of his king and queen. Marcello dove directly into the ravioli. "It's okay," he muttered. Amalea tried hers hesitantly like she'd traveled to an exotic land and someone had tried to feed her live monkey brains. She reluctantly injected a crumb-sized portion into her mouth.

"*Ma*, this isn't right," she said.

It seems that they took it less as a sweet gesture and more of a challenge, like *you* think you can make pasta for *us*, motherfucker?

Amalea cleared her throat. "When you put the flour and eggs together you have to mix it like this," she did a motion with her hands like she was punching a toddler in the face. "Not like this," like a limp-wristed diva from the top of a float. "And seriously, you need to drink more wine. You look like you just got out of an internment camp, all pale and too thin."

Got it.

When I served the second course of rosemary potatoes and roasted chicken, Marcello's face lit up. "These potatoes are really good! I tell Amalea to put onions in hers too but she won't. They're better this way!" He smiled at me. Amalea shot me a glance that read, "Bitch, don't you even think about taking that compliment. *I will end you.*"

After lunch, Marcello and Amalea declared that they wanted to go look at apartments with Francesco. I stayed home because it felt way too weird to be involved. On one hand, I'd be living there too, on the other, it wasn't "our" apartment and I didn't feel entitled to an opinion. I was sad that things were unfolding this way, that my fiancé was off looking at apartments to buy without me, that nobody was happy that we were getting married, that my ravioli was a disaster, and that our relationship seemed to be dripping in some kind of weird scandal. And I couldn't quite figure out how I felt: on one hand, I'd been taught to respect elders. On the other, to what extent?

When they came back a few hours later, I was way too devoted to feeling sorry for myself to give the right amount of social effort. Logically, I knew that moping around wouldn't solve anything but I'd totally lost my ability to be a cheerful person.

"Why is she so quiet?" they kept whispering to Francesco as we walked through the center of Florence. Francesco shook his head.

While they were window-gazing, he scolded, "Knock it off! You're making everyone really uncomfortable!"

The gray skies and humidity that day only added to my foul mood. I glared at the water droplets rolling down a cement wall covered in love-letter graffiti, the most common graffiti in Italy. It read: "Silvia, Ti amo, amore mio, per tutta la vita." Silvia, I love you, my love, for the rest of my life. It was written next to an old alley full of trash, and I hated that stupid wall and fucking Silvia because I needed to hate something.

However, something good and unexpected came shortly after. Marcello and Amalea decided not to get an apartment after all. Once we mentioned that we might leave Florence and rent it out the conversation came to a screeching halt.

"You can't rent out your apartment," Marcello objected, "I am *not* buying you an apartment so a stranger can stay there." And just like that, we were off the hook, the house was out, and yet the wedding was still on. What happened to our children being homeless? I wondered. But I wasn't going to push the issue.

The following morning Francesco and I lay in bed talking about the apartment situation and getting married. The next thing I knew we were having sex, without blankets because it was already one hundred degrees.

Francesco whispered in my ear, "*Ti amo*, you—"

Which is probably why neither of us heard the doorknob turn.

Over Francesco's shoulder, I watched, in horror, as Marcello appeared in our room. "Franci," a nickname for Francesco, "*ma, que*"

I screamed. Francesco somehow threw covers over his naked bum, and his father bolted out, slamming the door behind him. I heard commotion in the living room. Francesco stumbled into his clothes and ran downstairs to catch his parents bursting onto the sidewalk below, sprinting from our apartment to their car. I glanced out the window overlooking the street in time to see them awkwardly hug Francesco before speeding away.

Francesco came back inside and sat down on the edge of the bed. He held my face in his hands and asked gently, "Are you okay?"

"Did your dad see my vagina?"

"Probably?"

He was visibly distressed and I *wanted* to feel bad for him but I couldn't, because we were way too old for his parents to come barging into our bedroom unannounced. It's one of those "I wish that didn't happen" but also "that's what you get" sort of things.

I shrugged. I mean, things couldn't possibly get worse than your fiancé's dad getting a glimpse of your vulva, right? Wrong.

24

There's No Place Like Home
(for Trauma)

Christmas 2011

Francesco and I went to Utah for Christmas. We had reservations about going, since the last time Francesco came to Utah my mom ran off and got married, my dad refused to meet him, and I left him on a curb. But I missed my own culture, my mom's open-mindedness, my dad's cooking, good Mexican food, general efficiency, my friends, and my brothers and sisters.

Mom and Brian greeted us at their home on Christmas Eve with a bottle of wine and an assortment of wildly processed snacks like Doritos and Cheese Whiz. "Jingle Bells" blared from the speaker and the house smelled like pine cones. Francesco was both fascinated and horrified to learn of a cheese that one could squirt out of a bottle and he watched me eat it as though I were chewing on the head of a live mouse.

My little brother Dakota came over to meet Francesco for the first time and they played soccer in the backyard together. Later that night, Dakota and his girlfriend went on a date so Francesco and I babysat my nephew at my mom's. All evening Francesco just followed me around in a constant state of panic going, "But can his head come off? You're not holding the baby securely enough! What if he dies?" And I whisper-yelled back, "His head is not just going to come off, Jesus! Does that happen in Italy?"

My mom and Brian cornered Francesco in the kitchen and asked him dozens of questions about his job, his family, and his life in Italy. It made me happy that they were finally getting to know him.

"Francesco, I really like you," Mom said. "But if you hurt my daughter, I'll kill you. In a real way. But I really do like you."

Brian smiled, "I agree."

On Christmas morning, we exchanged gifts in the living room under the tree. I got a face cleanser brush and a new purse. We ate breakfast, drank coffee and it felt nice to be nestled in familiarity, in a place where I knew what to do and what to say and didn't sound like a person raised by squirrels like I did in Italy.

After our fifth cup of joe, Francesco and I started packing up our stuff to head to my dad's house. Mom stood up and said, "Wait, before you guys leave, come with me," gesturing for me and Dakota to follow her.

"I've got a special Christmas gift for ya," she said inside her room. We sat on her bed and she handed each of us a small box to open while my mom clasped her hands together in barely contained excitement. I peeled back the tissue paper on mine and nearly keeled over from shock. I looked quickly at Dakota to tell him not to open his but it was too late. His smile faded, and his hands began to shake. I looked back down. A framed picture of me, Dakota, and our dead brother Mitch, who had been Photoshopped into a recent picture of me and Dakota.

"Mom," I whispered, my eyes flooding with tears.

"Do you like it?" she smiled.

"Mom—" I tried to speak.

"Why?" Dakota sat on the bed and began to sob, his shoulders heaving violently. I set my box down and hugged Dakota to me tightly. "It's okay. It's okay. We all miss him. I love you."

My mom bit her lip. "Oh no! It's not good? I'm sorry! I just thought you guys would want a picture with you all together!"

"Mom, thank you? But he's *dead*. We can't keep him alive by cropping him into all of our family pictures. This is just, so, creepy and dark."

Dakota wiped his eyes on his shirt sleeve. "Mom! You're so weird!"

Then we all erupted into awkward laughter through the tears.

"I'm sorry," Mom sighed. Dakota and I shot each other oh-my-God glances but patted her on the arm to cheer up.

I walked out into the living room and handed Francesco the "gift." He glanced down and his eyes grew wide with horror.

"*Dio mio! Madonna!* Are you okay?" He bolted up and hugged me.

"Bury that in the bottom of our luggage. Please." I whispered.
He nodded and headed for our bags so we could drive south to where my dad lived.

In a wealthy neighborhood of giant suburban mansions, Francesco drove around the block for the tenth time.

"Can we please just go to your dad's place?" he asked.

"Just go around the block one more time," I pleaded.

Francesco pulled over. "Babe, it's going to be fine! I promise!"

"It's not going to be fine! You don't know my dad. Look, okay, just don't back down from him if you disagree with something he says; he hates passive people. But be polite, he hates bad manners. He doesn't like anyone without strong opinions and he especially hates it when people kiss his ass.

But he also hates it when people are argumentative and think they know everything. You just need to be yourself but don't do that thing that you do with your own parents where you just let them say whatever they want. He'll view it as a character flaw. He's going to be looking for anything and everything he can to hate about you."

"Okay babe, that's okay. It's not a problem, stay calm, it will be totally fine."

"Francesco, in college he once told me that passive people deserved to die. He's not like other people's dads."

"Got it. Can we please go to his house now?"

"Ugh. Yeah, I guess."

We walked straight in through the front door which was always open, giving Francesco a clear view of my dad's taste—the Persian silver tea steamer on top of the lion-foot credenza, ornate Italian dining room table, red Persian carpets, and a very bizarre oil painting of a Middle Eastern man with his harem. Sebastian, the family Shih Tzu, came running at us as fast as his nubby little legs could go, barking hysterically. He slammed on his brakes when he realized who I was, sat down and wagged his tail.

"Little monster," I said lovingly, and bent down to pet him. I smelled saffron in the kitchen, which meant that my dad had been cooking.

"Baby? Is dat you?" Dad called out from the living room.

"Yeah," I hollered back.

In the kitchen, my stepmom Kathy was making coffee.

"Hey guys!" she said warmly. She hugged me and then turned to shake Francesco's hand. "You must be Francesco! So nice to finally meet you!"

My dad was on the couch in the living room. "Come give Daddy a kiss, baby," he yelled without turning around to look at me. I walked over and kissed him on the cheek.

"Dad, this is Francesco," I said, then whispered, *"Please* be nice." My dad cranked his head around.

"Hey, you," he said, eyeing Francesco, "come sit here," and motioned for Francesco to take a seat next to him on the couch. Kathy shot me a this-is-going-to-be-interesting glance. Francesco took a seat next to my dad and politely introduced himself.

"So," my dad began, "what do you think about Israel?" He was referring to something he'd just seen on the news. I went back to the kitchen to get a cup of coffee and put some distance between me and anything insane my dad was about to say. Possible topics could range from the importance of probiotics, cherry juice and garlic to the impending collapse of society as we knew it. I heard Francesco politely disagree with something but couldn't make out what it was. Kathy leaned on the counter next to me.

"You nervous?" she asked.

"Yeah. Who knows how this could go?" I said.

"I'm sure it will be fine," she smiled. But I knew she was only saying that to be nice; surely knowing him as well as she did she was thinking the same thing as me.

After what felt like days, Dad took a pause from talking with Francesco to ask me, "You hungry baby?"

"Yeah, I could eat."

Eating makes my dad happy. Enthusiastically eating his food makes his entire week, which was easy to do because he's always been a really good cook. He'd made basmati rice, *ghormeh sabzi,* salmon, vegetables with feta, lavash bread, and turkey *kubideh.* He explained each dish to Francesco.

"Persian food is the healthiest food in the world! It's mostly vegetables and yogurt. Yogurt is very important for digestion. Did you know that, Francesco? Probiotics prevent cancer. They are very good for you!"

Francesco nodded, "Yeah, that's true. It's really good for you."

"That's right, boy!" Dad said, setting a heaped plate of food in front of him.

Over-feeding is my dad's way of being generous and hospitable but it's also a test. If Francesco didn't eat the food as if he'd been served edible gold, my dad would decide to hate him and there would be no coming back from it.

Francesco ate two platefuls, and when my dad came back around to pile on thirds I waved my hand over his plate.

"Dad, he's going to get sick! Three plates are too much."

My dad puffed out his chest and thrust his jaw forward. "It's *Persian* food. It digests faster than other food. It's okay, baby."

"Lunch was incredible. Thank you so much, Azar!" Francesco said.

"Of course it was good, buddy. It's Persian! We've been making this food since your people were still in caves." He guffawed and slapped the counter. Francesco chuckled.

When we left later that night, Dad kissed me on the cheeks, looked at me and said, "I like him, baby."

I felt a huge wave of relief. It was difficult not to like Francesco, he was different from me in that way.

In the car heading north on the freeway back towards my mom's house, Francesco put his hand on my leg. "I really like your dad," he said, "he's a really unique person and he's funny."

"Do you feel like you're going to barf?" I asked.

"Yes. I ate so much food! Oh my God!"

"You have to tell him no. That's a thing you have to learn early on. I've never met anyone in my life with a stronger personality and if you don't say no, he'll feed you until you actually die. And who knows what else could happen, honestly."

"Noted."

"But he told me he liked you. So at least one set of parents is on board with us getting married." I was slightly jealous that my dad liked Francesco. Why couldn't I be likable, damnit?

"He did? Wow, that's great. And babe, don't worry about my parents. They'll get on board eventually or they won't. I want to marry you and that's all that matters."

"Should we set a date now or do you want to wait a few more years?"

"Let's set a date. How about next fall?"

"Perfect," I said.

25

Pirates of the French Riviera

Spring 2012

Back in Italy, Francesco and I sat outside at a bar on Via San Gallo, drinking a few glasses of wine while recalling our recent trip to Utah and throwing out ideas for our wedding before becoming overwhelmed and staring off into the distance. We came to the conclusion that we needed a little "we" time to bond in the midst of all the wedding, holiday, and family drama. We hadn't been on a real vacation since a little trip to southern France with friends a while back, which was *fun* but not necessarily relaxing or romantic.

For example, one night in Arles, I'd drunk way too much Bordeaux one night at dinner and tried to fulfill a childhood pirate fantasy. After midnight, I drunkenly dragged Francesco out into the streets to "explore." We wandered down to the cruise ships docked on the river and I decided out of nowhere that I absolutely had to get on the ships. Francesco watched in horror as I sprinted down the dock in my leather miniskirt and sandals and tried to scurry up the side of a ship, but I couldn't get a foothold so I just kind of looked like a lizard trying to scramble up wet glass. I tapped on windows and tried to "yoooo-hoooo" my way inside to no avail. Around the time that I should have given up, I spotted a group of men on deck a few ships down, sitting around a table drinking. I approached their ship and mimed, "Me + drinking = yaaay!" at the captain but the two other men on the boat shook their heads no. But I was determined. So I forced Francesco to climb over a rock wall with me (despite my heels) to spy on the crew. In my drunken state, I felt very *sneaky*, but in retrospect, the crew most likely watched me awkwardly clamber over the wall with the grace and stealth of a manatee.

I peered over the wall and the captain was staring right at me, so I slowly raised my hand like I wanted to be called on, and waved my fingers. Then I popped up, gave him a huge smile and screamed, "*SALUT!!!!*" Francesco at this point was sitting with his back to the wall on the ground, imploring me to stop. "Can we *please* just go back to the hotel? I'm *begging* you!" But then the captain turned to speak with the other men, who all nodded their heads, and finally waved me and Francesco over. I left Francesco in the dust, hopped over the wall and barreled down the dock onto the ship where five crew members were waiting, bemused.

The skipper disappeared and came back with beers for me and Francesco. We sat down at the table and introduced ourselves as best we could. None of them spoke good English and our French was even worse but we all managed to get by with gesticulations and cell phones. They showed us photos of wives, children, and random excursions; I showed them a picture of Oliver. The men pointed to their wives and children with sad eyes:

"Many weeks, no see."

I pointed to Oliver: "He pee a lot."

When the sun came up over the horizon we stood up to leave but they begged us to stay.

"Come on! The guests come now! We next city! You come, you! No pay!" When I agreed to stay and live on the ship, Francesco politely escorted me off, lecturing me about how I couldn't just decide to live on a French Riviera boat whilst shitfaced. We stumbled back to our hotel with fond memories of our new friends and a reminder that language isn't as necessary as kindness.

I wanted to go somewhere outside of Italy again because I always felt more like myself. The stakes were different. In France, away from Francesco's home base, I didn't have to worry about making him look bad, embarrassing him, or offending his friends and family. I could let my hair down and be ridiculous and he could do the same, which was important considering how stressed we'd been for the past six months.

"What about France again?" I asked, dreamily.

"No," Francesco said, "we're broke. Somewhere local."

"Fine!" I harrumphed.

"Tuscany?"

"Sure!"

We settled on a weekend in Chianti.

Despite being a hop, skip and a jump from one of the most beautiful places on earth, we rarely ventured into Chianti, partly because we spent most of our free time in Cumino with Francesco's parents. The landscape——cypress trees amid billowing grass juxtaposed against vineyards as if it had been styled by gifted oil painters——and the cheap delicious wine was exactly what we needed to get a little R&R even if it were still on Francesco's home turf.

"Chianti it is!" I held up my glass of, well, Chianti.

When we arrived at the medieval bed and breakfast a few weeks later, we took a stroll through the hills on the property after checking in. A few minutes in I found wild boar shit, which reminded me of being a kid and spending time on a farm and hiking the mountains near my home. I felt like a super tracker and ran up the hill following the boar doodie and hoof tracks. Francesco told me to stop stalking the animals because he found it weird. I waved him off and kept going until we'd found an olive grove and I tried to eat an olive but it tasted like bitter death and nothing like the fruit I put on my pizza.

After a little flirting, we got romantic under an olive tree, but while we were kissing the tree bark dug into my back and I kept seeing branches out of the corner of my eye that looked like vipers, so periodically I'd jump and scream, "SNAKES!" scaring the shit out of Francesco. A friend of mine once told me that vipers slither up the olive trees to mate and sometimes fall from the branches onto helpless passersby. We eventually gave up.

I thought about how one thing I loved about my relationship with Francesco was that I could be my weirdest and most vulnerable self around him because he was so accepting. The fact that it was special made it hurt even more when I felt like he expected me to hide that part of me around people he knew, like his parents, so I'd seem like a more desirable mate. It felt like regression. As we left the olive grove and headed back to our room, I wondered if there would ever be a time where he could be proud of every part of me, even around people he wanted to impress.

We went to a little village nearby for dinner. In the city center, five lonely apartment buildings lined one deserted street. The windows were dark even though it was well after dusk, and sitting under a single lamp at the end of the street was an old man having an inappropriately long conversation with his bored Labrador.

"Dog!" I pointed and Francesco held his breath for a second because since our trip to Sicily he'd got a little stressed out anytime I point out a dog in public. We popped into the only bar for coffee and learned that we didn't need to search any further because it was also the town bakery and restaurant, so we stayed for dinner and dined outside in the empty square. The highlight of our dinner was our waitress, a hilarious woman from Morocco, who made us laugh and fed us three hundred bags of chips while we waited for our food to come. Since becoming an immigrant, I noticed that I took solace in the company of other foreigners because we could often find common ground in the shared experience of otherness, the same way I'd flocked to outsiders back in Utah.

It had been a long while since I'd felt so free and relaxed with Francesco, and watching him joke with our waitress I remembered why he was so important to me: his warm personality that could get along with anyone, that genuine laugh which radiated from a deep part of himself, and his total absence of ego. In these moments where I saw him as the rest of the world saw him, I felt like my heart might burst. That intense rush of oxytocin that gets lost within the context of a relationship, often falling through the cracks of disappointment, hurt feelings, and plain old taken-for-grantedness.

After dinner, I convinced Francesco to start a fire in the fireplace in our hotel room because it would be romantic but I forgot that he hadn't grown up camping in the Rocky Mountains like I had. It took him an hour of intense laboring and forty rolls of toilet paper to get the fire going, and for a moment I'd given up on the idea and crawled into bed. But shortly after he jumped up, banged his chest and bellowed, "FIRE! I created FIRE! My-a babe wanted deh fire and I gave air deh fire!" He was very proud of himself and all at one with his caveman. I pushed the bed in front of the fireplace so it would be like camping.

"Do you want to go to Cornucopia?" Francesco asked.

I nodded and we burrowed under the blankets together and fell soundly asleep. Often when I would get super stressed out or upset, I'd pull the blankets over my head and Francesco would climb under with me and we called it "visiting Cornucopia." It was like our break from the world. It was the only time in my life when I wasn't an actual child where I did stuff like this. Even now, years later, when I'm really upset, Francesco will still ask, "Do you need to go to Cornucopia for a minute?"

The next morning we visited a vineyard, where the family who invented a very important Tuscan wine still lives today. We paused to look out over the garden and take in the fresh outside air. There wasn't a lot of greenery in Florence, a city of stone and terracotta, which was strange for someone like me, who came from a city defined by mountains that you could always see no matter where you were. Without the mountains on the east, how does anyone know where they've come from or where they're going? While Francesco and I wandered around the gardens, he tried to speak in an Old English accent and pretended to be aristocratic, but I'd already decided that this was *my* castle

"This is awesome huh babe? I mean, could you imagine living here?" Francesco asked.

"Yes. I can. In fact, I finally feel at home," I answered. "I'd totally reclaim this place, fix the drapes, and kill whoever built this wall. I mean seriously! Do you know how easy it would be to breach the front wall? An army of humans, or trolls—nobody is safe!" I'd recently read a book on Joan of Arc and fully embodied her strategic genius.

"You know, the scary thing is that you used the word 'reclaim,'" he joked. "So, could I live in your castle?"

"No. No, you can't. Wait, actually, can I *finally* have a pet capybara? I would name him Dwayne and he would be glorious." I'd been asking for a pet capybara ever since I found an Instagram account of one swimming in a pool and leisurely eating lettuce while sunbathing. They essentially look like giant guinea pigs, a rodent the size of a bulldog, but more refined and I *really* wanted one.

"*Dio mio*! Yes. *Fine*. If you own a castle and you let me live in it then you can finally have that stupid giant rat you want." I glared at him for calling Dwayne a giant rat.

"You can have that tower over there." I gestured to a far-off structure, "But you can't live in the main part, that's for me and Dwayne."

"Whatever. So you belong here with this family, huh? Are you like the long-lost daughter or something?"

"This family? Ew no! These guys have been living here for like thirty generations and they're all rich and probably can't talk with commoners, so basically everyone inside is possibly super inbred because they don't have a dating app for old-timey aristocrats. In fact, I'm sure it's very exciting at this point if someone is born without tentacles. The octopus clan. No thanks."

"Riiiight," Francesco said.

"Follow or perish," I commanded, and set off to inspect the grounds, imagining what it would be like to rule a castle or maybe get married in one.

Raw

26

Easter Vampires

March 2012

Before I lived in Italy, I thought that my family was crazy because they were divorced, remarried, and generally bonkers. I admired how close Italian families were, or what I perceived from the outside, and wished that I could somehow be more like them because my family wasn't all that close in the way that I wanted them to be. When I met Francesco I was really scared that I wouldn't be accepted into his family's close circle because I was damaged, but the longer our relationship went on the more I saw that "normal" families were totally fucked up in their own, unique way. Where my parents were firm believers in sink-or-swim parenting, Francesco's were closely following the my-child-is-a-marionette style. The child-parent relationship from afar resembled stalking, and up close, love seemed to be delivered via incessant nagging. Sometimes, it was like watching a hen peck a worm to death: slow and cruel, until eventually the worm stops wriggling, goes limp and accepts that it's going to be devoured.

It was Easter weekend. The streets in Cumino were packed with a procession of Catholics carrying an emaciated statue of Jesus on the cross.

Francesco and I were in bed in the guest room at his parents' house. Oliver had just woke me up by dropping a wet stuffed elephant on my face, repeatedly. We could hear Amalea in the kitchen banging pots and pans and wielding a wooden spoon at her husband, so we snuck outside with Oliver to skirt the chaos for a moment and breathe a little before Francesco's sister arrived.

The procession had passed and the streets were now eerily empty because everyone was home getting ready for lunch. We stopped on a patch of dead grass to let Oliver pee on every inch of the surface, as he trotted along merrily. We watched him lovingly, held hands and exhaled in preparation for the hours to come.

"My mom is going to freak out soon, so prepare yourself," Francesco muttered.

"Okay," I said.

Back inside the apartment his elder sister, Julia, who looked exactly like a mix of Francesco and Sophia Loren, had arrived, along with her husband Alessio and daughter Emma. Francesco's mom paced in circles in the kitchen screaming, "Lunch will never, ever be ready," and, "This is a disaster!"

Everyone in the kitchen froze, became stone, pretended to play dead.

I put my hand on Amalea's shoulder and tried to be helpful. "Well what help you need? What we can to do? Everything is in place!"

She swatted my hand away. "Someone has to cut the bread! But I'm too busy!" she huffed.

I volunteered Francesco: "He can cut the bread."

She banged her hand on the counter, shouting, "HE DOESN'T KNOW HOW TO CUT BREAD!"

And then we all just kind of stood there confused, wondering if it were really true: can Francesco not cut bread?

Then she said something like, "Go to the church." So Francesco and I left with his sister, Alessio, and Emma towards a nearby church.

Emma grabbed my hand to walk with me. I'd known her since she was three and I was as much a part of her life as Francesco. She was five years old now and I adored her. She'd recently figured out that I spoke a different language than her, and tried to teach me dialect using her limited vocabulary. She was a better teacher than most of the adults. I stared at the empty jam jar that Julia carried, and Emma saw me looking at it.

"*Vaso*," she explained. I kissed her hand and wondered what Julia planned to do with the "vaso." We stopped in front of a church.

"What are we doing here?" I whispered to Francesco.

"My sister is filling her things with holy water." Julia entered the small Catholic church with the jam jar. The rest of us stood just outside of the white doors.

"The jar? She's filling the *jar* with holy water? That doesn't sound right at all. It seems kind of *unsanitary*." I imagined her dipping her old, sticky, strawberry preserves in the marble fountain thing, and it just seemed so wrong. If I needed holy water, I would be pretty pissed about someone putting a jar in it. Everyone knows holy water is only supposed to come in old, mystical apothecary glass.

"Yeah, a jar for lunch," Francesco said, as though I were the weird one.

"Because your mom invited vampires?" I asked.

He turned and gave me one of his what-the-fuck-is-wrong-with-you looks and then he translated to everyone else what I had said, and they all turned and gave me the same look. I wasn't the one dipping dirty strawberry preserve containers into everyone's holy water and gathering religious weapons.

Back at the apartment, Francesco's mom was still angry that Francesco didn't know how to cut bread. She clunked the jar down on the living room table along with everything else she had made for lunch, which was basically enough to feed the seven of us four times over. We took our seats. Francesco's dad reached for food and the mom yelled at him. She stood over the table, grabbed the jar in one hand and a sprig of rosemary in the other. She said something in Italian, then dipped a sprig of rosemary into the jar and sprinkled the water all over the table.

Francesco turned towards me. "She's blessing the food," he explained.

I nodded. Then his mother turned to me, smiled, screamed, "*Battesimo!*" and threw the strawberry-tainted water into my face.

"Ack!" I cried out as beads of water dripped down my cheeks and ran into my eyes. She made the sign of the cross in front of my face then took her seat, a smug grin inching across her face.

Francesco leaned over and snorted, "She baptized you!"

"I'm still not converting," I said, all soggy and annoyed.

"I know," he laughed.

I held my throat, pretending to choke like demons do in the movies when someone throws holy water on them. Francesco just rolled his eyes and told me to stop it. Everyone dismissed me and started eating while I sat there with water dripping down my face, wondering how one goes about wiping off holy water. Religious or not, I didn't want to take any chances with bad luck.

Amalea brought course after course of food: three appetizers, two pasta dishes, lamb, rabbit—and if she'd had the opportunity, she'd probably have clubbed a baby seal or two— followed by three or four different desserts, nuts, and fruit. We ate until we felt sick.

Francesco cleared his throat. "So, I think we've decided to have two weddings. One here and one in the US. We want to do the US wedding first, next fall."

Amalea straightened up. Marcello went quiet. Julia smiled and said, "That's great!"

Francesco continued, "We'll have the wedding outside in Park City, Utah. And we'd love it if you guys could come but if not it's okay because we'll have a wedding here, too, if you think that's a good idea."

"So, the wedding in Utah will be outside?" Amalea asked. "Not in a church? So it's not a *real* wedding, it's an American party!"

Francesco shot me a glance, then looked at his mom. "No, it's not in a church."

Her face relaxed. "Ah, okay then. If that's what you want."

I interjected in English, "Wait, I don't think it's a good idea to lie to them." The entire family looked at me, wondering what I was saying in my funny language.

"I didn't lie. I told them we're getting married outside in Utah, which is true," Francesco replied. "If she doesn't believe it's real because it's not in a church, well, there's nothing I can do about that."

I shook my head in disapproval.

"SPEAK ITALIAN!" Marcello yelled.

After lunch, Francesco took a nap. I protected Oliver from Emma, who had witnessed her grandmother douse me in water and had been inspired to bless Oliver, repeatedly. He couldn't understand why a tiny human kept throwing water on him and shrieking, "*Santo spirito!*" He eventually hid under the bed. I distracted her with crayons, and she labored on a portrait of a man nailed to a cross.

"Is that Jesus?" I asked.

"No, Zio Francesco."

And why wouldn't she crucify her uncle? She filled in her picture around Francesco's corpse with fifty smaller crosses, crosses for flowers, crosses for stars. I drew a tree. She added a cross to it.

"That's so Roman of you, kiddo," I said in English.

"*Ma, che?*" she responded, stroking a long tendril of hair around her face.

Shortly after crucifying the family, Emma fell asleep. Bored, I went to the kitchen to offer Amalea help cleaning up but she shooed me away. I held up my hands.

"Okay, I give up," I said in English. I leaned against the doorframe to watch her furiously scrub a pan, making the ruffles on her apron shake.

"Thank you for lunch," I said. "Oh, I mean, *grazie per il pranzo.*"

She slapped the air. "It was not so good," she replied in Italian, then looked over at me. "You don't have to always thank me, it's a strange thing to do it. I love to cook for my family."

27

Your Boobs Suck! and Other
Observations

April 2012

"I swear I will kill you! OR MYSELF!" our new landlord downstairs shouted into the phone at his ex-wife. The screaming and threatening was a daily thing, almost as though his morning agenda read: wake up, drink coffee, threaten to kill self to ex, shower, repeat. Through the balcony doors, birds chirped and Oliver watched them. In the apartment upstairs, someone played the piano and a man sang opera in a deep baritone voice. They practiced for hours, the same song over and over again.

Francesco and I were five months away from our wedding in Utah, or the "American party" as his parents referred to it. We'd been engaged at that point for two years and had finally picked September 25th, 2012 to tie the knot. This is why we'd just moved to a new place in the Campo di Marte neighborhood in Florence. Francesco insisted we live alone if we were going to be married as if we were adults or something. I suppose it was good timing because Jenny planned to go back to North Carolina and she stayed at her boyfriend's place most of the time anyway.

I loved the new area; it wasn't in the center of Florence but it was a bustling neighbourhood and the locals were friendly. I knew the woman who owned the café across the street, and she greeted me and Oliver by name in the morning when I'd swing in for a cappuccino. I'd lean on the bar and we'd chat in Italian about our day or she'd roll her eyes at her boyfriend and we'd smile knowing smiles. And it occurred to me one day that I'd finally become like that redhead I'd envied so many years ago on my first trip to Florence.

In addition to the lovely café and barista, our apartment was new and furnished with Ikea furniture instead of musty leftovers from someone's dead grandma. For the first time in years, my bedroom didn't smell like a funeral home and I didn't have to wonder how many sex puddles had seeped into the mattress before mine.

I wasn't happy to see Jenny go. She was my closest friend in Florence, even though we rarely hung out because of work, boyfriends, and life. We'd put our design company on hold so we could relocate it to the US and sell online in the future. We'd been doing well in high-end stores in Florence, but it wasn't enough and being foreign made it unnecessarily harder than it needed to be. Our ROI was shit. One thing we'd both learned: immigrants do not have it easy. From standing in sweltering immigration offices in lines two-hundred strong for hours to begging office workers through reinforced glass for forms and more information to maintain our resident status or *permesso di soggiorno* (stay permit). We had to be twice as careful when making deals with shop owners, and almost always got the short end of the stick because we weren't legally protected. In Italy, we'd found that most of our foreign acquaintances were often paid much less for their work than their Italian coworkers, we were constantly overcharged in cafés and always felt like we were on the outside looking in. I understood why she was leaving and had started to think about it myself.

I was lonely in Italy. I missed my friends, my family, and the simplicity of belonging. I started a travel blog as a way to connect with others and to reclaim my voice and sense of humor (I really needed someone to get my pop reference jokes). I wrote about my life in Italy, the day trips to wineries and feeling like an outsider, and it felt great to vent but even better to just sit down and hash out my feelings about all the stuff going on in my life.

Our apartment and neighborhood were fantastic but there were drawbacks to the new place. I no longer had a roommate that acted as a built-in friend, and our homicidal landlord was home twenty-four-seven, which meant we couldn't leave Oliver home alone, ever. See, Oliver had separation anxiety and when we left he'd cry and whine. The landlord would call after exactly twenty seconds of this. So, Francesco and I had to take Oliver with us anytime we left the apartment. In Florence, everyone takes their dogs everywhere from cafés to clothing stores and nice restaurants. But Oliver wasn't like sweet Florentine dogs, he was more like a methed-out baby goat, hopping and parkouring himself down the street to smell, see, or pee on everything. We were tied to our home. We tried training but our trainer said that his anxiety seemed "genetic"; we'd hired at least a dozen different pet sitters but they'd all quit, most often because Oliver would shrilly yip-yap and howl at their front door like someone was killing him until we arrived.

"He's a sweetie," they'd say, "But he cried for four hours straight and everyone in the entire building hates us now." Once when my friend Elizabeth watched him, he became hysterical when he saw Francesco and I drive away, and projectile-shat all over her brand-new leather couch. I couldn't go to the grocery store, work from a café, nothing without bringing Oliver. So, I basically just stopped leaving my house. Trapped in my thoughts all day, every day, I was not in a good place mentally. Definitely not in the right frame of mind to be entertaining Francesco's mom.

Amalea was coming to Florence to do a "tour of the churches," and conveniently Francesco had to work all week, which meant it was my job to literally scrub the tiles with a toothbrush. I suspected she was *really* coming to conduct a thorough investigation of our life and I did not want her to have the satisfaction of spotting even one speck of dust or grime.

Only a few minutes after she'd walked in, she ran her hands over my bookshelves and along the radiators to check if I'd dusted; I watched her put her nose up to the tiles in the bathroom to check for soap scum. She went through the cupboards and pulled out biscuits and Illy coffee, filled the percolator with water, twisted the top in and set it over the flame of the gas range.

"You still doing that thing? That job?" she asked while rummaging through our fridge.

"Copywriting? Yes."

"So you just sit here and write words all day?"

"Yes, more or less."

"Hmm. Well, you know, you should quit and get a *real* job teaching English."

I responded in English, so she couldn't understand, "Wow, yeah! Teaching sounds way better than writing, the thing I went to school for and love."

She raised her eyebrows, confused. "Speak Italian. You know I don't understand it when you talk like that."

I smiled and nodded.

Having his mother in Florence without Marcello was supposed to be a bonding experience for us, according to Francesco.

"Just try to get to know her," he pleaded. I wanted a relationship with her but it was a little hard to open up around someone who appeared to beg God to kill you on a regular basis. Still, I tried.

Francesco, Amalea, and I went for a walk in the shopping quarter, drank a coffee or two, and popped into half a dozen churches where Amalea crossed herself, knelt down, and splashed holy water around. I thought, No wonder she has such a great figure, she spends all day doing lunges.

The three of us had dinner at a local restaurant. Amalea and I laughed at Francesco blushing over a woman breastfeeding in public, her engorged breast in open view, her famished, suckling infant latched onto it. Francesco diverted his eyes, his face turned a million shades of embarrassment, and then we had to move tables because seeing a stranger's boob was too much for him. I'd noticed that public breastfeeding was as normal as breathing in Italy. I thought it was pretty badass the way the women were proud to feed their babies, and how everyone else was proud of them. They'd often just pull out the whole boob, pop it in their baby's mouth, and carry on with the conversation as if a tiny person wasn't dangling off of them.

On the walk back to our apartment Amalea told us stories about growing up in the south of Italy during the fifties.

"My mother was a field worker. She wore large dresses so she could pee standing up while working."

"How did she not pee on her dress?" I asked.

"She just didn't," she laughed.

I felt like for the first time we were getting along a little. Maybe, just maybe, she wouldn't hate me forever and we'd be one big happy family. I would have liked to have had a family where I felt like I belonged. It would have been nice to have parents who were as involved as my friends' parents were, growing up.

It was six in the morning when Amalea banged on our bedroom door. I checked my phone. "Why is she up so early?" I groaned. Francesco rolled over towards me with "ugh, make it stop" eyes. It reminded me of when Marcello walked in on us having sex. "Well, at least she's knocking," I whispered to Francesco.

"Come in," I called.

Amalea flung open the door and dove into our laundry basket like a cobra striking a mouse. I rolled my eyes and fell back asleep.

Two hours later Francesco and I stumbled out of our room. All of our kitchen cleaning supplies were out and the apartment smelled like bleach as if it had been cleaned by little nurse elves on Adderall. Francesco's mom worked diligently at the ironing board, her elbow sawing back and forth with so much vigor that her tiny frame shook.

"*Buongiorno*," I mumbled, and looked at Francesco. "It smells like a hospital in here. And we don't even own bleach."

At about that time I'd reached the ironing board and I saw what she was so determined to de-wrinkle: one of my black, bedazzled thongs. Next to it were about ten others that had already been strong-armed into paper-like flatness.

"Oh, shit," I said in English.

She turned around. "Buongiorno. *Vi ho fatto un caffè*," she said, pointing to the coffee on the table.

I half-smiled and switched to Italian. "Thanks, but why you do this, with, uh,"—I forgot the word for thong— "my things for the here?" I gestured to my crotch.

She looked through me to Francesco and asked, "How did you sleep?"

Francesco went straight for the coffee.

I walked over to him as he stuffed a cookie into his mouth, and spoke in English. "Hey, so, um, can we talk with her about boundaries? Anything that touches my vagina and goes up my ass is definitely off-limits to her." I expected Francesco to emphatically agree. He did not.

He spat crumbs everywhere, "Stop saying vagina and ass!"

"Oh, sorry. My *lady bits* go there. Please, I'm begging you, tell her to not do our laundry. It's *fucking weird*."

Francesco bit into another cookie. "If it makes her happy just let her do it."

"You really don't understand women. We don't *like* cleaning, dude, it's not in our genes to enjoy housework. Maybe she feels like that's what she should do to make you happy or maybe she's doing it to try and show me how to be a better woman. But she's not thrilled to be cleaning my panties."

Francesco smiled. "No, she likes it! Italian women love it."

I rolled my eyes and went over to Francesco's mom.

"Amalea," I touched her arm, and tried to beam in Italian, "you don't make work here. You no slave! You make vacation, so nice! I do it!" She smacked my hand when I reached for the iron.

I recoiled and held my hand.

"These are things you should be doing! You should be doing this!" she barked.

"I need to iron my thongs?" I asked in English so she wouldn't understand while holding my slapped hand away from her. "I've got better things to do, lady."

Seemed like we were back to our old ways of disagreeing and being frustrated with each other. I wondered what she hoped to get out of it.

Amalea narrowed her eyes to focus on the task at hand, while occasionally shaking her head at us disapprovingly. I drank coffee and sulked while she examined my sluttiest undergarments, holding them up to the light to carefully inspect them. I wanted her to stop but didn't know how to make her. Talking with her didn't seem like it would get me anywhere, and I couldn't tackle her and physically wrestle my underwear away from her even though I'd thought about it. Francesco was no help because he seemed to enjoy having his mom slave over him.

"Francesco," I said in English, "it feels an awful lot like she's trying to make a point. Also, she's not going to like me if she knows that I own a black lace thong with faux pearls that run up my bum. You're ruining our chances of her ever liking me by letting her do this." Realistically I don't think she cared at all if they had pearls or lace or a strap-on attached. She cared about wrinkles, and she cared aggressively.

Francesco just looked away then waltzed over to his mom, who was now sweating, to deliver suggestions on what he wanted to eat for lunch. I felt a quiet rage build inside of me.

That afternoon we went for a walk to absorb some sun and mix with the locals, who were out to do a *passeggiata*, a stroll around in their best outfits, an old tradition stemming from the days when parents paraded their eligible daughters around the city, like a prized bovine, in search of suitors. Oliver dragged me down the street while Francesco listened to his mother, who was critiquing every article of clothing on every single person's body. A pantsuit looked really nice, a patterned dress did not, and don't even get her started on the horror of a woman's shoes not matching her purse. I watched the pigeons shit onto the cobblestone in abstract patterns, totally entertained, until we took a turn and stepped onto a street lined with wedding shops. Francesco started down the road apprehensively. We still didn't feel comfortable talking about our

American wedding because of how she felt about us getting married in general.

Amalea glanced at one store window full of pink and peach satin objects, like an elderly Utahan's estate auction.

"These colors are nice," she said.

I cringed.

When we passed a wedding shop with a window packed full of gag-inducing puffy cotton-ball-type gowns, I said to Francesco in Italian,"Me no like it, big dresses like that."

"Me either," Amalea added.

"Why? I do," Francesco said, lighting up. It wasn't surprising that he loved the idea of me crashing down the aisle in something that should be lit on fire instead of worn.

"You need this covered to here," Amalea said, and made a motion like she was slitting her own throat.

"I need a dress that goes up to my face?" I wondered.

She nodded rapidly, "Yes. Because you can't wear strapless."

"But I like no arms on dress," I smiled.

"No. No, no, no! It will be ugly on you." She scrunched up her entire body and shook her head to get the traumatic image of me in a strapless dress out of her mind.

I rubbed my arm. "Because I have a tattoo?"

"No. Not for that. Oh God! Honestly I don't know *what* we'll do with you. I mean, what can we do? JUST LOOK AT THIS!"

She lunged forward and grabbed hold of my boobs faster than a frat boy at a kegger. I pushed her hands down slowly, popping each boob out one at a time.

"Mamma, that's enough," Francesco said to her in a hushed voice.

She grabbed at them a second time, cupping them tightly. I looked down, horrified to see her tiny hands clamped onto my chest again.

"Look at these! I don't know. I DON'T KNOW! We have to feed her! She needs to eat more pasta! She needs to eat more! If she eats more they'll get bigger!"

I turned my torso to passively remove my boobs from her grip again. "Listen," I said in my shit Italian, "if I put more fats on me these remain the same. They no change. Once I made me to have one big ass but these they stayed the same!" I motioned back and forth between the left and right boob. "*Saaaaame.*"

She fanned the air like she was waving an imaginary insect away.

"Don't ask me then. I don't know. You're going to look terrible in a wedding dress. You need bigger... don't ask me."

Then she moved to walk a bit faster than us.

I turned to Francesco. "Is she being serious?" I asked.

"Yes. Just *ignore* her," he sighed.

"What's wrong with my boobs? I like my boobs. I think they're fine. Are they really that bad?" I peeked into my shirt.

"WHAT? NO! I love your boobs! Damnit!"

"Wait, did all of your ex-girlfriends have huge boobs?" I put my hands on my hips and stared him down, joking.

"I hate my life right now," Francesco said facetiously and walked away with his head down.

* * *

A few weeks later we went to Pallacio, a small city where Amalea was born just twenty minutes outside of Naples, to visit Francesco's paternal grandmother, Nonna, whom I absolutely loved. I'd only met her once before at a birthday party for Emma but she was really nice to me. She'd kissed my face and held my hand for a super long time like we were childhood besties. Plus, during that first encounter, she screamed at Francesco's father and called him a brat. She told me stories about what a little monster Francesco's father was as a child, always skipping school, getting into fights, and throwing massive tantrums. I'd never been to her home before, a two-level white plaster house, complete with window planters overflowing with pink flowers. Nonna greeted us at the door wearing a housedress and slippers like the adorable queen that she was.

"Oooh!" she said when she saw me, then grabbed my hand tightly and planted a kiss on each of my cheeks. Her living room smelled strongly of old lady, and was modestly decorated in typical seventies fashion, with a green armchair, a cream couch with big orange blossoms, and black-and-white portraits of her grandchildren taken during their Holy Communion. She summoned us to join her in the kitchen at her round table.

"I'll make coffee," Amalea said, briskly walking towards the stove. Francesco's grandmother whirled around.

"NO! Sit down. I can still make coffee for my guests in my home." At least, that's what it seemed like she said. She spoke a dialect that I couldn't understand even remotely. But Amalea froze mid-step, turned, and took her place at the table. The look on her face told me that she'd been reprimanded. *Isn't this an interesting turn of events.* Nonna made espresso with her ancient, slightly rusted percolator over the raging flame of the gas stove, then sat down to join us. Halfway through a good story about her dead husband, she paused to ask when we were getting married.

Amalea jumped in. "But I don't know what she'll wear because *look!*" She leaned across the table to jab her pointer finger into the flesh of my right tit. Nonna shrugged, I jerked back from sheer shock, but Francesco had had enough of it. He reached across the table and firmly swatted her hand away.

"Those are not for you! Do not do that again! Just stop it!"

I stared at Francesco, slack-jawed. He was never assertive with his family. Amalea blushed and lowered her head. "Ah, *va bene*," she said, chastened.

Nonna showed us black-and-white portraits hanging above her staircase—Italian family members from as far back as one hundred years ago.

"These are amazing," I said in Italian. I turned to Francesco and Nonna. "Right?"

Nonna touched my face. "Sì, sì," she grinned.

Francesco put his arm around me and whispered in English. "These are really cool. And, I'm sorry, babe."

"It's okay. Thank you for sticking up for me. And, well, I mean it could be worse than your mom groping me like some horny adolescent, right?"

"Oh? How?"

"She could still be pretending that we aren't getting married."

"Ah, now that's true."

28

An American Party! (Wedding)

September 2012

On my wedding day in Park City, Utah, at a beautiful cliff-side venue that my dad had reserved for half price by offering the owner "Persian recipes in exchange for a good deal," I stood in the small dressing room under the jaundiced glow of yellow light bulbs, as my eight bridesmaids tried to yank my wedding dress over my head. I was in my underwear, arms in the air all "hallelujah," while small, smooth hands pushed and poked and grazed my abdomen, trying to fight white poof into place. I saw only white and smelled the faint chemical smell of "Made in China" organza.

"Ew! Ew! This fucking thing! Suck it in, goddamnit!" said Michelle, a friend I'd known since we were teenagers.

"Was this dress made for a mouse?" my maid of honor, Dani, asked.

I heard my friend Bobbi grumble, "Stupid, stupid, pretty dress," in a shaky voice while she pawed at my bodice, trying to angle it "just so" to slide it over my ribcage. I heard more grunting, felt the dress strain until it suddenly gave way and popped into place.

"Finally! I can see!" I laughed.

I turned to Bobbi and saw her lip quivering.

"Do *not* fucking cry. My makeup will literally drip off. Somebody get this woman alcohol!" I surveyed the women around me, absolutely certain that I had the coolest, most badass bridal party ever to exist. A whiskey bottle appeared in our dressing room and was passed from hand to hand as someone yelled from the back of the room, "It's from your sister, Ellen!" Violetta, who had flown in from San Francisco, filled plastic cups with whiskey. My dress was on but now they couldn't zip it up. In just one week of eating brunch, burritos, and almond-milk lattes with one pump of vanilla, I'd gained five pounds. Giselle, my longtime friend and former editor, held the dress together so that Dani could zip it.

"Ay, shame this dress. Let out all your air," Kuhle called from the corner, where she was pulling on a bright purple princess gown. I exhaled. Zip. Sighs of relief all around. "I can't breathe!" I protested, gasping for air, "Is this normal? Can I die?" Everyone looked around and shrugged. *Great.*

A man yelled outside the dressing room, "You guys are already twenty minutes late! Let's get this thing going! Francesco is already out there!"

My sister Chloe snapped a photo with her iPhone of me in my giant white princess gown and an American Spirit cigarette between my fingers. Alix, our photographer, darted around the room wildly snapping pictures. A whiskey shot was shoved into my hand.

"To your wedding! We love you! I cannot believe you are getting married!" Giselle yelled. Manicured paws shot up into the air holding plastic cups of whiskey.

"Thank you so much. I love you guys so…" I trailed off, my throat tightening. It felt so good to be home, in the center of a cluster of my closest friends. It made it difficult not to break my own "no crying" rule.

"Shut up and drink!" Michelle ordered. She winked at me before tossing back the liquor.

"You look so pretty," Violetta giggled, bringing out her dimples. "This is so exciting!"

I paused in front of the mirror to take it all in. The giant cotton-ball dress that I never thought I'd wear in a million years (I'd have chosen a skin-tight, red gown) that I wore for Francesco, the white birdcage veil that I'd bought in a small boutique in Italy with Amalea. I felt like an imposter. For a second nothing seemed real, me in that dress, in a room full of friends who I missed, who I hadn't seen for over a year. They stood around, powdering their noses, adjusting their boobs, saying things like, "I hope you get sexed so good tonight after all of this work," reapplying lipstick as if the world hadn't turned, never skipped a beat, as if I'd never moved away. This world was so different from the one in Italy, where I felt isolated and out of control.

"Are we ready?" I asked everyone.

"Let's do this," said Dani, and quickly left the room. The rest of my bridesmaids followed her.

Francesco's parents had chosen not to come to our wedding in the US, mostly because they still didn't think it was a "real" wedding. I wished that they'd come because I could tell it made Francesco sad that they didn't. But luckily, all of Francesco's good friends showed up for him. The groomsmen, all imported from Spain and Italy except for two of my brothers, my step-brother James, and Dakota, were lined up next to the open doors downstairs with my bridesmaids, ready to walk. My father, drowning in a tan suit four sizes too big for him, kissed me on the cheek and grabbed my arm.

"Do I look okay?" I asked.

"You look beautiful, baby," he said.

My vows, which I'd written on lined journal paper, were in my sweaty hand, so I casually turned away from my dad and jammed them into my bra.

As we stood there waiting, Dad looked sideways at me. "Is it true that your maid of honor is a lesbian? Kathy told me—"

"Yes, she is and WHO CARES?"

"Really!"

"Dad, seriously, I need you to be quiet."

My dad turned to me, his eyes serious and a little sad. "I don't understand why they make deh fathers do dis job. It's really, really unfair. What if I don't want to give you to him? What if I just punched him instead?"

I heard my cousin Sarah, our viola player, begin the music. My dad was visibly nervous and it was making my shoulders tense up and my throat tighten.

"Dad, you love Francesco. This is not the time to go on a rant about your son-in-law. Seriously, you crazy person. Shhh."

"Well baby, he's a great guy but—"

The violin music changed to Wagner's wedding chorus. My anxiety fell away as the warm familiar wave of whiskey spread throughout my body and into my head. I took a deep breath and we stepped outside, up a stone staircase and onto the aisle lined with rose petals that led to Francesco. I could smell the dough from the pizza cart we'd hired, the one with the brick oven, and it smelled like Italy. My dad booked it down the aisle, practically dragging me. Friends and family craned their necks to see us aggressively power-walk towards Francesco like we were there to kill him. My mom snapped photos of us with her 1993 Kodak from the front row, looking very official in her Hillary Clinton pantsuit. The officiant Jakob, one of my best friends, waited patiently flanked by the wedding party. My ladies to the right in neutral dresses, the guys to the left in slim-cut gray suits (very slim, accentuating toned glutes and man packages for all to admire).

Francesco stood next to Jakob with his hands clasped in front of his body like a senator campaigning at a political rally. A grin of epic proportions spread across his face when he saw me galloping towards him. My dad deposited me in front of Francesco, kissed me on the cheek, and strode off to find his seat in the front row next to Kathy.

Standing there, slathered in makeup, hair frozen in place, I was five all over again and playing in Mom's closet, wearing the one dress that she owned and her neon-pink blush. I wasn't used to being so made up, so on-display. I flashed a *"Can you believe this?"* smile to everyone around me and withheld the urge to high-five my bridesmaids. Francesco, on the contrary, was completely composed, like he was born to wear his tailored Italian suit. He ran a hand through his messy hair and mouthed "Hi"; I waved back erratically. Our guests were quiet, patiently watching and waiting for the show to begin. For months I'd been scared of standing in front of all of those people but it wasn't so bad because I felt completely supported by everyone around me and could not wait to marry Francesco. My heart raced, my cheeks flushed, because I was excited but also drunk. I looked to Jakob and whispered, "Now what?"

He laughed, "Well, now I marry you."

Jakob delivered a monologue about "the importance of acceptance," and how both of our "friends and families should be open and accepting because close friends and family make for a happier marriage and a better life." I hadn't told him much about the problems I'd had with Francesco's family or my dad in the beginning, so I was surprised that his speech was so on point.

I mouthed, "Thank you," to Jakob and he mouthed, "Love you," back.

Then Francesco pulled a stack of index cards out of his jacket pocket, stood up tall, and cleared his throat.

"I still remember the first time I saw the sea. I was little, maybe three or four. It was very hot that day, and I was wearing little shorts, a white t-shirt, and flip-flops. I was holding my sister's hand and we were walking down the tree-lined street that, further on, would lead us to the beach. And then I saw it! I remember that it was the biggest thing that I had ever seen. I was amazed and astonished, I couldn't breathe or talk. I just stood there in silence, contemplating the beauty and the immensity of nature.

"These things stay with us forever. We tend to lose those feelings as we grow up, we tend to ignore them because we get distracted by so many other things. We don't get surprised anymore and are not as lucky as we once were when discovering new things. I want to let you know that I am lucky, because every time I look at you, every time I listen to you, every time I touch you, I return back to that time and I remember that day twenty-five years ago when, as a child, I was surprised and filled with love, happiness and the will to live. Next to you, I feel alive."

Francesco's eyes glistened. "I love you," he said, then he carefully organized his cards and slid them back into his pocket. He clasped his hands in front of him like a politician again. I could hear sniffling in the line of bridesmaids behind me.

I smiled sheepishly at Francesco. "I guess it's my turn?" I said, laughing nervously.

I reached into my boobs to find my wedding vows that were buried somewhere deep in my strapless bra. People in the audience chuckled when I pulled them out and straightened the crinkles. I steadily read my vows, something about being drunk at a bar and finding your other half.

Then it was over. We kissed, said, "I do," people cheered. I could feel my face twitch from the sheer effort my muscles were putting into keeping it together. *I'm married, weird.* The following five hours happened in a sangria haze and I can only remember a few moments here and there. The sun began to set right after the ceremony. We posed for pictures and it was so cold that half of my bridesmaids turned into hobos as they pieced together random articles of clothing for warmth—old sweatshirts, biker boots, blankets, scarves wrapped around their legs, anything warm. We ate artisanal pizza and salad at the farm tables under the stars. Francesco walked around to each guest individually, patting them on the back, shaking hands or hugging them, saying, "We're so happy to see you here." I guzzled three glasses of white wine while I huddled at a table with Cousin Sarah.

We moved inside the cabin to get down and dirty on the dance floor. My good friend Hacker manned the DJ booth in the front of the room, and in the corner sat a massive vat of white sangria courtesy of the Spanish groomsmen. For the next four hours, Hacker blasted everything from '80s pop and rock'n'roll to Danzig, and we made the dance floor our bitch. Kuhle taught my stepmom to "cut the cake," which is a mix between air-humping and booty-shaking all the way down to the floor and back up.

At one point I stopped and looked around and the room reminded me of that one scene in *Dirty Dancing* where Baby accidentally wanders into the dancers' party and the music blares, "DO YOU LOVE ME? DO YOU LOVE ME? NOOW THAT I CAAAN DAAANCE.?" Nicki did the cha cha, Dani swayed and dipped with her hands in the air. My youngest brother Casper, who had been our ring-bearer, and my youngest sister Jasmina, who was a "flower dude" (being the gender non-conforming eight-year-old that she was), were break-dancing in gray suits. My mom and Brian slow-danced together to fast songs. At one point, Bobbi and I played air guitar on our knees. We sang "Mother" by Danzig into our invisible microphones, "If you wanna find hell with me, I can show you what it's like... till you're bleedin'!" It was our anthem song from our bartender days. Francesco tossed me around to "I Can't Help Falling in Love With You" by Elvis. During this, our photographer managed to snap a very classy picture of Francesco lifting me into the air, revealing my bare ass and white thong. It was exactly what I wanted, unbridled fun. The kind I felt like I couldn't have in Italy.

Francesco's groomsmen grabbed a microphone and headed to the center of the dance floor. Our Spanish friend Alejandro gave a beautiful teary-eyed speech: "Misty and Francesco taught me love. If it weren't for them I wouldn't be with the amazing woman that I have in my life now. My life is complete because of the advice they gave me and the example they set." Francesco and I were very touched. Everyone else was mostly confused. Bobbi leaned over and whispered, "Is he okay? Why is he crying?"

Dani, my maid of honor, went next. She reluctantly took the microphone, unraveled her speech, then crumpled it back up and threw it across the room.

She looked directly at me. "I can't. I can't. I really just fucking can't. I *fucking* can't. You know I love you. I do, but I can't stand up here and cry and read my fucking speech. I just can't." Then she turned to my dad— "Sorry for the language,"—then looked back at me, "I seriously fucking c—"

Bobbi walked up to Dani, took her microphone away, picked her up, and carried her off, in six-inch platform heels. Then the lights dimmed, the music came back on, and the dance floor came alive again.

While I watched Kuhle dance with Francesco's friend Luca on the dance floor, I realized I'd been wrong about weddings. I'd always hated weddings because they seemed like choreographed expressions of love meant to impress people or display exhausted traditions with outdated symbolism. But I couldn't imagine celebrating such a big day in any other way. I also kind of understood why Oliver peed on stuff. In a way, marriage is like metaphorically peeing on each other. And it was awesome. And also scary. I worried that my relationships would change or that people would treat me differently. I wanted to be married but I still wanted to be *me*. Just like when Francesco and I started dating, I was uneasy about what this would mean in terms of my identity. Did this mean I had to start brushing my hair and wearing yoga pants to brunch?

Francesco and I left the reception around midnight. We stayed at Hotel Monaco in downtown Salt Lake City, where we found rose petals on our bed, and a gift basket of "natural" Lush bath products from my bridesmaids with a note that read, "Fuck it out, y'all." The hotel left an exceptionally pervy wedding-night basket with massage oils and vibrating sex toys.

Francesco poured us a glass of champagne. "I'm so happy I married you, my wife," he smiled. "To us!" He raised his glass. Then we tried to consummate our marriage but we were really tired, and instead high-fived each other for effort, and fell into a deep, corpse-like sleep.

The next morning, I woke up feeling disgusting. My makeup was caked on, I was hungover, and had trembling hands from the low blood sugar. I hobbled into the bathroom to take a quick shower while my new husband (HUSBAND!) called for room service. We drank mimosas, cheering once again for the incredible feat of getting married, proud as though we'd returned from battle. I ate French toast, and Francesco smiled at me merrily. We were finally married and it was *awesome*. For about ten minutes.

Francesco's phone rang just as I'd swallowed the delicious last drop of my heavily sugared coffee. "It's an Italian number," Francesco beamed, "It's probably my family calling to congratulate us!"

"*Ciao!*" he said, excitedly. But his joyful expression melted away instantly. I could hear yelling on the other side of the phone and Francesco's face contorted into a painful grimace.

"Okay. Ciao." He hung up.

"What happened honey?" I sat down next to him and put my hand over his.

Francesco's head hung low, and he stared at our hands. "My parents are really mad at us. My dad was screaming because our guests posted our wedding photos on Facebook. They demanded that we call everyone and ask that the photos be removed immediately." He bit his lip, watching me out of the corner of his eye.

I threw up my hands and responded a little bit louder than I meant to, "Of *course* people posted photos! We just got married!" I tried to tone down my yelling, lighten the mood, "And did you see my Running Man last night?"

He grabbed fistfuls of his hair. "It's not funny babe. They're *really* mad. They said that the town is going to gossip because we got married in the US first. They're embarrassed. We have to tell everyone to remove the photos."

I stomped my feet and growled, "No."

"Babe," he spoke quietly, "we have to."

"No. Fucking, no." I paced back and forth at the foot of the bed. "This is our wedding we're talking about. We're not going to hide *our wedding*. We're a multicultural family and we're having two weddings, and everyone

277

already knows that. It is not a *secret*. How could they call and yell at you the day after you get married?"

My voice was shaking. I was roaring at Francesco, even though it wasn't his fault. He felt ashamed and I knew we would never get that elated moment back, ever, and for a moment I *hated* them for it. I hated them so deeply that I had to stop myself from declaring that I wouldn't go back to Italy. I *never* wanted to see them again.

"I'm so sorry…" he whispered.

"No, I'm sorry. I'm sorry for yelling." I said, fighting to lower my voice, "I'm sorry that you feel bad and that your parents can't let you be happy for even five fucking minutes."

I flung myself onto the bed and stared at the ceiling. We'd only been married for a few hours but somewhere deep in my core, I wondered if we'd made a mistake. I wouldn't stay silent forever. Francesco must have known how I was feeling because he grabbed me and pulled me across the bed into his arms, and held me on his chest for a long while.

Bare

29

The Hedgehog Left the Table

I pressed my face against the bulletproof glass in the Italian consulate in San Francisco.

"I've been married for less than forty-eight hours," I whined to the consulate officer, a thirties-ish Italian woman with wild curls and kind eyes, "and I'm here and my husband is already back in Italy." I sighed, for emphasis.

Suddenly she was interested. She brought a hand to her chest and gasped. "But no!" she said, heavily accented, "He had to return to Italy without you the day after the wedding? How can this be?"

"Yes," I nodded slowly, "he had to work. I came here with my friend to apply for my spousal visa so I can go back to Italy." I made doe eyes at her, "I miss him."

"That is heartbreaking! I'm so sorry. You must be devastated." She held her hand over her heart like she was preparing for the pledge of allegiance.

"I mean, yeah, I'm definitely bummed."

She frowned and bit her bottom lip. "I'll see what I can do," she said, with a face that read, "LOVE SHALL PREVAIL ON MY GODDAMN WATCH!"

I thanked her and wandered out of the consulate to find Violetta standing on the sidewalk, with her face tilted up towards the sunlight in an expression of pleasure. She felt me looking at her and opened her eyes, "Hello, honey. How did it go?"

"I don't know. I just have to wait. Apparently I live with you in San Francisco for a minute."

Now that we were married, I couldn't go back to Italy until I upgraded my expired student visa to a spousal visa. The necessary paperwork wasn't all that complicated, but I'd read that it could take weeks if not months to process and there was no guarantee it would go through.

The day after our wedding, shortly after being scolded by his parents, Francesco flew back to Italy because he'd somehow exhausted his forty paid vacation days and had to work. I drove to San Francisco with Violetta to camp out in her guest room while I applied for and waited on my visa. Everything happened so fast, I didn't even get the chance to refer to him awkwardly as "my husband" before we'd been separated. It felt downright criminal. Though I couldn't complain, Violetta and I had been having a great time for the three days I'd been there, enjoying wine-tasting sessions and late-night art exhibits that featured "free pancakes!" And, it was probably better that I took a break from Italy and Francesco's parents to recharge and regroup. Some days I found myself staring off in the shower, imagining a million different scenarios where I shook off the debilitating anxiety that manifested in their presence and verbally destroyed them.

I was in the middle of one of those fantasies—one that I took great pleasure in, where I calmly stated all the reasons I found them to be intolerable—when my phone rang. I saw out of the shower; it was a call from the consulate. My heart sank. The consulate was technically closed

281

to the public that day, and I'd been waiting for less than a week, so surely they were calling to tell me that I'd messed up the papers somehow.

I stepped out, sopping wet, and put the phone on speaker.

"Hello?" I answered, searching for my towel.

"Misty?" I recognized the voice as the kind woman on the other side of the bulletproof glass who had felt sorry for me.

"Yes."

"Your visa is done. You can come to pick it up and get home to your husband."

"*Really?* Holy shit! Thank you so much!"

"*Niente, cara.*"

When I arrived at the consulate, I was greeted by a screechy "NO! CLOOOOOOSED TO THE PUBLIC," by a rotund woman on the other side of the glass. The nice officer, the one who called me, wasn't there.

"I was told I could pick up my visa today."

"Nooo! Cloooosed." she repeated, slightly less yelly this time.

"A consulate officer just called me not even one hour ago. Please, would you mind asking your coworkers?"

She rolled her eyes and crashed through the door into the back, where I heard arguing in Italian. Someone was saying that they were closed and I should have to wait till the following week like everyone else. But then I heard the one officer, the one who had helped me, bark,

"This woman just married a few days ago and *her husband* is already back in Italy. She needs to return to him!"

Then silence as the others undoubtedly caved in. When it comes to family, food, or love, it's never much of a fight with Italians. Once, Francesco was allowed to bring a metal blade on an international fight by citing, "My mamma gave it to me to make marinara sauce." The airport security woman in Rome nodded and said, "Oh, it's for *i pomodori?*" (the tomatoes). "Okay." And she helped us jam the sharp steel into our carry-on.

The curly-haired officer stepped out from the back, waving my passport above her head, open to the page with my new visa. She slid it under the bulletproof glass.

"Get back to your love and have a safe trip, *cara*," she said. I thanked her profusely.

When I stepped outside and called Francesco, he screamed into the phone as if he'd just won season tickets to Roma games.

"NO WAY! NO WAY! Please get home. I miss you so much and Oliver is being an asshole. Probably because he misses you."

I booked my flight to Salt Lake first to gather the rest of my luggage and say goodbye to my friends and family, and then another plane to Rome two weeks out. As soon as I got the confirmation email, though, I wished I hadn't. When I thought of Francesco I got a compulsive urge to steal a helicopter to speed up the process to return to him. But I felt deeply sick to my stomach when I imagined being back in Italy. What exactly was I going back to? For months and months, my time in Italy had been marked by loneliness, anxiety, and the emotional terrorism dealt out by his parents. Italy made me incredibly insecure. I hated the soap-opera desperate woman I'd become and it wasn't pretty. But I didn't want to admit out loud that Italy made me miserable because I wouldn't accept defeat. What kind of a *loser* couldn't make Italy work?

I stepped into Rome airport, smelled the stale air and watched a group of Italians argue over a gate number. For a minute, I felt how I had as a student, a tourist, many years ago. I saw what outsiders see, people who haven't struggled as an immigrant within the borders or discovered that they were basically a tumor in the bowels of a dramatic family unit. It felt new. Francesco came running towards me outside of the baggage claim, picked me up and squeezed me so hard that I nearly peed my pants and had to playfully swat him away.

"Where's Oliver?" I asked, looking around.

"At my parents' house. We're gonna stay there for the weekend," he said.

"Great," I smiled ironically.

Why wouldn't I want to go straight to their apartment after they ruined our post-marital high instead of spending time with my new husband alone after a month apart?

I waited for the usual panic to take over, the fight-or-flight terror that made me want to run as fast as I could and hide somewhere dark and quiet for the rest of my life. I waited and waited, and it didn't come. Surprisingly, I caught myself wondering if they'd be different now that we were married. Love me, hate me, I didn't care much either way. I had an annoying poodle who I adored and a smart, sexy, occasionally annoying *husband*. Apparently, a month with friends and family who loved me in spite of myself had validated me, reset me a little. I hoped that we could be a normal family now that we were married, and that my new confidence might last this time. Francesco was also excited to see his parents, to show them wedding pictures and tell them everything that had happened, because he hadn't seen them since the wedding either.

When we walked into their apartment, Oliver bounced with manic hysteria. He leaped three feet high, like a kangaroo, crying with puppy delight, and then barking at us as though to say, "I love you guys! You're back! But seriously, go fuck yourselves!" We really had no other choice than to hug him first. We kissed my in-laws in the small foyer of their apartment as always and exchanged a few hundred pleasantries about the length of the plane ride before I could excuse myself to the bathroom to shower away the airplane grime.

After I felt human again, we sat down for lunch and while we munched on baby broccoli, anchovies, potatoes, and salami, his parents tackled village decorum.

"So, now that you've done this in America," Marcello began, "we need to plan the Italian wedding soon. People are going to start gossiping." This would have been an opportune time for us to make it clear just how much we didn't care about the gossip but instead we focused on the food in front of us.

Amalea added, "Yes, we found a church that is nice; we'll go look at it after lunch."

Marcello popped an anchovy into his mouth and spoke with his mouth full, "We need to find a restaurant and book it quickly."

Francesco put his hand on my leg, "Okay, we can do that. Do you want to see pictures of the American wedding?"

Amalea changed the subject and started clearing the table and Marcello paid closer attention to something uneventful on the news. Despite their obvious disinterest, Francesco went to grab the MacBook. He set it on the table between the wine glasses and opened to the file of our wedding photos.

"Look!" I pointed to a picture of Francesco and I kissing in front of a backdrop of gray silk and antique lace. Marcello glanced at it then turned back towards the TV, turning up the volume, flooding the room with pasta commercials. Amalea glanced at a few pictures, scrunched up her face and mumbled that she didn't like them. Francesco kept his eyes down. He closed the computer and stared at the wall. My palms grew hot and I fixed on the back of Marcello's head like I was trying to cause him physical pain with my eyes. I could feel my pulse quickening as I looked from Francesco's crestfallen face to Amalea, who was fiddling with the lid of the coffee pot The person that I was in the US, the adult me, would have said something, would have told them that they were hurting their son. But at their table, I knew I was powerless because speaking up would only provoke them, and Francesco would be thrown in the middle. A few deep breaths and happy thoughts—*it doesn't have to be forever*— helped to dissipate my murderous rage.

I put my arm around Francesco, and said in English, "Look, they're just hurt that they weren't there. Ignore them."

He forced a smile. "Yeah, you're probably right. But it was their choice not to be there."

There was a tiny part of me that could understand where they were coming from. I mean, this was their child and he'd gone off to another country to marry a woman that they didn't particularly like. They felt out of control, and no doubt like they were losing him, and not just to any woman, but one who hated to cook. I paused to wonder if I'd react the same way to photos of my child in a wedding I wasn't a part of, even if it were my choice not to attend. After some careful reflection, I decided that no, no I wouldn't because that would make me an incredibly selfish *asshole*.

Marcello turned around. "Maybe go out and find a restaurant you like today," he said.

Francesco perked up a bit, almost as if hoped that our Italian wedding would somehow redeem him in their eyes. I wondered how he could tolerate it all.

After lunch, Amalea took us to a few florists and boutiques that took care of the *bomboniere*, wedding favors, and the *confetti*, candied almonds. Traditionally, in Italy, wedding favors are these little glass figurines of doves or hearts, objects that collect dust on forgotten shelves in the homes of every grandma. Francesco and I agreed on something more functional, and Francesco's mom and sister had a great idea about gifting an espresso maker and some coffee.

In a wedding shop, I pulled small moka percolators off of the shelf, turning them over in my hands before putting them back. They came in white, gray, red, and black, some a stronger stainless steel, and a few cheap aluminum ones. I heard a shop assistant approach Amalea behind me to ask what we were searching for. Amalea called me over and said with a dismissive wave in my general direction,

"This is my son's *ragazza*." This is my son's *girlfriend*. Amalea turned to Francesco and casually explained in passing that she didn't recognize our marriage. I froze. In three years, that was the first time I'd ever had to literally bite my tongue to stop myself from saying something I'd regret. Speechless, I masked my feelings with a weak smile to the shop assistant, set down a little silver percolator I still held and slinked out of the shop to stare into a filthy puddle so I could feel sorry for myself. The November rain really highlighted my inner gloom. I completed the whole scene by folding paper from my notebook into a ship to sail in my pond of despair. Francesco is going to come out and see this, I thought, and it will break his heart, me in the rain, with my lonely paper ship sinking into the muddy abyss.

Instead, he came out horrified, "What the fuck are you doing, weirdo? Oh my God! EW! Stop huddling near that pond. Are you-a *trying* to catch a disease? You get the pneumonia!" As usual, Francesco had repressed all normal emotions in the presence of his family. And he had that look on his face, the one that said, "Why can't you feel nothing, too?"

I abandoned my ship to sulk in the car. The confidence I'd had when I arrived earlier was gone. I wrestled between feeling empty and robbed to trying my best to be fair.

On Monday morning back at home in Florence, I made myself a coffee and plopped down in front of my laptop to write some web copy for a client. I tried to concentrate on the task at hand: identify pain points, figure out the value proposition. Why would anyone want or need this product or service? But the phrase, *don't recognize your marriage* kept creeping up like a wafting dog fart that would reignite my inner psycho. I couldn't shake the feeling that things were never going to change and for the rest of our life together, we would be robbed of simple joys. What would happen when we had kids and we didn't baptize them? Or worse, what if we didn't have kids? My friends back in the US were becoming increasingly concerned. Nicki told me to stop visiting Francesco's parents, to slowly push them out. And even though it was super appealing, I couldn't do that. That whole "choose one or the other" thing just seemed like it would breed a bad case of resentment. Francesco deserved to have a good relationship with his family, just not at the expense of my happiness.

I worked myself into a frenzy in our tiny kitchen, pacing back and forth in front of the computer with my coffee sloshing onto the white marble. *She'll never respect me until I stand up to her.* But part of me worried that maybe I deserved to be treated like crap because I was horrible for Francesco; maybe he did deserve better, maybe she just wanted me to leave him so then he could marry someone that was right for him. Someone who spoke his language, someone who knew how to cook lasagna, and took great joy in ironing sheets and towels. Or maybe I was totally justified in being sick of the bullshit, and all this doubt took root in my anxiety. I didn't know. I jack-hammered my butt into the chair and typed out an email in Italian that sounded like it had been written by a drunk pimp raised by Dr. Seuss:

Look, I have understand the's problems so many with me you have. Me think that after three years, me you hate, you make the's problems for always Francesco. What you want of me? I so sorry I am not the woman Italians. I have the understanding that you no like me. Me I have want of you me to make a pleasure for you but I think it no possible. So stress we have you plus me plus everyone. Impoverished Francesco he is sad. His life I make bad; his life I make sad. His ex-girlfriends you preferred but he no liked those ex-girlfriends.

Me you want to go to the United States? Me you want I left Francesco? This you want of me? I go if me you tell to leave. Me, I do anything for Francesco to make contented even if my heart make frown.

I was shaky and sweaty when I hit "send," and immediately regretted it. "Agh! Why did I just do that?" I squealed to Oliver, who opened his eyes slightly from the couch, yawned, and flipped onto his back with his four legs straight in the air. I knew that I'd just opened the gates to hell but a very optimistic side of me hoped that it would open up the dialogue: she could tell me her concerns, I could address them, and we could come to some sort of understanding. And frankly, I was tired of being a bystander in my own life. My slightly improved but still intermediate Italian didn't really convey any kind of cohesive idea but maybe she'd get the gist?

I paced the kitchen, grabbed a bottle of wine and chugged it straight from the bottle like a sailor. Then mumbled to myself, "Well, dumbass, no wonder they don't want you for a daughter-in-law."

She wrote back almost immediately:

I have no idea what you're talking about. You've imagined everything because you are mentally unstable. Maybe you should look at how you're acting, and stop hiding inside of yourself, hedgehog.

Hedgehog? Why a hedgehog?

When Francesco came home from work he found me sitting at the kitchen table still glowering at the email, a half-empty bottle of wine next to me.

"Babe?" he asked softly, resting a hand on my shoulder.

"Your mom called me a hedgehog," I said, still staring straight ahead.

"Why would she call me a hedgehog?"

"Huh? When did she—"

289

I turned to him, "Okay, don't be mad, but I did something stupid…"
I told him about the email.

He stood there, doing this weird thing where he pinches his own face, for what seemed like an eternity, vacantly staring at the ceiling.

"You shouldn't have done that," he said, then shrugged, "or maybe you should have. I don't know anymore. I don't know how to handle any of this." He leaned over my shoulder to read the email I'd sent.

Francesco chuckled, "Your Italian is really terrible, babe. Did you drink the wine before, or after?"

"Har-har, asshat." I rolled my eyes.

"I don't know why she called you a hedgehog. Because they're shy animals? You're definitely not imagining any of the shit that has happened."

"It's like we live in 1825 and a cross-cultural relationship is just a giant fucking faux pas if there ever was one. Why is this so hard? Why can't they just love me, so we can sing and dance together and have picnics? And camp."

"We are Italian. We don't camp. I don't know what we should do now. Don't write back, I'll call my sister for advice."

"K."

Francesco called his sister. Throughout the years she'd often sided with Francesco and offered him little glimpses of rational support. I wasn't particularly close with her because we couldn't communicate very well and were fundamentally just very different people, but she'd always been nice to me and I liked her a lot. When Julia answered the phone, she immediately told Francesco that she'd already heard about the email from Amalea.

Francesco started yelling, "My WIFE did not make shit up. Everyone knows how Mamma feels about her. Everyone! They are ruining *everything!*"

"Mamma said that all of this is her fault because she left the table during lunch," Julia said.

She was referring to an incident that had occurred months ago with Oliver that I hadn't thought about since because in no way did it occur to me that it could have been a big deal. At the time of said incident, we were having lunch at his parents' home with his sister's family when Oliver took it upon himself to start raping our niece's leg. After fifteen minutes of everyone screaming, "Oliver, NO!" and him refusing to give up on dominating her kneecap, I excused myself from the table to take Oliver into the bedroom where I remained with him for twenty minutes because otherwise he would bark and scratch at the door and ruin everyone's lunch. It seemed the only polite thing to do. Apparently, it was not polite and I had offended *everyone*. I had no idea.

Francesco hung up the phone with a sigh. "You shouldn't have-a left-a deh table, babe…"

"What? How does this relate to your mom not recognizing our marriage? Also, I thought I was being polite. You never came in to tell me I was doing something wrong. In the US if a baby is crying or something, we take it away. Temporarily. We don't end the baby. But we remove it from the room."

I didn't understand the connection between my email and excusing myself from the lunch table. Then I realized that I was dealing with a goddamn *genius*.

"HA! Classic red-herring move!" I blurted out.

"Fish?" Francesco crinkled up his nose.

"Red. Herring. A formidable adversary, if I do say so myself." I considered using the same strategy by replying back: "Goats drink goat milk in the spring. Bob ate an orange. Caffè latte!" But I thought better of it, mostly because Francesco told me I couldn't, with an appalled expression that I had to respect.

"So now what?" I asked him.

He grabbed the bottle of wine and took a swig. "Now, I guess we wait."

In an effort to find a solution, a way for us to peacefully coexist, and to get some sort of validation from the world, I asked around for advice. An Italian friend of mine, Chiara, said that her behavior is "standard for a small southern village," and that Amalea would continue to use a "paranoid and insane strategy to try to take the higher ground politically." I had no idea what that meant but it sounded terrifying. Politics? I called my friend Nicki back in Utah, who told me emphatically, "Never, ever go to their house ever again. This shit is emotionally abusive. It's eating your brain. Stop going there," which had become her go-to advice. One of Francesco's Florentine friends just looked bewildered and said, "But none of this could have possibly happened. Are you sure you didn't confuse it?"

My options were limited. I could fake my death, move to South America where I'd train Dwayne my capybara to be my butler and pool boy. He would wear a monocle and we would live happily ever after. Or, Francesco and I could pretend like *nothing happened*.

Francesco voted for the latter because "capybaras are gross." Instead of talking it out, he acted as though the conversation had never happened, and avoided his parents' house for a few months to let things settle down. And I agreed to let it go, let bygones be bygones, let the hedgehogs remain where they lay. I would, as parents tell their young children, "be the bigger person." I felt very grown-up and a little bit like a martyr because I had been so quick to *let things go*. I wondered if anyone else found me to be thoughtful and saint-like. And I totally was being selfless, except for the fact that I wanted to be vindicated, which wasn't very saint-like at all. In the meantime, we focused on wedding invitations for the Italian wedding, six months away.

30

And Then the Hairdryer Ate Her Head

December 2012

"You better watch out, you better watch out. You better watch out,yoooou better watch out. Nah, nah, nah, nah, nah, nah, nah, naaaah." Francesco danced around the kitchen singing his terrifying rendition of "Santa Claus is Coming to Town" to Oliver. Francesco loves to sing American Christmas songs, much to the horror of anyone nearby. He doesn't know the words and he refuses to learn them. For this song, all is lost on him except for the caveat, "You better watch out." That particular line is super creepy even within the context of the song, but when merrily sung over and over again it becomes a haunting warning that Santa has stopped taking anti-psychotics and is coming for your kids.

We'd been cleaning all morning. Dani, my best friend, and Kat, her fiancée, were coming to visit for Christmas. When we picked them up from the airport I made a joke about something nonsensical and then wondered if this was something I've always done. Do I make jokes? Do I normally hug people? Am I acting weird? I thought back over our fifteen years of friendship; what am I normally like? My words felt forced and fake and I could barely figure out what to do with my body. What is wrong with me? When I initially decided to move to Italy to find myself, I hadn't planned on losing myself in the meantime.

However, sitting across from Dani and Kat at Giuggiolo, our favorite restaurant, I felt more confident. I held my head a little higher and called the waiter over to order table wine for all of us, instead of having Francesco do it. Dani shared a few anecdotes from her job in NYC. Kat, a comedian, writer, stripper, and champion of "happy sluts," told us about her first time stripping in Australia and how the scene differs in Thailand and New York.

She flashed her pageant smile and said,

"I get tired of the weird questions like, 'What's a girl like you doing in a place like this?' It's ridiculous to assume that strippers are all junkies with daddy issues." She ran her hand through her messy shag and adjusted her oversized wool sweater, "People are actually surprised that I have a college degree, that I'm engaged, and a lesbian. What people don't understand is that stripping isn't a career choice for 'broken' women; truly, it's the purest form of capitalism."

After dinner, Francesco went home to watch Oliver so I could go out with Dani and Kat. The three of us strolled through the cold, wet streets, bundled up in layer upon layer of clothing. A girls' night on the town reminded me of being in school. I missed those days, and the nostalgia awakened the old me, the fun and careless one. When men called out to us as we passed by, I turned and yelled, "No, we don't want to come home to your mother's apartment," in Italian. I suddenly spoke Italian with abandon, though just that morning, I'd stammered to explain to a shop assistant that yes, I was *really* married, and no, I didn't think that thirty-one was way too young and yes, my parents were just fine with it because women in their thirties in my country are not considered child brides.

Since Dani's arrival, the suffocating cloud of self-doubt had lifted and I could see glimpses of how I used to be. The wave of sexy self-assurance forced me to wonder, why am I still in Italy? I had moved to Italy for personal growth and, while I did grow in art school, ever since then I'd found myself shrinking, becoming smaller and smaller to be less imposing to those around me, and I didn't even know why. I'd given away parts of myself that I'd always liked, parts that I liked because those parts weren't normal. *God, how do I get back to who I was?* What I didn't consider at the time is that it was perfectly not weird that I fell apart the way that I did. Glass shatters easier once it's already cracked. And when I arrived in Italy I was basically a *kintsugi* masterpiece.

White Christmas lights draped above our heads like a joyful street valance. The glow from the ever-present water that pooled in the cobblestones created a luminous insect effect like the city was being swarmed by fireflies or fairies. We walked through the annual German Christmas markets in Santa Croce, drank hot spiced wine, paused in front of a small pig roasting on a spit, and admired the hand-blown glass ornaments. Then we turned a corner and ran into a group of people I knew through Francesco. I hugged Luca, one of Francesco's best friends. Hugo, a tall Swedish man, had felt deer antlers that flashed and twinkled on top of his blonde head.

"Come to the bar with us," he said, "Today we're celebrating the incredible idea that a university would give me, of all people, a Ph.D."

We followed the group to an empty bar near Sant'Ambrogio. After a number of greyhounds, I believed myself to be a motivational speaker and pinned Luca against the building outside while we smoked.

"Look, Luca," I said, resting one hand on his shoulder while balancing my hand-rolled cigarette in the other, "if you want something, you've just got to go for it. You know?" Then I stepped backwards and fell into the gutter.

Luca helped me up just as a young Senegalese street vendor came by with more Christmas-themed hats. I bought one for all of us so we could be festive and staggering, *together*.

Around 2 a.m. we found ourselves at a club I'll call SLOB, a figurative cesspool of degenerates, with a few clueless nineteen-year-old students floating among the chlamydia-infused slop. I was loaded so I went straight to the dance floor to shake my ass. Dani, Kat, Hugo, and the group joined me and we quickly overtook the floor, blinking hats and all. Then, just as some dubstep began playing, Dani and Kat kissed, and we were swarmed by rapey assholes that must have slithered out of the wall crevices. In order to protect them, I hopped around them with my teeth out and my hands above my head like a rabbit. In my drunken haze, it made *perfect sense* because who would try to molest girls surrounded by a giant bunny? Then Hugo joined in. A six-foot-three Swedish bunny is apparently terrifying so we quickly took back the dance floor, pressing the weirdos into wallflowers. Unfortunately, just as we'd regained the territory, our friend, a Yale law alma mater, crawled up on stage to wrap his leg around the stripper pole. He slipped and fell the five feet to the dance floor, flat onto his back. I ran over to him, worried that he'd knocked himself out or broken his neck. But before I reached him he'd already clambered to his feet, laughing. And we decided it was probably time to go before one of us actually died. Plus, we had to drive to Cumino the next day for Christmas Eve and the last thing I wanted was to be painfully hungover and trapped with family on the holidays.

* * *

Less than thirty-six hours later, Francesco and I woke up in his parents' guest bedroom to a thick Neapolitan dialect echoing in the foyer. In the US, I usually spend Christmas Eve at my father's home with my six siblings. I wake up to "Jingle Bells" blasting on the room speakers, my youngest brother or sister standing eerily in the doorway at 6 a.m., "Come on! Santa came! WAKE UP!" I slip out of bed in my pajamas and hobble downstairs where my dad or stepmom is waiting with coffee in the kitchen. The entire family eventually takes a place around the tree and we celebrate consumerism together.

"Oh shit," Francesco groaned, "I can hear my nonna. People are already here."

Francesco and I shot out of bed yelling, "Oh shit! Oh shit! Oh shit!" We stuffed ourselves into mismatched clothing. Francesco was hysterical, "Babe, put on a dress. Find a dress! A DRESS!"

In the living room ten minutes later, Nonna attacked me with very slobbery grandma kisses. She grabbed my hand and said, "I have a gift for you!" then dragged me to the living room where she pulled a cellophane-wrapped and ribboned bottle of Pantene Pro-V from her purse. She pushed it into my hand, petting my arm. I hadn't washed my hair in three days, so, *touché* grandma. I loved Nonna, even if she thought I needed help with my hygiene. I hugged our niece Emma, and my sister-in-law and her husband. I went into the office and woke Dani and Kat, who were asleep on the pull-out sofa.

Amalea, who had already been up since the crack of dawn, zipped into the living room with a tray of espresso. She set it in front of me, Kat, and Dani. Then she arranged a few gifts on the table.

"Open these. *Buon Natale*," she smiled.

"Shouldn't I wait until everyone has something to open?" I asked.

"No."

Gifts are not a thing in Francesco's family and his parents usually open them with the same level of enthusiasm reserved for a colonoscopy. I opened the presents and realized the theme for that year was: *Bitch, get in the kitchen.* The entire family was in on it. Francesco's sister got me some kind of cauldron, his mother gave me an apron and tea towels, and Francesco bought me a Snuggie. They thought they were helping me into kitchen slavery, but in reality, they just gave me a beginner witch kit. Dani periodically pointed to me and giggled at my apron. Francesco's mom also gave me an endless supply of pink, bedazzled pajama sets. I thanked her profusely and wondered why she'd shopped for me at the Disney store. I told Francesco that they were anti-grandchildren pajamas, a cuddly form of eugenics. He rolled his eyes and assured me that his mother was not trying to stop us from having sex by making me look ridiculous. "No dude, she's just trying to make amends with you," he smiled.

"Oh. Really?" I said, surprised.

Later that evening I walked by the office and saw Amalea struggling to blow-dry her hair with one of those terrible round brushes. I thought, Hey, I know how to do a blow-out! And I skipped over to her and asked if I could help because I was trying to be affectionate, because it was Christmas, and because Francesco said that she was trying to be buddies.

She put her hand up defensively like a crossing guard.

"No, no, grazie." She eyed me suspiciously and took a step back.

I took this as an intimacy issue, a barrier that was stopping us from being the best of friends, so I forcefully insisted by wrestling the brush from her hand and snatching the blow dryer away.

"I help! I make okay!" I reassured her with a pat on the shoulder. I blow-dried her hair, using the round brush to nicely shape her old-lady bob, happy that we were finally bonding.

She watched me carefully in the mirror. Francesco walked by and gave me a thumbs up. I grinned enthusiastically.

"See!" I said, "This it is a way a faster!" I beamed in Italian.

She smiled with her mouth but her eyes were set on me. It was right about then that I turned the industrial blow-dryer a little too much at an angle. It made this horrible garbage-disposal noise, then it hacked and coughed and died. I smelled burning. When I tried to set the blow-dryer down, I yanked Amalea's head violently backward.

"AAAAAAAACK!" she screamed.

"Oh, God. Oh shit. Shit!" I panicked.

Two full inches of her hair were lodged inside the motor.

"Get it off!" she shrieked in Italian, flailing her arms around.

The hair dryer had sucked all the way down to her scalp. It was stuck to her head.

"Oh shit, oh shit! No! FRANCESCO!" I yelled. I looked at Amalea's face in the mirror. "It's okay, I think. I make better! I make better!" I tried to tell her in Italian.

I breathed deeply, more to calm myself than to calm her. I slowly sat the brush on the dresser, got a good grip on the blow-dryer and yanked it gently in different directions. Her head jerked around, her arms outstretched in front of her as she tried to turn, but I didn't want to face her in case she tried to head-butt me or something so I kept stepping to the side to stay behind her.

"Francesco!" I shouted as loud as I could, "The fucking dryer ate your mom's head! I fucking need you! *It ate her head!* OH MY GOD HELP!"

By the time he ran into the room she'd wrangled the blow-dryer away from me and was pacing back and forth, tugging at the dryer. I followed behind, reaching towards her, apologizing profusely and offering to help. After a very long time, we decided the only thing we could do to free her head was to cut it out. Two inches of hair, gone. Her chic bob now had a patch of matted fuzz shooting from the top of her head, as if the crown had sprouted ready-to-harvest wheat.

She stared at herself in the mirror for a second then spun around to face me.

"I am so sorry!" I said, panting, my heart beating out of my chest.

She shook her head and said, "It's nothing, my hairdresser can fix it. I'm just glad you don't want to be a beautician."

Francesco laughed. "You can hardly tell, Mamma," he lied.

She smacked him on the arm and left the room.

He wrapped me in his arms. "Oh, honey, at least you tried," he said. "How in the hell does this kind of shit always happen to you?"

31

Things Have to be Destroyed
to be Rebuilt

March 2013

Francesco and I were in Cumino again, this time to get his parents' approval on the wedding invitations I'd had designed, finalize the baskets for the wildflowers, and agree on the number of courses at the restaurant Francesco's father had chosen (ten or twelve). Almost immediately, things were off to a rough start. The second we walked in the door, I watched in horror as Oliver dripped a muddy, gelatinous Black Death goo from the rain-soaked street onto Amalea's polished parquet. Ignore the mess, I told myself, stay engaged in the regal affairs of their home to avoid triggering a meltdown. We shook hands, said hello, kissed on the cheek, made awkward, drawn-out small talk while clutching all of our luggage (it was the same treatment for everyone: strangers, friends, family, and the Queen of England, and after three years I still found it odd that everything was so *formal*).

We went through the motions while Oliver leaped, flipped and spun on the other end of his leash, covered in filth, and I could feel my anxiety increase with every hop. If he managed to break free, he'd bound into the living room and go straight for the white couch. Then Francesco's parents would murder him and I'd be forced to retaliate, which would make Francesco very upset. So as soon as there was a lull in the conversation I excused myself to go to the restroom to clean him, which seemed probably fine because things seemed to have settled down a bit, or so I thought.

When I emerged from the bathroom five minutes later, darkness had been cast over the mood of the apartment, which had somehow shifted drastically from "Welcome thee to my humble abode" to an ominous "The power of Christ compels you."

"What's wrong with everyone?" I whispered to Francesco in the kitchen, where he was eating alone at the table. Amalea wasn't hovering to dish out neighborhood gossip and Marcello wasn't pulled up to the table to snack on our dinner while commenting on the many ways we didn't understand food. They'd retreated to the office together where I could see the gentle flicker of the television through the door crack.

"Why did you take Oliver into the bathroom when we got here?" Francesco asked.

"He was dripping muddy water all over the clean floor?"

"That doesn't matter. My mom can clean the floor. You can't just say hello for two minutes and go to the bathroom because now they are furious and you should know how they are by now." Turns out that our little bonding experience with the hairdryer hadn't lasted long, and we were inexplicably back to the same ol' song and dance.

When Francesco took Oliver outside to pee, I stuck my head in the dark office to thank Amalea and Marcello for dinner, because I thought Francesco would stop being mad at me if I made some sort of attempt to fix things. They both turned to me without responding then focused back on the TV, so I went to the guest room to lie down.

Francesco stormed into the room and said, "Why are you in bed?" He dried Oliver off and threw the stained towel into the corner. "You should have gone into the office to watch a movie with my parents!"

"Oh. But there wasn't anywhere to sit. I went in to thank them for dinner but they ignored me, so I didn't think they wanted me to cuddle with them. I'm not going to cuddle them against their will. You need consent for cuddling, Francesco."

"They didn't talk to you because *they're mad at you*. I don't understand why you don't understand that."

I pulled the covers over my head.

"What? Do you hear yourself? What mental gymnastics are you performing to make sense of this?" I peeked over the covers with just one eye.

Francesco groaned and flopped into bed with his back to me.

"Just try harder tomorrow, babe. They're my parents."

I wanted to be happy with my new husband but I was done being sorry. And maybe that meant that we would never be able to be happy together. Maybe my hopes were hollow. I struggled to breathe and started to cry, and a small part of me wanted him to wake up so I could be like, "Look at what you did, motherfucker!" But then I abruptly stopped myself. I did not move to Italy to collapse into a pit of self-loathing and phlegm. I stared into the dark, feeling the tears and snot dry on my face. There was no way to fix it. As far as I knew from Italian friends, I wasn't violating any cultural customs. These weren't really *Italian* things, these were rules specific to Francesco's family and therefore impossible to navigate without a lifetime of grooming.

The next morning, I found Francesco in the kitchen making coffee with the Bialetti percolator. The apartment was empty. "Good morning!" he said, handing me an Americano. I felt relieved when he gave me a big hug and kissed me. Francesco chanted, "Go, baby, go! Go, baby, go!" while I did the Running Man in my pajamas. Oliver ran circles around me until Francesco scooped him up to kiss his face and sing a song to him, bouncing him in his arms. This was the little family I loved and for a moment my heart was full. Then keys jingled in the front door and I ran into the bedroom to get dressed so I didn't get shit for wearing my flannel pajamas outside of the bedroom.

I pulled on my clothes, determined to make sure that the rest of the weekend was bearable. I would be cheerful. I would smile. They were going to totally love me based on cheerfulness alone. I would be *aggressively* happy.

Francesco opened the bedroom door and asked, "Can we show my mom the invitations you made?"

"Yeah," I smiled until it hurt my face, "they're right over there; go ahead and show her babe. I'm getting ready as fast as I can so we can leave whenever your mom is ready to go finalize the flower order!"

He took the cards into the kitchen. I pulled my hair up into a bun then joined them. They huddled next to the table chatting in Italian, holding the invitations up one by one for close inspection.

I leaned against the ancient gas stove about a foot away from Francesco and Amalea. I smiled as hard as I could to show that I was there and fully engaged. They spoke too quickly in dialect for me to understand most of it but I made out a few small words like "nice" and "strange." I hoped she liked the invitations. I'd made them with vintage white Italian paper with gray calligraphy and evergreen details, which were perfect, in my opinion, for a spring wedding.

Oliver unexpectedly barreled into the kitchen and slammed into my leg. He bounced off, sat down and looked up at me like, "What the fuck just happened?" I laughed and bent down to ruffle his head. Francesco scooped up Oliver and moved him away, then shot me this look of pure hatred that I'd never seen before. I burst into tears right then and there, so shocked by my own crying that I looked around wide-eyed like, *My face broke! What do I do?* I dramatically ran to the bathroom, arms flapping behind me like an injured bird. I felt unhinged, completely out of control of my own emotions, like I'd finally just gone nuts. Staring into the mirror I whispered, "You've lost your fucking mind," while noting how tragically cute I looked with my runny mascara, messy bun, slightly pink face. Amalea pounded on the bathroom door.

"You need to learn to smack Oliver in the mouth like people smack their children."

What the fuck?

She said something about my "mental problems" then stormed off down the hall. Marcello came home and started arguing with Amalea in the kitchen. I snuck into the bedroom to hide because I was ashamed. Francesco came in a moment later.

"Honey, I didn't mean to lose my temper. I'm sorry but my parents are like this. They get offended by *everything*. You have to stand right next to me when I explain everything, you have to listen to every word, and nod enthusiastically; you can't pet Oliver while they are talking."

I started out calmly, "Francesco, they have rules on when we're allowed to drink coffee, for how long I walk around in pajamas, what outfits I'm allowed to wear, how I speak and when I'm allowed to speak. There are sexist rules about the women waiting on the men, and my all-time favorite, the rule that says I have to iron towels even in my own home." My voice rose as I began to feel sure that I was in the right, "And now there's a rule that states I'm not allowed to pet Oliver, my own fucking dog, when you're explaining STATIONERY! Seriously, how is this not fucking crazy to you?"

"It *is* crazy. Why do you think I moved to Florence? But I grew up like dis. I'm used to it." He took a huge breath and I noticed that his English was becoming increasingly spotty. "And because if-a you don't explain everything deh think you don't like-a deh wedding. It's-a just how it is. There's no point in complaining because they are like this, they are old, and they will never change. I don't know what else to do, *amore*. Nobody is happy."

"I don't want to focus on making them happy anymore. I feel like this was all a mistake. There's no way I can spend the rest of my life like this, Francesco. I can't do it anymore, no matter how much I love you."

He stared at me in disbelief, anticipating what I might say next. The word "annulment" floated on the tip of my tongue but I managed to keep it there, locked into place.

Amalea screamed and threw a pot of spaghetti or something in the kitchen. Marcello screamed back. Francesco's eyes widened and he flew out of the room straight into the argument. I heard his dad's deafening voice, "American piece of shit!" and Francesco's voice grew into a hysterical shriek. I couldn't help but feel like I'd missed something. Glass shattered, there was a crash, his mother was crying. Francesco was berating his parents so passionately that I was sure someone had been mortally wounded in some *Clash of the Titans* shit. Furniture fell. Bang. Boom. BANG.

My hands were shaking but I managed to stuff my clothes into a suitcase as fast as I could. My focus sharpened, my breathing grew steady. I spent fifteen years with a verbally abusive stepfather who'd repeatedly served time in prison for assault and battery. Screaming ignites something deep within my core that prepares me for war. The last thing that I needed was to physically attack his pocket-sized father. Then Cumino would *really* have something to gossip about: that time I tried to choke my father-in-law to death on the balcony underneath the granny panties blowing on the line.

Francesco, the agreeable son, the golden child who always kept his mouth shut, who feared to upset his mom and dad, was now berating his parents, in a fit of rage. He appeared in the bedroom red-faced, disheveled, his voice quivering,

"We are leaving right now! NOW!" he barked. His hand was bleeding and red trails ran from his knuckles down his fingers.

"Oh my Go—"

"NOW!"

I cradled Oliver in my arms and kept my head down as we made our way to the front door. Marcello stood by the door and yelled at us to never come back, Amalea grabbed at Francesco's clothes and begged us to stay. There was blood smeared on the wall, where Francesco had obviously punched it. The walls in Italy are *cement*. Who punches cement? We ran to the car in a torrential downpour, our clothes and hair soaking wet as we flung ourselves inside and peeled out of the parking lot.

The rain only added to the drama as we rushed north on the freeway towards Florence in uncomfortable silence. Oliver's ears were pinned back in fear and confusion.

Francesco's iPhone, set to some flamenco music, filled our sad Fiat with party music. He ignored multiple calls. When he finally exited the freeway to get gas I answered the phone while he stood in the pouring rain, surrounded by the rotten smell of the methanol he pumped into the tank.

It was his sister. "Where is my brother? What happened? Why is the wedding off?" she asked worriedly.

"I don't know what happened," I responded, "Everything was okay then I petted Oliver and I created a lot of problems."

"No, they're angry because Francesco canceled the wedding when you were crying in the bathroom," she said.

"Wait, what?" I asked. So *that's* what I'd been missing.

Francesco hopped back into the car to find me on the phone with Julia. I held it out to him.

"Honey, take it. Your sister is worried. And why in the hell did you *cancel* the wedding?"

"I didn't *really* cancel it. I said something like, 'Maybe we should call the whole thing off,' it's not like I even meant it or it was a final decision. I was pissed and just said it out of anger."

He argued in rapid Italian with her for twenty minutes while we sat in the parking lot.

"I never want to see them again!" he roared and hung up. I felt conflicted, part of me tingled with joy at the possibility of being free from them, but the other part of me knew I couldn't let him fight with his family like this because he'd hate himself for the rest of his life if he cut them off. I knew how painful the entire scene must have been for him. But I also knew that he could be stubborn and was pretty far gone by that point.

"So, you went all Incredible Hulk on the wall. How's your hand feel?" I teased him.

"It hurts."

"You couldn't find something softer to punch? Like the couch?"

"I was mad."

"Clearly. Well, I hope you didn't break your hand. We'd probably have to amputate it."

"Ha."

"Why did you cancel the wedding?"

"I was mad. My mom was upset and I just kind of lost it for a minute. I'm getting really tired of trying to make everyone happy. They are always mad about something and I just don't know how to handle it. I've never gotten mad at them before, I learned early on to just keep my head down and do what I'm told. It's easier that way. But I don't want you to have to be a part of a family where you're being bossed around and yelled at all the time. I know it's making you miserable."

"Maybe that's the problem," I said, "maybe we should just let them feel how they feel and stop worrying about it. Let them be mad sometimes. They're not going to wilt or disown you. And don't punch walls, you angry chimpanzee."

He laughed, "My parents were really shocked. I've never had an argument with them before."

"It's not healthy to never get mad. Thank you for defending my honor."

"You see!" he smiled, "Nobody says mean things about my *amore*." He puffed up, super macho. I reminded him that while his father loved him maybe he didn't know how to express it in a productive way. If the situation were reversed, and it had been me that fought with my parents, he would have made me go back to fix it. Sometimes people disagree, they fight, they move on. It didn't have to be the end of the world. This was a new learning experience for me too because I was too proud and my dad and I often went months without talking after one of our big fights.

We were almost at Rome when he turned his car around and headed back to Cumino.

His mother opened her apartment door with maraschino-cherry eyes swollen from crying. All of the lights were off in the apartment, either to save electricity or for dramatic emphasis. We passed the office where his dad was on the phone, talking calmly, merrily even, to a friend. We walked into the dark living room where we all took a seat. Francesco and Amalea stared at each other for an eternity before they both started speaking at the same time.

"You canceled the wedding!" Amalea wailed.

Francesco began, "I was just mad for ten seconds, I didn't mean it. It was obvious that I didn't mean it."

Amalea turned towards me with tears in her eyes. "I don't have any problems with you. Yes, in the beginning, I did, but now I don't. You just imagine it all."

"Mamma, that's not true," Francesco said. "Please, stop putting this on her. You told me you didn't want me to marry her, you asked me to find an Italian woman instead. You told everyone we know that you didn't like her. And you certainly don't act as though you like her. If we're going to talk, let's be honest. Even if you don't have a problem right now, you can't make someone feel unwelcome in your home for years then expect them to feel welcome once you decide you're over it. It's not fair. She knows *everything* that you've told everyone about her. It's impossible for her to do anything right here. You guys are always yelling at her."

"She takes offense to everything!" Amalea said. "I didn't see the point in telling people you were already married when we're planning a wedding. In my eyes, you're not married until I see it." She was referring to the incident a few months ago where she introduced me as Francesco's girlfriend instead of his wife.

Francesco translated for me because I couldn't speak fast enough. I cleared my throat and looked her dead in the eyes.

"I understand that this is hard for you that your son chose to marry a foreign person. I understand, I really do. But since we've been married, we haven't even had a chance to be happy. Francesco feels ashamed because of how openly miserable you guys are. We *are* married. There's nothing wrong with having two weddings; we know other Italians who have married foreign people and had two weddings."

Marcello marched into the living room to watch the conversation with his arms folded across his chest.

Then he jumped in and said, "Amalea should not have called you his girlfriend. Marriage is sacred and that wasn't right. But we don't have a problem with you. You just sit there and you never talk! You can't act like that in *this family*. You have obvious self-esteem issues."

Francesco raised his voice, saying "She's different than you guys. Her culture is different, it's the opposite, really. And she doesn't speak Italian fluently and she doesn't speak dialect yet. Instead of getting to know her, you spend all of your time trying to shove your own culture down her throat. I do not *want* her to be Italian. She does not need to be like an Italian woman. If I wanted an Italian woman, I would have married one."

Francesco and his parents started yelling at each other at the same time.

"She needs to be Italian!"

"No!"

"Yes!"

"No!"

Then both Amalea and Marcello turned on me, "You need to be Italian, not American, not *Persian*! You can't speak English to Francesco in our house anymore. You have to care more! You never yell at Francesco and you don't tell him what to do! You don't talk enough to people in the street!"

Francesco yelled over the top of them about how I can't be Italian because I'm *not Italian*. Realizing that we were fighting a battle that could not be won in this way, I had no option but to yell,

"Okay. Fine. Okay!"

They all stopped arguing.

Marcello nodded, "Okay."

Francesco went to talk, "But babe—"

"It's okay, let's just let time resolve this."

"Okay," he said, begrudgingly.

Amalea smiled and nodded matter-of-factly like she'd just been nominated for an award. "*Sì*," she said, then in an attempt to speak English, "ES ZOKAY!"

* * *

At a large round table in a pizzeria, surrounded by Francesco's friends who bore horrified expressions, I chewed mozzarella and listened as he related the drama of our afternoon.

"You got in a fight over what? They called you a what? They said that? Surely you misunderstood!"

I soaked it up. Yes, it was true, it was so sad and woe is me.

"But the wedding is still happening soon, yes?" Sergio asked.

"Yeah, and hopefully things will get better now." Francesco said, rubbing his neck and grimacing.

In a way, our relationship with his parents was like a condemned house that had been constructed with rotting two-by-fours. Some structures have to be destroyed before they can be rebuilt.

32

Hungover and Chapel-Bound

May 5th, 2013

I woke up in a complete panic in a small hotel room in Cumino the day of our Italian wedding, feeling absolutely devastated. I grabbed my cell phone: 8:30 a.m., just in time. I'd had ten too many glasses of wine, vodka soda, and any other bottle of booze I could get my face on. I wiggled my fat toes; they were engorged and blistered from the platform stilettos I'd worn like a real fucking idiot the night before. My body was no longer dewy and soft; instead, my muscles had turned to jerky, my dry mouth begged for water, and my eyes had transformed into itchy, hot, parched sand dunes.

"Guys, wake up," I whispered to my friends, Giselle and Michelle. They'd flown in a week ago from the US, to "support me" through the Italian wedding, and were passed out next to me with puffy red faces. They stirred and resentfully opened angry bloodshot eyes that read, *This is bullshit, I'm dying, get married without me.* My other bridesmaid, Violetta, was somewhere down the hall in another room with her new husband, Alex. Francesco's best man Loris and his partner Antonia had thrown Francesco and me a huge party to celebrate our wedding and we'd stumbled back to our hotel around 6 a.m. Two hours of sleep, three hours till the wedding.

"You guys," I sat up, groaning, and yanked off my bra that was somehow backwards and upside down, "how the fuck am I supposed to get married this afternoon? I'm pretty sure I'm actually dying. Can one of you just pretend to be me?"

I pushed my blankets and a pile of clothes off of me. Our room looked and smelled like Skid Row had been there—half-empty cups of alcohol, hodgepodges of makeup, bras, underwear, and bags everywhere. A posse of people would be arriving in our room any minute and we were still covered in a film of cigarette tar and Fernet.

I stepped out of the shower to a knock at the door. Michelle answered it, and then popped her head into the bathroom, "Babe, it's the hair guy, Get out here because he doesn't speak English." I greeted Fabio, the local hairdresser I'd picked, with a kiss. My hair was still wet and drippy. He worked at a salon that seemed to do mostly old-lady hair but I adored him because he was sweet and yelled at Amalea for being "naggy and annoying" when I went with her to get my hair done. He spoke dialect and moved his hands wildly, his words mimicked by enthusiastic facial expressions, so we could get by just fine without speaking the same language.

I pulled on a delicate white satin and lace nightgown that Amalea and Marcello had gifted me a few nights prior, in front of my Iranian aunt and horrified dad who were in town for the wedding.

"A wedding gift for you," Amalea said as she presented it to me.

Marcello slapped his knee and laughed, "Now, don't wear this too often, Francesco needs to get some sleep! Francesco! Translate that! Ha-ha!" When Francesco reluctantly explained what Marcello was saying, my dad's face turned crimson, and a variety of other colors I'd identify with hell before his expression finally settled on sheepish grin.

As I entered the room in my slutty yet virginal gown, Fabio grabbed my hand and twirled me around, exclaiming, "Oh! That is beautiful!"

"Thank you," I curtsied.

His assistant, a gothic woman dressed like a Marilyn Manson fan, introduced herself as Paola with a crooked smile. I settled into a chair in front of a mirror. Giselle shoved a cappuccino into my hand. I sipped the foam, locked eyes with the wall, and prayed that the universe would stop me from drooling. Paola handed Fabio nineties glamour tools: a ginormous crimper, pink foam rollers, and two million safety pins. He yanked back on my hair, ripping through the tangles. He held some baby's breath (the world's creepiest flower) up next to the side of my head, nodding approvingly to himself.

"Now, what do you want darling? Like this, or like this?" He piled my hair on top of my head, then brought it down lower. Up again, then lower.

"Can we do a low bun, a bit messy, like I just spent all day having sex?"

Fabio threw back his head and guffawed, batting me with his hand.

"After sex! HA! How naughty! You're a fun bride! So fun!" (He later told all of Cumino that he had a really fun morning with the American woman who wanted sex hair.) While Fabio curled my hair, Giselle and Michelle wandered around in their robes, sipping champagne and dabbing on makeup here and there. Then there was a knock at the door and the concierge dropped off strawberries, chocolate, and more champagne. Fabio finished my hair just as our photographer, Alix, flew into the room like a tornado, straight off the plane from Utah. She'd captured our wedding in Park City, mostly pics of me smoking while adjusting my thong, and we liked her so much we hired her for the Italy wedding too.

"Hey, nice to see you again," Alix said, dropping her camera bag, snatching my wedding dress off of the wardrobe hook and disappearing back out the door. She returned a few moments later to snap shot after shot of us finishing our makeup, eating strawberries, or squishing our own boobs. Alix took a few pictures of me looking out of a giant window in my tulle-covered bridal underwear, towards the local monastery (Amalea had pointed it out to everyone the night before as "the place the Americans bombed").

"Am I allowed to flash the monks?" I wondered out loud.

"Yes, they need something to think about when they jerk off in between their conversations with Jesus," Michelle said.

"That's probably true," Giselle agreed.

Violetta came into our room just in time to get the wedding dress over my head. Luckily, unlike the Utah wedding, this time it fit right away, albeit tight as hell.

I took a deep breath in the mirror. Violetta held up her glass to toast, I threw mine back and then quickly drank two more.

"Careful honey, you're going to be drunk," Fabio warned.

I set my empty glass down. "That's the idea."

"Why you look so nervous?"

The butterflies in my stomach had turned into vicious bats. I nearly gagged.

"Fabio, I'm not Catholic," I said cautiously so I wouldn't offend him. A few months prior, Amalea had discovered that we could have a "mixed" ceremony, one that allowed heathens to marry Catholics. I had reservations, mainly that neither Francesco nor I were religious, and that I didn't like the Church's stance on gay marriage. Especially because we had gay friends attending the wedding and I felt like shit asking them to sit in the church, knowing that they weren't welcome there. But the mixed ceremony allowed Amalea and Marcello to uphold appearances and hold onto tradition without my having to compromise my own values (that the belief in a higher power is cool but giant conservative institutions merited the same kind of caution as a nuclear bomb). I wouldn't be required to say anything religious but Francesco, the confirmed Catholic and altar boy, would have to have a long conversation with Jesus and Mary.

"What does it matter if you're Catholic or not?" Fabio asked, sweetly.

"Well, I've never even seen one of these weddings. I have no idea what to expect at this thing and everyone is going to be judging Francesco and his family if I mess up. And I *always* mess up. It seems pretty impossible for me to get through the day without embarrassing everyone."

The fear was totally rational since I'd learned the day before at a quick run-through that the ceremony wasn't a simple "you stand here, he stands there, say your vows and be done" thing. Instead, it was like memorizing choreography from a Jazzercise video. You go left, he goes right, you meet up there, go up on stage, bow, turn, get off stage, plié, turn, kneel on a thingy, sit, stand, sit, backflip, dismount, do the hokey-pokey. And it would be in Cumino-accented Italian with the entire village standing by, so I'd have *quite* an audience if I couldn't get the words or moves right.

"Oh, who cares about these people and their gossip?" he said, touching my arm soothingly.

"Since when do you care so much about what other people think?" Giselle asked, adding a pin to her French twist.

"Since, I don't know?" I adjusted my non-existent boobs that were being squeezed to death by my torture device of a dress.

"This scared chick is not the person we know," Michelle said as she fluffed my gown. "I've never seen you act so insecure in the fifteen years I've known you. This place is making you crazy. I really wonder if you should be here for much longer."

"Ignore the world. If these people have something to say they can say it to me," added Violetta. "You're perfect; if they don't like something, screw them." Everything Violetta said sounded very convincing because of her confident delivery and sultry Russian accent. "Screw them" sounded like "I'll kill their family."

"What if it gets worse?" Giselle pointed out, a serious note in her voice.

"Jesus, I don't know," I answered. "If it gets worse then I'll have to strangle myself or leave Italy. I've thought about it a lot already, I promise I'm not blind to everything that's happening. I haven't given up yet because I want to feel like I tried my hardest before I just completely lose my shit and move home. You know?"

Violetta caught my eye in the mirror as she lightly pressed a mauve lipstick into her full lips. "Yes, that makes sense, and we all love Francesco. But, just be careful not to sacrifice your own happiness. Women do that a lot, no?" She gave a final scrunch to her dark waves and tossed her head back. "Are we ready?"

Downstairs my dad and Aunt Zhara waited for me in the lobby along with my cousins. I'd met her for the first time that week because she'd never traveled outside of Iran. We spent the day together in Rome, and even though we'd never met before you'd never know it. She immediately took my hand, kissed my face, and when I was tired shoved my head into her bosom, saying, "You're tired, sleep," while I suffocated in her cleavage. She took Oliver's leash from me and laughed loudly as he dragged her through the Roman streets, and when we paused to look at the Colosseum she pulled out handfuls of candies rolled in rose petals.

Dad hugged me and kissed my cheeks then admired my wedding dress and hair.

"You look gorgeous, baby," he smiled, "You got that from me."

"Naturally, Dad." I rolled my eyes.

It helped with the nerves to have my friends and family there, a little support went a long way.

"Should we go?" he asked.

Giorgio, a neighbor, and friend of Francesco's family, pulled up outside the hotel in a black Bentley to take us to the church, and my friends and dad piled in. The car was adorned with white ribbons on the mirrors to signal a bride was inside.

"Do you want some gum, baby?" Dad offered. He looked concerned.

I shoved three sticks of Winterfresh into my mouth and chewed rapidly, observing a group of fashionably dressed teenagers pass an elderly man making wooden chairs on the sidewalk. I took a few deep breaths and clenched my jaw.

"Baby, what is the matter vit you?" my dad asked, frowning at me. "You look very nervous."

"I *am* nervous! I don't know what I'm supposed to say or do. I'm totally going to trip and fall on the priest. What if I squish the priest to death?"

"It's not going to happen, baby. Just calm down."

I nodded and chomp-chomp-chomped my gum like a starved goat up to its ass in hay.

Children ran up to our car to peer in at me and old men smiled and waved. It was an adorable distraction. We drove through the hills, past fields of poppies, and abandoned stone houses overtaken by vines and moss until eventually arriving at our small chapel in the middle of nowhere.

We'd already been married and I'd already worn the same dress, so I wasn't expecting a big reaction from Francesco but when I glided up to him outside the church his eyes danced and a huge grin spread across his face. Amalea made herself tall and statuesque to show off the perfection of her black gown, her long neck and tipped-up chin drawing attention to the slender silver snakes weaving around her collarbone. Francesco looked like a politician again but this time in a slim black Hugo Boss suit. He mouthed, "Pretty!" to me and I winked at him. In the distance, someone yelled that it was time to get started. Francesco locked arms with Amalea and they stepped forward into the chapel together. A lump rose in my throat but I looked at my friends, Giselle, Violetta, Michelle, Jerome, Jakob, and Grayson, who were all standing in a group waiting to be told where to sit. I wasn't this "scared" person. I picked up my bouquet of wildflowers and took a confident step forward.

The priest led Francesco and me through the whole song and dance, then finally, at the end, to our seats in front of him. I felt a huge wave of relief to just sit down. I didn't fall so I considered the whole thing a victory. Until Amalea tracked down a tissue from the back row and had it sent all the way to the front of the church so I could spit out the giant ball of gum I'd been absentmindedly chowing down on the entire time.

The ceremony was much shorter than I expected—we had cut out all of the religious stuff like my promise to obey, since being bossed around by a person who often can't even find his own underwear is where I draw the line in life—and it was over before I knew it. Francesco and I signed a church document in a book made for giants, then we were pelted by four hundred pounds of rice that got stuck in my hair, my boobs, and my underwear. It was fun, except for the stinging pain of the rice bouncing off my eyeballs and chest, and the fact that rice is toxic to birds so I was thinking, Birds don't eat it! Fly away! the entire time. Plus, for the rest of the day, every time I peed a handful of rice would fall from somewhere. I hoped that nothing would wander too far north and sprout.

In the garden at the restaurant they served cocktails and six thousand hors d'oeuvres, little bite-sized things like melon balls wrapped in prosciutto served on fountain-like tiered silver trays. I spotted my dad next to a pastry tower, totally unaware of how Italian weddings work, double-fisting everything he could get his hands on into his mouth. I teetered over to tell him that we were having a real dinner that would last for at least six hours inside the restaurant.

"Are you serious?" his eyes bulged out of his face, "Baby, I'll die!"

"You should probably go force yourself to throw up," I advised.

In the restaurant, Francesco and I were put on display at our own table twenty feet in front of the others, like our own private fishbowl. The decor was charming, unlike some of the other fluorescent-lit, art deco restaurants in the area. The dark wood tables and exposed brick walls lent a bit of rustic charm, along with the small vases of white wildflowers and silver candelabras on all the tables. Francesco and I sat down and almost instantly the wait staff burst through the kitchen doors, dispersing to each table with wine and mixed antipasti in a well-rehearsed, impeccably timed dance.

I turned to Francesco. "Doesn't this totally remind you of that one scene from *Beauty and the Beast* where the household appliances burst through the double doors and get shit done to a beautifully choreographed song?"

"No? Should it?"

He then excused himself to check on the fun table where all of our American and Spanish friends sat, putting his hand on each person's back while he leaned over their shoulder to thank them for coming. I rearranged silverware at our little table alone while our guests gawked at me in between their bites of prosciutto and buffalo mozzarella—the peculiar American woman with her tousled hair and plain cotton-ball dress, chugging glass after glass of wine. I understood their interest; I watched people with intensity and fascination usually reserved for stalkers.

My father, aunt, and cousins were at the nearest table, scream-speaking Persian. Every few minutes they broke into fits of roaring laughter. From experience I guessed that they were talking about fat-assed sheep or the famous characters of their small village in Golpayegan like "the butcher," or maybe they were telling stories of my dad as a child, the family terror, who peed on the walls in revolt when my grandma left him at home. Meanwhile, my in-laws strutted ostentatiously between the tables, pausing to ask each guest if they were content. The feedback regarding the fifteen-course menu must have been good because Amalea's chin pointed progressively higher towards the ceiling and Marcello's cheeks flushed with pride. My father-in-law leaned down to every male in the space to make *Mad Men*-style jokes, the kind that hasn't been socially acceptable since the fifties. My mother-in-law laughed shyly at her husband, batting at him with her hand, "Oh stop!" She clearly still adored him when she wasn't fighting with him.

After the first course of *pasta con vongole* the DJ sang a famous Italian song, "Ma il cielo é sempre più blu." Francesco came running to fetch me from my little loner table and dragged me to the makeshift dance floor. He waved for our friends to join us and reluctantly they did. Grayson, Jerome and Jakob, along with Michelle, Giselle, Violetta, and all of Francesco's friends from Italy and Spain crowded onto the dance floor. Next the DJ moved onto an English song but he didn't know any of the words so he just improvised with mouth noises like karaoke. An older woman with watermelon breasts hoisted up to her chin tried to force my dad out of his chair for a dance. He laughed and shook his head, protesting, "No, no, I'm married!" My father-in-law and his Italian female friend had made their way to the center of the dance floor to do the Tuca Tuca, a dance from the early seventies that is a lot like the Macarena only you do it on the other person's body. They faced each other, taking turns tapping each other's thighs, sides, and shoulders to the rhythm of the music. I heard my dad yell, "Oh! The Italians are getting nasty now!"

Just after the third "first" course, Francesco stole a flower from a vase, threw it between his teeth and dragged me to the dance floor again for a sloppy tango. But I'd had too much wine, and stumbled through a promenade, tripping on my dress and nearly face-planting into the DJ booth. Then I slow-danced with my dad, who chortled at a little ninety-year-old pervert who ran cartoonishly behind Giselle with outstretched arms. When he finally managed to trap her for a dance he shamelessly stared into her breasts with an expression of pure satisfaction, and because she was a full foot taller than him her boobs were perfectly eye-level for the old creep.

After the dance, I headed back to the table to catch my breath. My skin-tight dress made it a little difficult to breathe and at one point I must have looked faint because Amalea came running over out of nowhere, yanked my zipper down, and shoved my back into the wall.

"Stay here so nobody can see your bra; you're pale and your lips are blue," she said and faced me until my color went back to normal. I sucked in huge gulps of air and concentrated on the twisted metal snakes on her neckline. She zipped me up again, saying firmly, "No more sitting down, it's too constrictive and you can't get air. If I'd known that your dress was this tight we would have found you a different one."

I nodded. "I told Francesco it was tight."

Amalea shook her head and said, "Well, sometimes my son is an idiot." She put her hand on my shoulder. "You did a nice thing today, to marry in that church. I thought you were just being difficult before when you said it made you uncomfortable but I could tell that it really did when I saw your face at rehearsal. But thank you for doing that for my family."

I smiled and nodded.

She blushed. "Anyway, this dress, *Madonna mia*, my son is really an idiot." She swatted the air and glided off to sing "Dimmi quando" with

Francesco and his friends who were swaying with their arms around each other, passionately belting out lyrics next to the DJ. Amalea linked arms with them and looked at her son with adoration as he sang to her. I hadn't seen him or his family that happy, ever.

I made my way outside to smoke a cigarette, or at least pretend to smoke one in order to get some fresh air. I concentrated on not spilling my Montepulciano d'Abruzzo down the front of my gown, Jerome pondered out loud whether or not two tiny Italian men inside were on "his team" or not, and Grayson chimed in that he'd been wondering the same. One of Francesco's Spanish friends, Alejandro, stroked his girlfriend's head and whispered *"guapa"* into her hair. He looked up and asked me, "Which wedding did you like more?"

I thought about it for a minute and just shrugged. Both weddings were a reflection of the cultural and personal differences between Francesco and I. Our American wedding felt impromptu and weird, more like a party to celebrate our love for youth and each other by writing our own vows and stumbling incoherently around the dance floor to Joan Jett. The American wedding felt free because we were allowed to be more selfish: no small-town gossip or reputation to uphold. In Italy, our wedding was elegant with an emphasis on aesthetics, a life-or-death adherence to tradition with a dash of flamboyance. Even Francesco's dad was really into the wedding decor and wanted to participate in all of it, which was pretty different from the US where a lot of American men, unfortunately, equate an interest in beauty with the exclusive world of wombs. I learned a lot about Francesco through his traditions and those of the humans that produced him. It suddenly made sense that he obsessed over what people thought of him, he was rooted in the little community, and he would be for the rest of his life. It also totally made sense why he practically fainted every time I wore shoes that didn't match my purse: a "bad" appearance was social suicide. The church and the restaurant were decorated just so and filled with guests in gowns and stilettos who dined passionately, moaning with every bite, critiquing each expertly prepared noodle. The dinner would be the talk of the town for months to follow.

Towards the end of the night, after nearly six hours of eating and dancing in uncomfortable clothes, we were all exhausted. The flowers in my hair were upside down and hanging on by a dehydrated stem. Francesco had a painful grimace on his face that he attempted to hide behind a superficial and slightly frantic smile. I wanted nothing more than to climb under my own dress and sleep but the celebration wasn't quite over yet.

Francesco and I were herded outside for a final champagne toast and to cut the cake, which turned out to be the biggest fucking cake I'd ever seen. Instead of their usual flat pan cake, the restaurant thought it would be nice to bake a multi-tiered cake "for Americans." It was the size of a Mini Cooper. After sawing at the bottom layer for five minutes in front of all of the guests, we realized that the entire cake, with the exception of the very top layer, was made of styrofoam covered in fresh cream frosting. Then someone shoved a green apple on a string into Jerome's hand and made him hold it in the air for Francesco and me to try and bite without using our hands. The guests cheered. Jerome whispered, "What is the goal of this game?" Francesco and I both shrugged. It seemed like a metaphor for marriage: nobody wins if you chew at each other's faces.

While we thanked guests for coming I switched my weight back and forth like I was participating in an invisible double Dutch. I felt like I'd just come off of a week-long crack bender. My ribs were bruised, my feet raw, and I had a rabid, pain-ridden wince on my face.

"Thank you so much for coming, thank you," we repeated a million times as we accepted wads of money stuffed into pretty envelopes in exchange for the espresso wedding favors in white linen boxes at the end of the night.

After midnight, Marcello and Amalea sat down in their apartment with a little black book and wrote down the name of every guest, along with the amount they'd given. The book contained every monetary gift they'd ever given or received from every family since the dawn of time.

"Why are you writing it all down?" I asked Francesco, "For thank-you cards?"

"No, we don't do thank-you cards here. What the hell are we thanking them for? We just fed them a six-hour meal."

"Jesus, I feel like someone should send me a thank-you card. That shit was painful."

He raised his eyebrows. "Everyone keeps a book like this," he said. "At least, everyone I know."

"Oh, so your family isn't just super weird about money?"

"No dude."

He explained that everyone kept track of gifts to maintain fairness. For example, whatever someone gave us for our wedding, we needed to give them in the future—up to the cent—when they or their children married. Giving too little would be an absolute scandal, giving too much is just showing off. It seemed like a lot of work.

We had survived two weddings and, most importantly, I was lucky enough to marry the same guy *twice*. Seriously, we killed it. And? We used all of our wedding money (that Francesco had tediously documented like the IRS) to flee to Thailand for our honeymoon two days later where I was bitten by an endangered poisonous monkey* and exposed to an impressive number of perfectly sculpted "ladyboy"** vaginas who liked to preface flashing me their lady cave with the declaration, "It's new!"

After years of our forbidden love, and disapproving jabs at my sucky breasts, we were finally able to relax on a beach in Phuket as a married couple, till death do us part. Probably at the hands of adorable asshole monkey.

*The slow loris is super endangered and a victim of animal trafficking because idiot tourists like me are all "Oooh monkey!" So they're pissed, and they bite. And, they're the only poisonous primate on planet Earth.

**These particular individuals introduced themselves as "ladyboys." I would call them women.

Stark

33

Immigration

June 2013

During aperitivo, as the sun began to set behind the skyline of apartment buildings and amp laundry lines, I drank a spritzer and watched an Italian child pee on a curb, hovering with the help of their grandmother, while Francesco and his friend Luca discussed the cause of Italy's economic collapse.

"Businesses can't succeed here, the unions are too strong," Francesco said while exhaling a cloud of cigarette smoke.

"We need the unions," Luca protested, "the problem is corruption."

"Corruption, yes, because our culture breeds that," Francesco said. Luca rolled his eyes in playful disapproval.

"I read a book a few years ago that accused all politicians of being aliens," I said. "It sounds crazy but I'm *pretty sure* they're all lizard people."

They both slowly turned towards me.

"What?" I asked.

It was all that anyone could talk about, the economic collapse of Greece and Spain, and the impending fall of Italy, too. In cafés, old men blamed immigrants, over Sunday lunch Marcello would lament, "Oh, *povera Italia!*" In magazines, journalists blamed the euro, *mammoni*, poor management at the hands of the media tyrant/man-whore, Berlusconi, who allegedly pulled Italy into the rumbling bowels of financial woe. There was no denying that bad things were happening and we could hear it all around us. American expats were leaving Italy by the thousands. Italians were emigrating at an even faster rate, in hopes of securing a more stable financial future somewhere else. Germany, England, and the United States were receiving Italian immigrants with open arms.

"But why are you staying here?" Luca asked Francesco, "I would leave if I could. There is no future in Italy."

Francesco and I had talked about leaving Italy a handful of times when things with his parents were especially rough. He suggested Germany, I suggested the south of France, and we both scoffed at each other's ideas. There were plenty of things we liked about Italy but admittedly money wasn't one of them. Being paid a livable wage in its supposed capitalism was harder than squeezing wine out of dirt. An average engineer in Italy made about the same as a Subway sandwich artist in Wyoming.

Francesco and I hadn't fought with his parents at all since our wedding in Italy but mostly because we were making the maximum effort. Francesco had upped his yes-man game, Marcello and Amalea had backed off a little, and I'd become almost pathetically desperate for the world's approval to avoid another blow-up. And I truly hated myself for it. I'd gone from struggling to find my voice with them to being practically mute and painfully agreeable because I thought I was protecting Francesco from the stress and pain of being trapped in the middle of two opposing forces. Somehow along the way, I'd forgotten that my needs mattered, too.

In trying to be "likable" —aka, not at all myself—I felt like a puppet, forced to perform in front of an ungrateful audience while being fisted in the ass. On top of that, Oliver continued to hold us hostage with his relentless yapping and separation anxiety, and our homicidal landlord still lived uncomfortably close. Alone in my Florence apartment, I'd developed a bizarre form of agoraphobia and every day I became more and more of a cave troll. I was horrified by the very prospect of having to leave because what if Oliver pooped in front of a store and I got screamed at or what if someone tried to talk to me and I couldn't find the right words, and why was everyone always staring all the time? These things would have never bothered me a few years ago; I'd have rolled my eyes or laughed at myself, but that was before the fear took over.

One day I was in our kitchen writing a blog post in my travel blog about our wedding in Italy when Oliver pawed at the front door to go potty. I took a few long, deep breaths, flung open the door and walked quickly outside. On the sidewalk I kept my head down, frustrated every time he stopped to pee on something. I rushed him along, scared that someone might speak to me. It was around noon, sunny out, so parents were walking their school children in their little dress uniforms that resembled a painter's smock. I zigzagged around the kids and prayed that Oliver wouldn't poop near a group of them because I would be embarrassed if they stopped to stare at me. I came around the final corner and my nervousness started to dissipate knowing that any second I'd be home.

Then something hit me on the head, hard. I whirled back, disoriented, the world blurred for a minute and I thought, Don't faint, Oliver will run away. Oliver was my best friend, he was my everything, so I held on as tight as I could to the leash in case I dropped to the ground. Something liquid and warm ran down my face, over my lashes, and down my cheeks in thick oozing streams. I looked down to see bright red puddles forming on the sidewalk. *Oh, no.* Oliver was in sled-dog mode, pulling as hard as he could to get me to move forward. I turned around and saw what had hit me: some asshole had left an electrical box open on the side of an apartment, and since my head was down I'd smacked right into it mid-stride. Blood seeped into my eyes as I stumbled down the sidewalk looking like the last scene of Stephen King's *Carrie*. Then, just as we passed a large group of people, Oliver spun in a circle, hunched over, and proceeded to squeeze out three sausage-shaped turds. Ten feet away an old lady stopped sweeping her storefront to shriek, "You clean it! CLEAN IT!"

I swayed uneasily while I fished a dog bag out of my pocket, Oliver pulled on the leash to bark at a dog across the street, blood dripped onto the sidewalk and onto his shit. I got my bag-covered hand around his final turd when a child and her mom stepped directly over my outstretched poop-seeking hand mid-cleanup. "Asshole!" I yelled in English. Tears welled up as I zig-zagged home with a fist full of dog shit, and it occurred to me that if I were hit by a car or mauled by a bear, I didn't have anyone besides Francesco to call. I was vulnerable and isolated. I wanted to go home.

Francesco came home early after I'd sent him an erratic text message about blood, to find me on the couch, mumbling about taking a flight to the US where people "probably wouldn't nearly step on a bleeding woman."

He sat down next to me and put his arm around my shoulders. "Honey, you look terrible, let's clean you up."

"I'm never going outside again! OUTSIDE IS MEAN!" Why did I sound five?

My depression and anxiety had worsened over the years, only I didn't know that's what it was because at the time I thought "depression" meant suicidal and "anxiety" just meant stressed or nervous when the reality is much more complex and sinister. I often found myself in the kitchen, repeating concerns I had over and over again out loud to myself in a never-ending loop, negative thoughts had started to crowd out any positive ones, and I'd lost fifteen pounds from my already small frame because food just didn't interest me that much anymore. Francesco had noticed that I'd become jumpy, too. Every day we'd walk past the same window where the same old man sat smoking a cigarette, and every day I'd squeal and rabbit-hop away from him, and every day Francesco would laugh and say, "You knew he was going to be there!"

We'd talked about what was going on with me, about the hypervigilance and the general sensitivity, but we both assumed it would pass. After all, I was strong and resilient, I'd been through a lot in my life and had managed to hold it together just fine. Right? No, not really. I'd just buried the trauma and my circumstance in Italy had revived it, and day by day it gnawed at me and weakened me from the inside out, like parasitic wasp larvae. Sitting there, pathetic and dazed, Francesco and I realized that things weren't just going to pass. I'd reached my tipping point and I needed to be somewhere that made me feel calm and safe, and where I could get help.

Unfortunately, importing a foreign spouse to the United States is famously difficult. I mean, any asshole can be born in the US but since the 2000s not even Ph.D. grads can get in from, say, Italy or London. In the eighties when my dad came, he practically skipped into the country, fist-bumped immigration and set up shop. We agreed that we'd start the application process for Francesco's visa so we could go to the US, even temporarily, sooner than later.

When we finally started the process a few weeks later, Francesco had to practically promise to give the US government his firstborn, cure cancer, and personally raise the economy out of the deficit. Dealing with immigration in any country is always a challenge but dealing with the US immigration services is like trying to run a marathon while a tiger shark munches on each of your legs. Also, you're blind. And deaf. And someone keeps randomly bitch-slapping you with giant hands.

When I got my Italian residency it took me a few days. I had to supply a marriage certificate, smile, wave, and say "grazie." Then decline a Facebook request from one of the senior employees who had gawked and winked at me the entire time I had been in the office to fill out the paperwork.

The US also made us pay thousands of dollars. Processing and denying immigration applications possibly sustain the American economy. The US Consulate General in Naples, for example, charged fifteen euro every time we called with a question. We couldn't talk with a representative without giving our credit card number.

I was confident, though, that we could handle the long American immigration process. We just needed to follow the directions, all inconveniently written in some government legalese. The first step seemed simple enough. We had to file something called an I-130 form and provide wedding photos, supplementary photos that showed a progression in time, a translated marriage certificate, birth certificates, passports, something showing that we lived together and had shared finances, and letters from friends saying we had really married and that he didn't pay me to marry him (but he should have), along with three-hundred euro.

These documents had to be filed in Rome. When the time came we slept at our friend Greco's apartment, woke up at 6 a.m., searched for somewhere to make copies for one hour until a nice elderly woman who owned a store selling paper let us use her copy machine. We were at the Rome immigration office by 8 a.m. and had to wait in line for well over an hour until we were called over to a woman who stood behind the kind of thick glass you'd find in a 7-Eleven in Los Angeles. "Slide your papers under," she said. She flipped through them, "We'll notify you." That was it. We were done by noon. A month later we found out via email that we'd passed the first round.

For our second appointment we had to be at the health clinic in Naples by 7:30 a.m. so the nurses could test Francesco for STDs, have his lungs x-rayed, and go over his childhood immunization paperwork. I'd told him a number of times to gather his paperwork but he insisted that he'd never had childhood immunizations.

"Because your mom was an anti-vaxxer in the eighties?" I wondered.

"No, because we don't do those shots in Italy," he said. Sounded fishy to me but who was I to know his country better than him?

When he failed to present his paperwork, a muscular woman with a strong jaw took him out the back to give him all of his immunizations.

"But what are they doing?" Amalea asked. She and Marcello had insisted on coming with us to Naples so we didn't have to "spend five euro on parking." I explained as best I could that they were giving him shots and she frowned. As soon as Francesco walked out of the nurse's room rubbing his arm, Amalea smacked him on the back of his head.

"You had these as a child, idiot, why didn't you just ask me for the records?" Then she muttered how everyone from a developed country gets vaccinations, crossed herself, and prayed to the hospital ceiling. I gloated at Francesco, who held the side of his head where she'd whopped him.

From the health clinic, we drove down the street to the US Consulate General, a massive, impressive building with an American flag the size of Portugal waving out front. In the paperwork, they'd asked us to arrive at 8 a.m. but they didn't actually open the doors until 9 a.m. so we had to wait outside in the rain for an hour, probably to highlight the hardships of immigration to inspire courageous stories for future generations. *When I came to America, I had to walk uphill both ways and stand in a tornado.*

At 9 a.m., we were ushered inside, like cattle, into a large empty office room with blue chairs lined up in the center. One by one, the two hundred-plus hopeful immigrants, including Francesco, were called up to a line of windows at the front of the room to be fingerprinted, then told to come back tomorrow at the same time for an actual interview with the officer.

We left the consulate and walked to a pizzeria to get three margherita pizzas to go. Naples is famous in Italy for its pizza: thin flavorful crust, simple red tomato sauce, and fresh, soft mozzarella, baked to golden perfection inside the fiery womb of a two-hundred-year-old brick oven. We ate the pizzas from the roof of the car. I looked out onto the sea on one side of the street and watched women walk down the sidewalk on the other side.

"But why are we here?" Marcello asked.

"Well," Francesco explained, "I need a visa to enter the US," and conveniently left out the part about us wanting to move there because when given an opportunity to complicate his life, he takes it.

On the second day, we arrived at the consulate at 7 a.m. again and stood outside in the rain one more time, soaking wet with chattering teeth for another hour. A building nearby was falling down and Francesco was really into it. He kept saying, "Babe, seriously, it's just falling down. *Look* at it!"

"Yeah, we're in the 'hood." But I was too distracted by the cold and the Neapolitans screaming at each other from the seats of their mopeds—"Go!", "Come on!"—in traffic to pay much attention to the buildings.

Inside the consulate, we made our way to the same disinfectant-smelling room as the day before. Once again we sat in the uncomfortable blue chairs to wait our turn for the immigration officers. One woman with a coarse bob called applicants up one at a time to slide their packets under the bulletproof glass. The room was somber and nervous like the waiting room at a hospital. For the most part, everyone was silent but on occasion, I'd catch the low buzz of families talking amongst themselves in their native language, which ranged from Persian to Zulu. The same manila envelope that contained financial proof that we wouldn't burden the American government could be spotted all around the room, resting on laps or being molested between nervous fingers. I was amazed that anyone had ever legally immigrated to the US. As a citizen, I had no idea it was so difficult to bring a spouse into the country. The financial bar is high, making it almost impossible to meet the requirements without a financial sponsor, and sponsors had to commit to a decade of support, even in the case of divorce. Before my dad signed the forms and faxed them for us, he'd told Francesco on Skype, "If you guys break up, I'll have you killed. Nothing personal but it will save me a small fortune." Francesco nervously laughed.

Three hours later, Francesco and I were called to the front to submit our packet to the agents standing on the other side of the protective barrier: us versus them. It felt criminal. Francesco slid the packet under and the agent with the bob pointed for us to go back to our seats. "We'll call you up again for your interview," she said.

There were three immigration officers working that day and one of them was an asshole who took great joy in declining people's applications with the kind of pizazz you'd expect from Satan. Every thirty minutes a different family would go before her and walk away crying, their dreams destroyed and their family separated for God knows how long.

We watched in horror as a little old Italian grandma positioned herself in front of the asshole immigration officer. I whispered to Francesco, "Oh, no, not a grandma! I can't watch this."

"Please hold up your right hand," the immigration officer barked through the glass. The elderly Italian woman ran her hand over her short gray hair and looked around for someone to translate. Her face was thin and wrinkled like crepe paper that had been crumpled into a ball then ironed flat over her skull. She wore sensible heels and a smart blazer that matched her slacks. She didn't speak any English.

The officer commanded, "Hold up your right hand!" waving her own hand around above her head.

The old woman mimed the officer with her left hand.

"YOUR OTHER RIGHT HAND," the officer spat. The old woman put up both hands like she was being accosted by the police. The immigration officer rolled her eyes, stood up and boomed, "YOU ONLY HAVE ONE RIGHT HAND!" into the loudspeaker that blasted out into the entire room, startling everyone.

I whispered to Francesco, "I hope you don't get her; Jesus, she's fucking insane." Around 2 p.m. our names were called by the asshole immigration officer and my heart sank. We approached the window cautiously like we were approaching a rattlesnake. The asshole officer had a permanent sneer and I noticed her Wisconsin accent when she growled, "Are you the petitioner?"

I smiled, "Yes I am."

She exhaled in a way that showed she already hated us. "What do you do in the United States?"

"I work as a copywriter. Freelance."

"Where do you live?" She made a note on one of the pages of our application.

"Right now I am staying in Italy."

She shoved our packet back under the window towards us and said, "We're declining your application because you are not domiciled in the United States. Go back to the US without him"—she motioned to Francesco like she was dismissing a bug—"and then eventually he can go to the US if he passes."

"I'm sorry? How long would I have to leave for?"

She shrugged. "Let's just say a *week* would be considered a *vacation*."

"Okay. But I still have all my American bank accounts, monthly bills, my mailing address, and residency. I pay taxes—"

She put her hand up to silence me. "Where are you standing RIGHT NOW? Where are your feet planted? In which country?"

"In Italy?"

"Exactly!" she said condescendingly, "So *no*. You have to go back to the US first then he can apply again without you." The horrible woman caught us off-guard. I hadn't expected to be treated so poorly by my own country while trying to *legally* bring my husband home. The woman completely lacked compassion and human decency and probably punched puppies for fun.

We gathered our things and bee-lined it for the door.

Francesco hung his head. We felt defeated. Thousands of euro, two twelve-hour days, weeks of preparation, vaccinations, and in less than one minute the immigration officer had flipped our world upside down like *that*, like our marriage wasn't real like we didn't matter at all as human beings. I hated that woman and prayed to the universe to give her genital herpes. Our choices were to stay in Italy throughout the economic collapse or be separated from each other for over a year. Leaving without Francesco was out of the question. We'd fought too hard to be together.

The next day I called an American immigration lawyer, Paul Saunders, who told me that the immigration officer who denied us didn't really understand the word "domiciled." He said that her interview was unfair at best and that off the record she sounded like "a real twat."

"Look," Paul said, "asking two questions then refusing to answer your questions does not constitute an interview and it's not the treatment that you deserve as a taxpaying American citizen. All of this bullshit reform has given these people unchecked power and some of them let it go to their heads. I tell you, it's just really unfortunate. You know what, you should ask your congressman to write a letter on behalf of you and your husband."

"You can call your politicians?" Francesco set down his coffee and bent forward to make sure he heard me correctly when I told him what I was doing.

"Of course. Can't you?"

"Oh, you're being serious? No, we can't talk to them. They're like kings here."

I nervously pecked out an email to my congressman, totally sure that he wouldn't help us because he was super conservative and kinda seemed anti-immigration. Surprisingly, his secretary responded within a few hours: "Congressman Smith would be more than happy to write the letter on your behalf."

Once I received the letter of support we scheduled another interview in Naples, feeling a little more powerful because we were packing a secret weapon this time. Let's try this again, you fucking demon, I thought.

The second time around I waited outside with Francesco's parents, who came again to save us that five-euro fortune. I wasn't required to be there with him and honestly, I worried that somehow I'd be the cause of rejection again. Amalea and Marcello still had no real idea why we kept coming to Naples because Francesco was being a misleading asshat. He told them that he couldn't return to the US without a visa since we were married. I felt icky to hide a partial truth from them but Francesco assured me that if he told them they'd just obsess and stress over it until we left.

Marcello slept in the car with Oliver since the weather was still mild. Francesco's mom and I drank espresso at a café next to the parked car. Every once in a while Oliver's head would pop up to make sure that I hadn't abandoned him, then he'd settle back down to nap some more.

Normally, sitting across from Amalea would give me stress but I was bolstered by a new kind of confidence. Francesco and I were leaving, and frankly, they could hate me all they wanted because I'd be gone soon. That little consolation had me sitting up taller in my metal bistro chair.

Amalea slurped her steaming espresso, then clunked it back down into the saucer. In Italian, she began,

"You know, if you moved to Cumino, near us, we would buy you an apartment. A *really nice* apartment." She rested her forearms on the table. "I think you guys would like a nice apartment, no?" She smiled.

Though a free apartment was tempting, I nearly choked trying to hide how repulsive the idea was to me. My eye twitched. "Probably we leave Italy somewhere because there are more monies outside of Italy." I said.

"Make him apply in Milan!" she answered, pointing at me. "The problem with you is you don't yell enough! Yell and yell until he finally does what you want!"

"Amalea, I no want to scream at Francesco. We just talk together about things and we decided together this thing. Also, you know better than anyone that he's hard-headed and doesn't listen if someone yells at him."

She smiled like she had a secret. "So, then, tell him that you won't have sex with him until he does what you tell him."

I burst out laughing.

She went on to tell me that Francesco is really passive, that he'll do whatever women tell him to do, that he's too sweet. I knew where she was going with this and what it would turn into once we left Italy. It would be my fault because "Francesco was too timid to stand up against his dictator wife." I completely understood why she might think of Francesco as passive. He's outgoing, silly, fun-spirited, easy to be around. Very few people see his temper or his stubborn, demanding side but it certainly exists. Additionally, he was raised in a super strict, super patriarchal family as the only son. It would be shocking if he weren't just a *little bit* entitled.

I blurted out, "Francesco's a good man but he not how you think he is with the womens. He's been with A LOT of womens."

Her eyes widened, "*Ma no! Impossibile!* My son? No. He's not like that!"

This was obviously a terrible decision but it was also a mild form of payback for all of her village gossip.

She looked away.

"No, I think you don't understand things because you're not Italian and you think that things like men not helping in the kitchen and men looking at other women is bad." She pointed towards her sleeping husband in the car.

"It's fine for men to talk about having sex with other women and to look at other women but it's not okay for women to do that."

I massaged my temples. "I no agree with you. The man not specials."

"No. You have to protect a man's pride," she replied, wiping dust from the table.

"Sorry?" I asked, louder than I meant to, "but what you are saying? The woman has the prides too. You have the prides. I have the prides!" Which sounded like a venereal disease and nothing to brag about.

"Maybe you're saying he was mean because, with his ex-girlfriend, the Spanish one, he didn't translate dialect for her."

I turned into a jealous pre-teen, flashing back, "Um. That girl had big teeth like a big dumb bunny! And he no loved her! He make the infidelity on her!" I regretted it immediately and thought, Jesus, what has that girl ever done to me?

"You have to be confused because my son wouldn't cheat," Amalea stated firmly.

I laughed dramatically like a cartoon villain, "Your son is a grand bastard!"

I knew I should stop but I couldn't because *it just felt really good*. I loved Francesco but it was totally true. He wasn't a poor, picked-on Italian boy being corrupted by the evil American.

"*Va boh*, he wouldn't have sex with someone while he was with you," she said.

I nodded. "I agree. Because I make him die."

Amalea shifted in her seat, uncrossing and re-crossing her legs, brushing off her gray blouse and black slacks. She dressed better than any mother I knew. She flawlessly mixed sexy with elegant, and her hair was always in a perfectly shaped, honey-brown A-line.

Amalea cleared her throat. "That is a problem with my son. He's so closed. He's never let us in his life, I feel like I don't even know him sometimes. Everything he says to us is superficial and he thinks that we're too stupid to know that. I hope he's better with you. You're always writing at home alone, he doesn't speak very much, and I'm worried you'll get too lonely. He's like my father. It's easy to get lonely with someone who doesn't open up very much."

She'd never said anything so open before and I wasn't sure how to process it.

I took a sip of my coffee, picked up the napkin and folded it into a small square. "He is very quiet but he's working on it. We'll be okay, don't worry."

She smiled and touched my hand briefly. It was almost like a normal human relationship except the part where I told her that her son's penis had had more action than a World War II veteran and then called his ex-girlfriend a rabbit. It was nice of her to worry about me. It was mostly because she didn't want us to get divorced, I think, but I was glad.

"Men are never perfect," she said. "You can't find a perfect one, you just have to find one that is okay and then mold them."

I laughed. "Are you happy?" I asked.

She blushed, "I don't know, now more than ever. Anyway," she gestured towards the car again, "you should sell your dog. He's too difficult."

"No. We like him."

She rolled her eyes then leaned forward across the table to examine my face. "Your face looks dirty. We have to take you to get those sunspots laser-removed."

I covered my lip, "Um. Okay."

She squinted. "You need to wear sunscreen."

Still covering my face I said, "I know."

She reached up and touched my hair. "I don't like your hair long. I really don't understand why you don't cut it short. I liked it much better when it was short."

I threw up my hands, "For the love of God, woman! Leave me alone for five minutes!"

She laughed, then, in her best attempt to speak English, said, "Okaya. Is zokaaaaay!"

I smiled. "Yes, it's okay," I said in English.

Francesco screamed my name and came running towards us, frantically waving a piece of paper in the air.

"I got it, babe! I got my visa!" he shouted above the traffic and distant construction work. I stood up when he reached our table and gave him a tight hug.

"I got it! I got it!" he laughed and waved the papers above his head. "But here's the crazy thing," he said, a little winded, "it expires in six months."

"So we have to move within six months?"

"Yeah."

He explained to Amalea in quick Italian that he'd got his visa. She smiled and nodded, though it was clear that she had no idea why it mattered. I winced a little.

"So how did it go this time?" I asked.

"Super easy. The evil woman wasn't there. The guy that helped me quickly sorted through my papers and stamped them. What have you guys been doing? Are you about ready to lose your mind?"

"No, not at all. We had a long talk about how your history of cheating and being an overall douchebag."

"*What?*" he froze.

"Well, she implied that you were essentially a puppet and I disagreed by telling her you'd slept with *so many women*."

"So, you told my mom that I'm basically a man-whore?" He smiled sheepishly, "That's not at all crazy."

"I'm sorry! I know! I'm an idiot! But they're going to blame me for us moving to the US if she thinks I own you. Are you mad?"

"No, I mean, it's hard for them to understand that I'm not the person they think I am. I'm not like them, I'm the opposite, really. I guess you could have told her worse things." He laughed.

"Oh, totally. You know, this whole thing has me thinking about how much I *wish* I controlled your life. That would be awesome. I'd rename you and put you in a bowtie."

"I don't. You're a dick. My life would be miserable."

"By miserable you mean awesome. Pierre. Do you like the name, Pierre?"

"Stop."

"Fine. Pierre."

"Shut up."

"But I love you, Pierre."

"I'm going to kill you."

"Apologize, Pierre."

When Francesco and I said goodbye to his parents the next day, Amalea surprised me when she pulled me in for a warm hug. She stepped back, looking at me the way someone would look at a family treasure that brought back fond memories, smiling a knowing smile. Then she hugged Francesco, shaking her head as if to say, "Oh, you, I know you, I know *things*." She turned back to me and caressed my cheek, then shoved a plastic bag into my hand full to the brim with six aluminum-wrapped eggplant parmesan sandwiches, a bottle of carbonated water, and a stack of plastic cups so we could drink the water "hygienically."

I was utterly confused. Had my mother-in-law and I finally bonded, while sipping espresso outside of a café, and discussing her son's wandering penis? Yes, because like she said, Francesco was a closed person and I'd let her in. She felt included, allowed inside the intricacies of our private relationship but most importantly inside Francesco's very private world. In my kitchen a few hours later, I thought of Amalea as I watched a sweaty and heaving elderly woman in a floral housedress beat a rug to death on her balcony across the courtyard. The woman paused, took a deep breath, and screamed inside the window leading into her apartment,

"Angelo, I'm killing myself to keep the house clean for you. The least you could do is come out here and keep me company." Then she picked up her paddle and *whack, whack, whack*.

34

But Will Everyone Love Our Balls?

November 2013

"You ready?" Francesco reached out and took my hand to pull me up from our kitchen table. "We need to leave. I'd like to get to my parents' house and unload the car before lunch."

We'd already said goodbye to the people and places that mattered to us in Florence: the café across the street; Mufasa, a Senegalese immigrant who sold lighters and such on the corner by our house; Angie's on Via dei Neri, where we'd met; my apartment in Piazza del Duomo numero 7 where we'd first "made the love"; and Giuggiolo, our favorite restaurant, where we'd had our first dinner together. On our goodbye tour, I remembered why I moved to Florence in the first place: the three teenagers piled onto one bike whizzing through the streets and singing loudly, the old widows who held hands in solidarity during their daily stroll around my neighborhood, the elderly men who always stopped me in the street to show me every picture they'd ever taken of their poodle Fifi, the smell of homemade sauce coming from apartment windows, the charming waiters who snuck ham to Oliver under the table. How had I stopped seeing all of the good in this place? *"Don't it always seem to go, that you don't know what you've got 'til it's gone...."*

I took one last look at our little apartment and I felt like we were making a horrible mistake. My stomach gurgled, my hands were shaking. Maybe it wasn't all vineyards and rainbows all the time but at least I knew what to expect. Our history was here, our relationship, everything that we'd built together thus far had been built on Italian soil atop so much history (and so many corpses). We'd never lived in the US together, what if things were vastly different? Did I want to return to the US and face everyone's expectations of me at home? The culture was different, the lifestyle, the people. What if we changed? What if I changed? What if Francesco hated it there? I couldn't bear for him to feel the same crushing loneliness or constant state of confusion that I'd experienced.

"Babe?" I turned to Francesco, panic-stricken, right before we shut our apartment door for the last time, "I should have tried harder to make it work here, maybe this is a mistake? Is this a mistake? Is this a terrible idea? Are you sure ab—"

"Dude, we just spent a month packing our apartment. We canceled our lease and we bought the plane tickets. We fly out of Rome in two weeks. We're leaving. At this point, it's totally set. Don't worry, everything is going to be alright."

"Are you sure?" I asked, still tense.

"How the shit could I know? I don't have special powers," he answered.

"You're so good at reassuring. That's one of my favorite things about you," I said.

"I'm not surprised."

The door clicked behind us. Francesco picked up our luggage, adjusted Oliver's leash, and we walked away from our life in Florence, maybe forever.

In the car, Oliver glared up at me from my lap, upset that I wouldn't let him sleep on the boxes and luggage crammed into the back seat.

"You can't sit there, Oli. What if we stop fast? You'll fly off of the boxes and out of the window. Or maybe get crushed to death," I explained to my baffled dog. "You have to stay here, and for the record, I don't like it any more than you do. Your elbow is in my belly button."

Francesco shot me a look of concern. "You're doing that thing where you have a full conversation with the dog again," he said.

"And? So?" I shrugged. "Are you some kind of expert dog scientist? Do you know how his brain works? Maybe he understands everything and chooses not to engage because he finds me terribly boring."

The first few days in Cumino, Francesco and I didn't do much but eat, get Oliver's papers ready for our flight, and sit around on the balcony. But, as each day passed and our departure date grew closer, I became increasingly on edge. Would I forget it all? I put my nervous energy into documentation, acting as a sort of paparazzo of the everyman, stalking the streets with my Nikon slung around my neck, shooting at anything and everything, "That man is crossing the street!" *Snap, snap, snap.* "That woman has a mother!" *Snap, snap, snap.* "Italians eat cake." *Snap, snap, snap.* Faced with losing it all, with saying goodbye, I scrambled to gather tangible proof of every detail of my life and the people of the cities we drove through to say more goodbyes: Cumino, Pallacio, Naples, and Sora. A couple screaming in the street, an elderly man riding a bike, the crazy pet lady at the weekend market in Cumino that sold tick-infested puppies, a pasta shop that made fresh pasta daily. I needed proof of it all.

Francesco took a different approach. Starting from our first day at his parents' house he attached himself like a starfish to the couch. I barely recognized him, he became this thing sprawled out in sweats on a sofa, in all of its slothful glory. Often, he didn't move for hours, rather, he curled up to nap constantly, like he'd reverted to existing in utero. He didn't do his own laundry because his mom was somehow there the moment he removed any item of clothing, practically catching it right before it hit the floor, then running it to the washing machine as if it were covered in Ebola blood. Francesco didn't cook or help do the dishes, he didn't get up to walk five feet to the fridge for wine. Instead, he'd scream, "Maaaamma!" and Amalea would rush to his side to retrieve whatever he needed because his arms had turned into limp noodles.

She'd smack him, "Stop being so lazy!" and scold him, "I'm tired!" And she was tired. The woman still worked full-time as a Bible teacher, teaching children that if they fucked up, Jesus would shoot them in the ass with a lightning bolt. Plus, she did all of the things a stay-at-home mom would do, too. She returned home for lunch around one every day to clean the kitchen, cook lunch, do the dishes, then go back to work. In the late afternoon, she'd come back home to cook dinner, do the dishes, and prepare lesson plans all while my husband and her husband watched lazily from their place of leisure. If I were to embark on a multi-course dinner, it would all come out of a can, and halfway through I'd probably just give up to cry on the couch with a bottle of two-euro Chianti. Francesco called his mother's magical abilities in all things domestic the "curse of the Italian woman," because "they are expected to do too much and at some point, they go batshit crazy." The family never talked about the way she selflessly labored for them to show her love. And as Francesco yawned on the couch from a long day of snacking and napping she'd iron his shirts until midnight.

I couldn't remember how I'd ever had sex with this giant man-baby. I felt sorry for Amalea. I got mad and screamed at Francesco to stop being an entitled asshole. This part Amalea liked, in theory. She smirked while I yelled at him, and on occasion, she'd jump in to smack him a few times. Francesco's father, of course, wary of women coming together for any kind of suffrage, grumbled about how women "should act," or threw a tantrum, anything he could to union-bust.

But in the end, Amalea rushed to Francesco's side because she missed him already and indentured servitude was her love language. "Italian children are spoiled," she'd often say while wiping the sweat from her forehead after carrying my husband to bed at night.

"I can't imagine why," I said under my breath.

My futile attempts to motivate Francesco to return to the land of the living were usually met with blank stares or weird hand gestures I couldn't understand. *What is that? Are you making a bird? Are you trying to deflect by confusing the shit out of me? Cause it's working.*

I wasn't sure how Francesco really felt about the move.

One day while we were dining on roast potatoes and *branzino* (head still attached, eyes fixated accusingly), Marcello said, "But don't you think we should have lunch before you go? In Pallacio at the summer house with all of your friends?"

Francesco perked up. "Oh, yeah! That would be great!"

Marcello turned to me, "What do you think?"

I nodded, "Yes, it seems great."

Marcello nodded that he approved of my answer and turned to Amalea to inform her that she'd be cooking for all of Francesco's friends.

I took a bite of the fish on my plate and realized immediately that there was a graveyard full of bones jabbing every inch of my mouth. I looked around to make sure that nobody was watching and carefully took the chewed-up, bone-filled gob out of my mouth and set it discreetly on my plate.

"Great!" Marcello said, "I'll start ordering the food!" Then he turned and stared at my plate. "There are starving children in Afrreeeekah!" he said accusingly, scooping up my chewed-up fish and shoveling it into his mouth, bones and all. Then he washed it down with half a glass of wine.

"Oh, God! Gross!" I said, trying not to gag.

Amalea threw back her head and laughed. Marcello said disapprovingly, "Gross? You're a disaster. We don't waste food here in *Italy*!"

I smiled, "Oh, so everyone eats food that someone else has spit out?"

"You spat that out?"

Amalea cackled even louder, Francesco scrunched up his face, "Ew, Papà!"

Marcello shrugged and chuckled.

It was decided. A day before we left Italy they'd hold a lunch, lasting around six hours, in Amalea's hometown of Pallacio, right outside of Naples, the kind of place where everyone knows each other, where all five business establishments (a café, restaurant, tiny grocery store, post office, and a pizza place) close from noon to 4 p.m. for lunch. During lunch the locals are at home with their families, the roads are post-apocalyptic, and the one or two foreigners who might pepper the streets are watched with suspicion from windows or doorways.

When Marcello and Amalea weren't waiting hand and foot on their man-sized infant son, they were obsessively party-planning. Planning the lunch was great stress. They were terrified of disappointing guests (all of whom thought of themselves as professional food critics the way of Gordon Ramsey). Marcello developed a four-day stomach ache from all the planning and could only hold down digestive cookies dipped in chamomile tea. I suspected that the reason he and Amalea were so focused on the lunch was to keep their minds occupied on something other than Francesco leaving. Marcello spent hours on the phone with every butcher to check the prices and origin of different cuts of meat, sent his friends out to look for deals in the local grocery stores, and pre-ordered buffalo mozzarella and wine. Francesco and I came home from grabbing a coffee to find lamb skulls floating in some giant cauldron on the balcony near my bra and nightgown. Marcello patted me on the back, "Look what I have there!" He smiled mischievously, "The bull testicles and cheese with worms from Sardinia will get here in the morning."

It seemed like everything had been planned perfectly, but Marcello still couldn't relax. The situation was serious, their entire reputation hung in the balance: would the guests enjoy their balls? I tried not to be judgmental. After all, they totally thought the stuff that I ate was weird, too. But then again, ew.

I turned to Francesco, "Have you *seen* testicles? They look like chewed-up bubblegum. I mean, no offense, but I don't even want them near my face when they are attached to you. Oh my God! Do you think there's invisible bull semen in them? Like a meaty donut puff with a cream center? I'm going to throw up."

"Can you please stop talking about my bubblegum balls? And who says that? You're like being married to a teenager," Francesco answered.

I mouthed the word "BALLS" at him.

My inability to cook Italian food had been a problem since I'd met Marcello but the week leading up to our departure it had turned into a goddamn travesty.

"Your job as a woman is to cook but you don't know *dick* about food!" he said an hour after he'd showed me his lamb brains and told me about the testicles.

I turned to him and said in English, "I seriously disagree. My vagina does not make me some kind of goddamn MasterChef, dude." Then I switched to Italian, "Francesco likes to do the cooking," I said with a simper.

The next day we repeated the same conversation, *twice*.

"You have to learn how to cook!" he began, with a mouthful of mortadella or salami.

"I don't like to cook," I replied for the hundredth time.

"YOU HAVE TO LEARN!" He nervously eyed Francesco, worried that he'd starve to death in the US if I didn't perfect a frittata soon.

"I don't like it. He likes it. He can do it." I gestured to Francesco, who remained focused on his red wine and fried red peppers, a daily lunch staple.

Marcello rolled his eyes and scowled at me for the rest of the meal.

On the third day, after he'd lamented for a particularly long time about my inability to cook, I broke down and offered to make lunch for the family the following day.

"*Cosa?*! *CHE FA? TU? Che voo di?*! *Eh? Puoi fa KIST?*" Which is part dialect, part heavy accent, and a lot of not Italian, which means something like: "What?! What can YOU do?! What do you say? Can you make THIS?" He gestured to a bunch of dandelion weeds he'd foraged from a nearby soccer field.

I gagged a little, knowing how many feral cats lived in that field. "No, I can't cook that."

Panicked, Amalea jumped in, "No! You can't! We have to use the beans because they're going to go bad!" She did not want me anywhere near her domain and she loathed foreign food.

I thought about it for a minute then said in Italian, "I make chili. It good and easy!"

355

They argued for a moment amongst themselves, Marcello saying I should make the chili, Amalea vehemently protesting, "*No*, NO!" In the end, Marcello decided that democracy was not his thing and he ruled in favor of himself and my making the chili.

The following day Francesco and I spent all morning chopping tomatoes, onions, and garlic, boiling the beans, and preparing a chili recipe I took from a favorite food blog. I am no cook but with Francesco's help, I thought it was pretty okay.

At the lunch table, Amalea looked over her meal with her mouth turned down like I'd plopped a bowl of rabbit shit in front of her. Marcello immediately plunged his spoon into the piping-hot chili and shoved it into his mouth. SLUUUUUUURP.

He sank another spoon into his mouth, the chili staining his white mustache.

"This is garbage. What is this shit?! You need to learn how to cook! This is spicy RAGU!" He talked with a mouthful of beans.

Admittedly, it kind of resembled spicy ragu. I mean, we only had one cup of beans so it was pretty much just sauce and meat.

"It's good!" Francesco argued.

"It's better than your minestrone," I said defensively to Marcello, who, for the record, is a *terrible* cook. His go-to dish anytime that Amalea can't cook is a slop made of plain water, frozen mixed vegetables, uncooked legumes, and usually calamari and oysters that he tosses in at the end for no reason at all.

"It *is* better than your minestrone," Amalea agreed.

"*KIST! KIST É MONNEZZA! CHEEELLLEEH!*" Marcello added in dialect, which means "This is garbage," while he mopped up the last bite with his bread.

Francesco said to me in English, "Well, you tried, babe," and he patted my leg.

"Oh, no, I totally won. He'll never tell me to cook again."

"Ah, true! Nicely played." Francesco laughed.

"What are you saying?!" Marcello demanded.

"Just that Misty should never cook again," Francesco said, conspiratorially.

"I AGREE!" Marcello pounded the table for emphasis and we all laughed.

After we finished the meal, Francesco and Marcello sat back in their chairs like kings because they had penises and felt too special to help clear the table. My father-in-law pointed to the sink and commanded that I do the dishes. When I refused, my mother-in-law stood up to take over. I went to her, calmly removed the sponge from her fist and dropped it into the lap of my husband/man-child.

"What-a the hell!" Francesco jumped as his crotch absorbed the dishwater.

"I love you, King Franny, but you're doing dishes. Your ass has been planted on that couch all week and your mom deserves a break. I have copy to write for work. Biatch."

"Bully," he taunted.

From the balcony table with my laptop open in front of me, I watched a passerby glance up at my panties on the line. I caught the lamb heads bobbing around out of the corner of my eye and turned my back to them. A light breeze rippled the water, causing the skulls to clank against the metal.

"Ha-ha! You're doing dishes! This is a woman's job. Your wife is out there on the computer while you do the dishes. Sorry, but I just don't know.

I don't know!" I could hear Marcello giving Francesco a hard time in the kitchen while he scrubbed away at some pans.

I put my headphones on, turned up The Knife, a Swedish electronic band, and leaned back into my chair. Across the parking lot, a family friend hung laundry on the line off her balcony, pausing to wave to me. The Frenchman, who lived next door, left the building with his chubby white poodle, and also stopped to wave at me and Oliver, who was sleeping near my feet. Across the street in a field littered with debris and garbage, teenage boys played with a ball where Francesco grew up playing soccer.

A knot formed in my throat. I would miss it, I would miss all of it. So many times I wanted to leave and never come back but now that in just a few days we were really leaving I saw things more clearly and everything seemed to be getting better. Was it getting better? Or had my attitude simply changed when I realized that I had choices? I no longer felt out of control or trapped, which made everything else seem so trivial. So, I didn't have any close friends in Italy, so what? So people yelled a lot, so what. So Francesco's family was a royal pain in my ass, I could handle it, couldn't I? When I didn't *need* their acceptance, when I could leave when I wanted, I felt secure.

The freedom of feeling in control of my life allowed for a moment of clarity, allowed me to appreciate our family for the comically insane characters that they were. Their home no longer felt like a place of overbearing in-laws who highlighted my inadequacy but a place with "quirky" in-laws who did "funny" and sometimes "obnoxious" things that were easy to ignore. I wondered if it was possible that I had a strange form of Stockholm Syndrome when I realized that not only would I miss Italy, I would really miss *them*.

35

Farewell, Amici

December 2013

At the farewell lunch, thirty of Francesco's closest friends and family were seated around big farm tables in the garage of their summer house in Pallacio. Before we started in on the first course my father-in-law brought in his precious bull's testicles. I passed but unknowingly everyone else ate them, and as soon as they swallowed my father-in-law shouted, "YOU ATE BALLS!" while he slapped his leg and laughed like a hyena. Because deep down, we're all twelve years old.

Amalea brought out *pasta al pomodoro* and lasagna, placing a portion of each in front of everyone at the table. Then I helped carry in various grilled vegetables, diced potatoes, olives, more pickled vegetables, and field greens that my father-in-law had surely picked from a random field nearby (in fear of contracting toxoplasmosis, the cat-shit disease Francesco had as a child,

I avoided this), and more pecorino, while Marcello set an entire zoo of grilled meat on the table. The guys ate themselves halfway to a heart attack and I kept thinking that there were starving people in the world and drank more because I felt guilty.

It was around this time that my mother-in-law, who was seated at the opposite end of our table, fourteen people away, yelled, "HEY! Your friend here, this Australian girl, she speaks Italian way better than you!" She was talking about my friend Lucy, who had somehow ended up seated next to her instead of me. Unable to hide under the table I did the next best thing and screamed back, "*E che voo?*" which meant, "And what do you want from me?" in Neapolitan dialect. I have no idea why but when a foreign person speaks dialect everyone gets *super excited* about it. When Francesco used American slang it just creeped me out because "Dat's-a right shorty!" just sounds weird with an Italian accent.

My use of their village tongue erased the fact that I was being an asshole to my mother-in-law; my father-in-law burst out laughing and roared, "This one is from Naples!" Then the old men started eating lamb brains served in the lamb skull, and I went outside to smoke again.

Moving wasn't permanent but it certainly felt like it. The previous night, we'd spent two hours stuffing our luggage with olive oil and eight pounds of parmesan cheese and I wondered, Wait, why are we leaving? Recently, I'd just met a group of expat bloggers online. Oliver was welcome in Italy, everywhere, and Francesco had a lifetime contract at his job and could theoretically work there until he died—a system in Italy that is a nightmare for business owners, but comforting for employees.

My time in Italy wasn't bad; it had shaped my career goals in the sense that I was no longer afraid to live the creative writer-artist life I'd always dreamed of but which had felt too self-indulgent to pursue. I knew that all that mattered to me was writing, and family, and travel. I'd met Francesco in Italy, the love of my life was *Italian*. Our entire relationship had existed there and I worried about what could happen to us in another country. He was the expert in Italy but he'd need to lean on me in the US. Would he be able to handle being forced to depend on me until he got the swing of things? Would he be bitter about it like I'd been?

I'd miss the vineyards in the summer, the brightly colored cement buildings, walking to aperitivo in the evening with Francesco, peeing in back alleys when drunk, seeing people bring babies into bars, and having sex under the olive trees while watching for vipers and wild boars. A very small, masochistic part of me would even miss catching my in-laws in my luggage, as I had that morning as they emptied it out and invasively re-packed it the "right way."

The afternoon before we left, Francesco and I were in the foyer of Marcello and Amalea's house with a group of friends and neighbors, making awkward small talk about cake and travel. It was time to tell everyone goodbye and I didn't want to do it. I burst into tears as I handed out the letters I'd written to a handful of Francesco's friends, then spent the good part of thirty minutes weeping into Luca's neck. Francesco's mother also began to cry, and before I knew it we were all crying. Except for Francesco, who was apparently channeling a robot. The house emptied one by one until everyone had gone and the sniffling dissolved into silence.

That night just before bed, Francesco and I managed to shove yet another jar of *piccante* sauce into our bag, along with some more cheese for my parents.

"Wow, we're really doing this," Francesco sighed.

"You okay?" I asked for the tenth time. "Is this a terrible idea?"

He smiled confidently, "No, I'm excited! This is going to be awesome, babe!"

"Man, I hope so. If it sucks please don't hate me." I twisted my hair.

"At this point, I just need to get out of my parents' house. Even Chechnya sounds good right now. But it's weird to think that in the morning we're starting a new chapter of our life."

We paraded Oliver through the airport parking lot, imploring him to "just pee, please! It's your last chance until we cross the Atlantic!" He was too anxious to pee. Instead, he bounced around obnoxiously while we tried to maneuver four giant bags across the asphalt. Moving from one country to another via an airplane was a terrible idea and bags fell over, sometimes on top of Oliver.

My in-laws were uncharacteristically silent. Instead of telling nonstop jokes or nagging, Marcello played with Oliver, kissing him and rubbing his head. Amalea held her head up high while helping us into the airport. She remained calm and dignified all the way through checking our bags. She was being very kind to me, despite my stealing her kid and whisking him off to another continent. We hugged, and kissed on both cheeks, then she turned to Francesco and embraced him tightly. She inhaled deeply, like a pump forcing air into a soccer ball, and then exhaled in sobs that echoed throughout the airport, clinging to Francesco's peacoat.

He smiled reassuringly like he's able to do in every situation. "*Non ti preoccupare Mamma. Ci vediamo presto,*" he told her not to worry because we'd see her soon.

His father hugged him, pounding his back loudly, "Be good," he said in dialect. Next, we hugged, he kissed Oliver one last time, then we went towards the gate with our carry-on.

We looked back as they exited the airport, Amalea with her face in her hands being guided out the automatic doors by Marcello.

"Oh my God, I feel terrible!" I said. "Also, do you ever feel like our life is a movie?" I tried to hold Oliver tight as he thrashed around. He'd seen something interesting near the security check and desperately wanted to get to it at all costs.

"Yeah, me too. She'll be okay, though. She'll come to visit, and we'll be back."

I sighed, "My mom cried over me once in college when I had a nervous breakdown and she thought I was going to die. I weighed ninety-two pounds. It was kind of gross."

He shook his head. "Your family stories make me feel better about my life one hundred percent of the time."

"Oh. So, you're welcome?"

We took our seats on the aircraft. Oliver climbed under the seat in front of me and rested his head on top of my feet. He'd always been an excellent traveler, but we were armed with heavy sedatives in case.

Francesco took my hand in his. "I love you," he winked. "Are you excited for me to be American?"

"I don't want you to be American. I want you to be you."

He kissed my cheek. "Are you pointing out that you're more accepting of differences than some other people we know?"

I smiled, "Absolutely."

"I knew it."

I winked back. And then I took a deep breath and closed my eyes.

Five years ago, broken and confused, I'd stepped onto the same transatlantic flight in search of an improved version of myself. And it would be great if this book ended perfectly with a lesson learned and a beautifully packaged summary of growth about the ways that Italy made me better. But I'd be lying to myself and all of you. Though it's true, I did grow a lot: the first year was the best year of my life, I made art and lifelong friends in school, I could now decipher between a table Chianti and a Brunello, and I could make pasta from scratch. I'd written every day and I knew that writing was something I had to do for the rest of my life. As an added bonus, I could speak a version of Italian that no longer resembled an animal crying out in pain. Inhale. Check. Exhale.

I'd learned a lot about resilience and love. Even though he was an enormous pain in the ass, Francesco was my soulmate, my other half, and despite all of the difficulties we had in our relationship he was always my first thought in the morning and my last at night. Before Italy I never thought that was possible. I learned that relationships weren't about two people being perfect, rather, they were about two people trying their absolute best to do right by their partner, every exhausting day, till death do you part. And boundaries, relationships are also setting boundaries and arguing about directions, until you die.

In some demented way, Amalea and Marcello had taught me that people can love strongly but display it in the least beneficial way imaginable. And that helped me understand my own family. There was no question that Francesco's parents loved him deeply, but they showed it by essentially pecking him to death with incessant criticism, which totally reminded me of my dad. I realized that my dad cared about me, too, but had a *painful* way of showing it sometimes because he just didn't know a better way. All of us can only do our best given the tools we have at any given time.

Several months earlier, during some of the darkest times battling with Francesco's family, when my self-esteem was at an all-time low and anxiety had turned me into a half-starved waif, my dad had unexpectedly dropped by Florence on a layover from his annual trip to Iran. I hadn't seen him for months, so I was over the moon to be able to spend time with him, even if it was only for a day or two.

At one point, we were chatting in the car and waiting for Francesco, who had vanished into the post office. Our conversation veered towards my youngest siblings, Jasmina and Casper, and the cute things they were doing. As much as I loved to hear him gush about them, it always hurt a little because my dad wasn't there for me consistently when I was little. And maybe my face gave it away because he looked at me in the rearview mirror and said, "I wish I'd had the same experience with you, baby." He looked away abruptly, as though he were ashamed.

I put my hand on his shoulder, "I'm not mad at you, Dad. I know that you and my mom were both young and just didn't know what you were doing. It's okay."

I meant it. I'd never been mad that he made mistakes; more so, I was upset that he'd never acknowledged them like they didn't matter. His shoulders relaxed a little and he turned around to examine my face, "I'm glad, baby. I'm really glad." And it's hard to explain but it felt like this heavy, soggy, life-disrupting burden lifted off of both of us and was replaced by forgiveness and love. Me forgiving him and him forgiving himself.

* * *

In Italy, I grew and evolved and regressed because here's the truth—real life is fucking messy. Sometimes no matter how much you want something to be amazing it's not. I wanted Italy to be a refuge, a way to start over but it wasn't. At least not then. Italy taught me that sometimes growth and change are painful and that our past always catches up with us, no matter how fast you move or how far you go to get away from it. No matter where you are, there you are, right?

So I guess my story is in part a cautionary tale about fixing your shit before you run away from your problems to marry a foreign hottie with an intense family. I moved to Italy to become a better version of myself. Instead what I needed was more self-love, self-care, and wine.

ACKNOWLEDGEMENTS

I'd like to thank the majestic capybara, all of you who have followed my writing over the years, my therapist, Katie, for keeping me sane, my family for being amazing and providing endless fodder (and for letting me write about them), my friends for their constant love and support, Italy for the trauma and healing, the art school for being a magical creative space and introducing me to some of the best professors and best people I know (including all of the amazing humans mentioned in this book under fake names). I'd like to thank my editors, Kiki and Lucy. Kiki, this journey started with you and your feedback. Lucy, thank you for your patience and encouragement. I could not have done this without you. And last but not least, I'd like to thank our parents who are perfectly imperfect.